CROSSING THE BOUNDARIES

A History of the European Baptist Federation

Bernard Green

The Baptist Historical Society
on behalf of the European Baptist Federation
1999

ISBN 0 903166 29 1

DEDICATION

To the many friends and colleagues
in the European Baptist Federation
whose steadfast faith and courageous witness
have been such an inspiration to me since my
first visit to Eastern Europe in 1970

CROSSING THE BOUNDARIES
A History of the European Baptist Federation

CONTENTS

Foreword by David Coffey
Preface
Abbreviations used

Part One - The Story

Part Two - Major Concerns

Part Three - The Way Ahead

Photographs

FOREWORD

It is a remarkable achievement to present such a concise overview of the European Baptist story and I warmly commend this 50th anniversary history by Bernard Green.

One of the helpful features of the book is the way in which the story of the EBF is set in a social and political context. The development of many European Baptist communities in the twentieth century is interwoven with the rise and fall of political regimes. It includes stories of terror, bloodshed and the violation of human rights and religious liberty. Here is evidence from our family history that the gates of hell do not prevail against the Church of Jesus Christ and in our jubilee year we should honour afresh those who did not love their lives so much as to shrink from death and 'overcome by the blood of the Lamb and by the word of their testimony'.

As someone who has been privileged to witness some of the major changes in the EBF over the past ten years I have been intrigued to find some common themes running through the story of the past fifty years.

There is the *power of fellowship*. In the opening chapter there is evidence of how international friendships between Baptists were an important foundation stone in the birth and development of a future European Baptist Federation. This characteristic of fellowship has been important throughout the years of our history and from my experience, without strong and trusting friendships I doubt whether the EBF would have survived the stormy waters of disagreement of the last decade.

There is the *concern for mission*. The unfinished mission agenda at the commencement of the century is almost identical to those facing Baptists on the eve of a new millennium and this should prompt us to enquire whether a Federation of Baptist Unions is the best structure we can offer in our fulfilment of the Great Commission. I have long questioned whether we have the appropriate organization in place to assist us in the task of evangelizing the people groups of Europe and have called for the creation of a European Mission Agency to co-ordinate the work of numerous mission agencies. I am encouraged that this urgent question is raised once again.

There is the challenge of *diversity without disunity*. I sensed that the family conflicts, about which there are many discreet hints by the writer, are sometimes less theological and more cultural in their origins. One of the major challenges for the coming years is how we address those issues which threaten to divide us and whether we will have the capacity to fulfil the biblical command of striving to maintain the unity of the body in the bonds of peace. Do not miss the thrust of Dr Martin Niemöller's words to the Berlin Congress in 1958: 'The Church is only free when it is not on the defensive, when it is not anxious about its own life but is God trusting and missionary in spirit'.

There is the continuing campaign for *human rights and religious liberty*. There are moving testimonies of how easily religious liberty, which has been hard gained, is soon lost through the political whims of a hostile government. Baptists need to maintain vigilance in this area of religious liberty and consistently bear witness to what an earlier generation referred to as 'the crown rights of the Redeemer'. We can demonstrate from a long record of patriotic Christian living in all our nations, that faithful citizenship need not be irrevocably tied to membership of a state church.

Inevitably a book like this tends to feature those who have served the EBF more publicly, but if you read between the lines of this history there is the untold story of thousands of men and women belonging to local Baptist churches across Europe without whom there would be no evidence of Baptist work and witness.

In December 1998 I travelled with Karl Heinz Walter to Kazakstan in Central Asia, the former Soviet Republic which was the location for the infamous Gulag camps. I could fill a book with the stories of pastors and church members we met as we travelled the country. As I write this foreword, I can visualize Raisa and Micha, the church members who provided us with food and accommodation; Evgenny the deacon who had exceptional skills as a driver on the ice-packed roads of Kazakstan; Pastor Frank and his wife Olga and the children of the Orphanage; young Baptists such as Natalia, Benjamin and Vera who not only served as our interpreters but opened windows of insight regarding Christian discipleship in the post-communist era.

A few weeks after our visit to Kazakstan I visited the International Baptist Theological Seminary in Prague for the first conference of Young European Baptist Leaders: what may be termed the 'Joshua generation'. They are the young men and women who will write the next chapter of our unfolding history. The promise to Joshua is God's promise to this new generation of European Baptist Christians as they face the unfinished task of bringing the good news of Jesus Christ to the peoples of Europe: 'Be strong and very courageous, for the Lord your God will be with you wherever you go'.

David Coffey
February 1999

PREFACE

During the research for this book I came across an article on the mission of the Church in a society which habitually sets up barriers and boundaries. Throughout the ages, families and nations, races and tribes, governments and ideologies, cultures and languages, even religions and theologies, have erected fences beyond which people have been forbidden to go. By contrast, the Bible portrays God as the One who is never bound by these partitions. He is the God of all the earth. 'The earth is the Lord's, and everything in it, the world, and all who live in it;' *(Psalm 24.1)*. We see this in the ministry of Jesus. He constantly deals with all sorts of people on and beyond the boundaries of society. He actively seeks to draw into his love those whom others exclude and avoid. By reconciling people to himself through the cross of Christ, God brings them together as one family in his kingdom of grace and peace.

When the Christian Church engages in God's mission there are boundaries to cross - social, national, political, racial, economic, ecclesiastical, ecumenical, linguistic, and cultural boundaries. The gospel declares that in Christ there is no distinction between Jew and Gentile, black and white, male and female, master and servant. God's eternal purpose is to bring them all together, from north, south, east and west, into one in Christ. This is our exciting, costly and continuous task until his Kingdom comes.

Twentieth-century Europe has frequently been a continent of strife and separation, frontiers and enmity. It has forced Christians into situations where they have been divided from fellow believers, and had to look upon them as enemies to be defeated. The European Baptist Federation came into existence to cross the boundaries and lead Baptists into reconciled relationships after years of war. They would then be able, in spiritual partnership, to work and pray for a new Europe. As I researched the life of the EBF I became convinced that this was a central theme around which to present the story.

Like most writers of history, I was faced with a huge amount of material. It could not all be included, and I recognize that I may have omitted events and issues which others would have included. For health reasons, I have not been able to travel around Europe during my research; nor have I had access to fax and e-mail facilities. This may have led to omissions of which I am unaware. However, many people have given considerable help by providing photocopies of documents, by patiently replying to letters and questions, and by agreeing to be interviewed when coming to England. To more than thirty such people I am most grateful.

The British Baptist Historical Society and Regent's Park College, Oxford have given constant encouragement and support. Karl Heinz Walter and his staff co-operated by supplying research material, and allowing Susan Mills, the College librarian, to photocopy minutes and European Baptist Press Service items. I am also grateful to the Prague Seminary for permitting two former colleagues of the Baptist Union of Great Britain, Pamela Neville and Dora Smith, to explore Gerhard Claas's files on my behalf. Roger Hayden and Faith and Brian Bowers have attended to the technicalities of editing, collating the index, assembling photographs, and preparing the book for publication. Karl Heinz Walter helpfully suggested some additions and corrections. Stella Hambleton, a former history teacher, also read each chapter as it was completed. To all these friends I say a warm 'Thank you'.

Of course, I bear full responsibility for the interpretation of events and documents, and for any errors and omissions. I sincerely hope that nothing I have written will offend. It has been written in good faith, as I have tried to reflect disagreements and differences of conviction as honestly and charitably as possible. It is my hope and prayer that this book will be a worthy record of fifty years of European Baptist work and witness, affirming the amazing grace of God at work among us, and encouraging future generations, as they carry this heritage forward, to go on crossing the boundaries in the power of the Spirit and the name of Christ.

Bernard Green
1999

ABBREVIATIONS USED

ABC/IM	American Baptist Churches/International Ministries
ABFMS	American Baptist Foreign Missionary Society
ABTS	Arab Baptist Theological Seminary
AUCECB	All-Union Council of Evangelical Christians-Baptists
BFT	Baptist Federation of Tirana
BMS	Baptist Missionary Society
BR-E	Baptist Response-Europe
BTS	Baptist Theological Seminary
B & T	Books and Translations
BU	Baptist Union
BUGBI	Baptist Union of Great Britain and Ireland
BUGB	Baptist Union of Great Britain
BWA	Baptist World Alliance
CBF	Co-operative Baptist Fellowship
CBIM	Canadian Baptist International Ministries
CCECB	Council of Churches of Evangelical Christians-Baptists
CCEC	Commission of the Churches for the European Community
CEC	Conference of European Churches
CIS	Commonwealth of Independent States
EBF	European Baptist Federation
EBC	European Baptist Convention
EBM	European Baptist Mission
EBM/MASA	European Baptist Mission/Missionary Actions in South America
EBMS	European Baptist Missionary Society
EBPS	European Baptist Press Service
EBTTC	European Baptist Theological Teachers' Conference
EBWU	European Baptist Women's Union
E & E	Evangelism & Education
EEC	European Economic Community
EU	European Union

FDR	Federal Republic of Germany (West Germany)
FMB	Foreign Mission Board
FTM	FEED THE MINDS
GDR	German Democratic Republic (East Germany)
IBCA	International Baptist Co-operation in Albania
IBLA	International Baptist Lay Academy
IBTS	International Baptist Theological Seminary
IME	Institute for Mission and Evangelism
NATO	North Atlantic Treaty Organization
SBC	Southern Baptist Convention
SBC/FMB	Southern Baptist Convention/Foreign Mission Board
SBC/IMB	Southern Baptist Convention/International Mission Board
SCM	Student Christian Movement
SITE	(a) Summer Institute of Theological Education
	(b) Seminary Institute for Training and Education
TAG/BWA	Theological Assistance Group/Baptist World Alliance
TAG-E	Theological Assistance Group - Europe
TWR	Trans-World Radio
UECB	Union of Evangelical Christians-Baptists
USA	United States of America
USSR	Union of Soviet Socialist Republics
UK	United Kingdom
WCC	World Council of Churches

PART ONE

THE STORY

1

THE BEGINNING

When the first world gathering of Baptists assembled in London in July 1905 the Baptist World Alliance was formally constituted. Its membership was to be open to any Union, Convention or Association of Baptist Churches. Its aims were to enable Baptists world-wide to express their oneness in Jesus Christ, their God and Saviour, and to develop fellowship, co-operative mission and mutual support. From the beginning European Baptists held a prominent place in its work. The first President was Dr John Clifford, a renowned British preacher and leader from London; one of the two Secretaries was the Revd J. H. Shakespeare who was General Secretary of the Baptist Union of Great Britain and Ireland. Among the twenty-four vice-presidents, chosen to represent the international nature of the Baptist family, were ten Europeans.[1] From then until the present time European Baptists have made a considerable contribution to the Alliance. They have also received much encouragement through shared resources and personnel in times of suffering, in reconstruction after years of war, and in missionary endeavour.

THE FIRST STEPS

Within a few months of the Alliance's birth discussions began about the possibility of an all-European Baptist Conference. The idea was enthusiastically welcomed, and plans were made for such an event to be held in Berlin in 1908. J. H. Shakespeare enlisted two gifted young ministers to help in organizing the conference. They had both come to faith and grown up spiritually in Dr Clifford's church in Paddington, London. Their names, James Henry Rushbrooke and Newton Marshall, were to become well known in future years.[2]

Berlin was an inspired choice for the venue, because this was 'Oncken country'. Johann Gerhard Oncken was a young German evangelical preacher, who sought believers' baptism from an American missionary in Hamburg in 1834 and formed the first Baptist Church in Germany. His missionary influence spread far and wide, until he was described as the father of German and Continental Baptists. The pioneering work of Oncken and his colleagues led to the growth of Baptist congregations from the North Sea eastwards to the Ural Mountains, and from the North Cape southwards to the Balkans.[3] There were, of course, other influences in the development of Baptist life throughout Europe, such as the Anabaptists of the sixteenth century, the Dutch Mennonites and British Baptists of the seventeenth century, and American, German, Swedish and British missionaries working with Baptist groups which came to birth in the nineteenth century.

It is important to recognize the nature of this process, because the facts show that Baptist churches and unions throughout Europe have genuine European roots. Frequently, Baptists in some countries have been, and still are, denied official recognition on the grounds that they are a foreign sect with an alien culture. Traditional churches such as the Orthodox and Roman Catholics, apparently fearing their popular growth, have caricatured them as a new and undesirable invasion in countries where they themselves claim to be the truly national church. Such a claim is false: the evidence clearly indicates that Baptists have been rooted in most European countries for many years.

This was obvious when many hundreds of delegates from sixteen European lands assembled for the first European Baptist Conference in Berlin from 29 August to 3 September 1908. Reports described it as an inspiring occasion. People who had suffered hardship for their faith found new heart through meeting with their brothers and sisters in Christ from other lands. For all who were there it was a living experience of the power of Christ and the Gospel to cross the boundaries of nation, language and culture. Among the decisions made were three requests addressed to the Baptist World Alliance: to recognize Europe as a primary mission field, to assist in the building of new churches, and to work for the establishment of a European theological seminary.

There was no intention that the Alliance should become a missionary body or undertake what was the proper responsibility of local churches or national unions. What happened was that a new close relationship was forged between European Baptists. Instead of working or struggling in isolation they would now be able to help one another and strive together to meet the deep spiritual needs of Europe.[4] A year before the Berlin Conference Dr Newton Marshall had described its potential in the following words:

> ...a Congress which is to witness to all Europe as to our faith and to gather together from all over Europe into a strong and united body those who share our name, and make plans for a forward movement in every country of Europe. This then we need above all things - that touch of God in our hearts that shall make us live the apostolic life, so that we too may do something for the Europe Christ desires to save.[5]

A second European Conference took place in Stockholm in 1913. The presence of over 3,000 delegates at the conference sessions and an estimated crowd of 20,000 at a public rally in the Haga Park showed how the enthusiasm generated in Berlin had grown. Whereas the former event had emphasized the claims of civil and religious liberty, and urged the importance of being loyal citizens in each country where Baptists lived, this one was distinctly evangelistic. Afterwards, a circular letter was sent to Baptist churches throughout Europe, reminding them of their calling to win men and women for Christ, and urging them to be 'centres of salvation and light'.

Without doubt, the closer bonds of fellowship and the stimulation of wider experience were mutually enriching. Differences of conviction inevitably arose, but these could now be honestly faced. At Stockholm J. H. Rushbrooke spoke about internal dangers which could hinder Baptist work. He warned against Baptist isolationism that failed to appreciate what they held in common with other Christians. He also discouraged a tendency for their insistence on the separation of Church and State to become an excuse for opting out of responsibility for public and social affairs. Thirdly, he pleaded for more tolerance and understanding between Baptists whose national cultures and politics were radically different. This was wise counsel, especially if, as appeared likely, proposals to create some form of European organization within the Baptist World Alliance met with general support. A third European conference was in mind for 1918, and invitations had already been received to hold it in Rome or St Petersburg.

EUROPE IN CONFLICT

Sadly, these prospects suffered a severe setback. For some time war clouds had been gathering over European politics. Discord grew with an irresistible momentum, until in 1914 war broke out between Britain and Germany. As the conflict spread, many nations were drawn into four years of mortal conflict with disastrous effects. The prime of Europe's manhood was decimated. Widespread destruction left ruin, hunger and poverty for countless people. Christians found themselves on opposing sides, taking up arms against each other. Within the Baptist family this must have caused untold agonies for those who so recently had stood hand-in-hand at Stockholm, singing 'Blest be the tie that binds our hearts in Christian love'.

After the war Europe was a radically different continent. Substantial relief and reconstruction were needed. Territories which had caused past conflict were annexed by newly created states, made up of different nationalities and therefore multilingual and multicultural. Confusion, despair, hatred and bitterness were rife, and turned out to be the seeds of further strife in coming years. In 1919 the Baptist World Alliance arranged for an extensive tour of Central and Eastern Europe by Dr C. A. Brooks, the European representative of the American Baptist Foreign Mission Society, and the Revd J. H. Rushbrooke of England. Their task was to discover the best ways of giving assistance to Baptists in the various lands.

In July of the following year seventy-two representatives from Baptist Unions and Conventions in the USA, Canada, Australia,

Britain and eighteen European countries met at Baptist Church House, London, to receive their report. In it Brooks and Rushbrooke listed six needs to be urgently considered at the conference:

- Relief of distress caused by the war.
- Provision of training facilities for ministers, evangelists and other church workers.
- Creation and distribution of all sorts of Christian literature.
- Financial aid for pastors and evangelists.
- Provision of church buildings and plant of various kinds.
- Co-ordination of European Baptist activities.

After several days of intense discussions, during which many present were able to give first-hand accounts of their own situations, five proposals were agreed for submission to Baptist Unions and Mission Boards around the world. The following are brief summaries of the proposals:

1. To plan relief for Baptist Churches in stricken areas.
2. To meet the urgent need for trained ministry in Eastern Europe.
3. To extend Baptist work in Europe, especially in view of the many casualties which had seriously reduced church membership and ministerial figures, and also the many destroyed church buildings. In order to avoid wasteful overlap, it was agreed to establish regional mandates for only one Baptist Union or group of Unions to operate in each country.
4. To make representations to relevant government authorities over religious persecution in Romania.
5. To appoint a full-time Commissioner to co-ordinate European work and act as a Baptist ambassador throughout the Continent.[6]

After approving all five proposals the delegates unanimously appointed J. H. Rushbrooke as the Commissioner.

A common temptation for Christian organizations is to become inward-looking and concerned mainly for self-preservation. The Alliance deliberately turned away from such an attitude by categorically stating that their relief work must go beyond denominational boundaries. In the spirit of Christ they offered help to all in need, irrespective of religious or racial differences. Significant steps had now been taken to recognize and express a corporate European Baptist identity. It was marked by a strong sense of fellowship through which shared experience, more travel and communication, and mutual support produced encouragement and confidence. Relationships which the war had shattered were steadily restored. Damaged church buildings were repaired and new ones built in many lands. Ten new theological seminaries and preachers' schools were founded, and the resultant increase in trained ministries led to effective evangelism and church growth. Many people came to faith in Christ and the number of believers' baptisms increased dramatically; so much so, that in the Baltic States the secular press began to comment on the spiritual movement in society. In Germany and Czechoslovakia programmes of publishing and distributing bibles, testaments and all sorts of Christian literature were undertaken.. The new Commissioner and other officers of the Baptist World Alliance openly championed the cause of persecuted Christians, notably in Romania and Russia. World Baptists mounted a massive relief operation during a severe famine in Russia during the early 1920s. By 1924 Baptist Churches existed in twenty-six of the twenty-nine European countries.[7]

No other denomination had such a comprehensive European presence. Two series of regional Baptist conferences in 1926 and 1930 played an important part in consolidating the rapid progress now being made. In one sense the First World War had been a terrible disaster leaving many unhappy memories and huge problems. Yet, in another sense, it providentially opened doors of unexpected opportunity for the healing of relationships and co-operative Christian mission. This strengthened Baptist work by giving the Baptist World Alliance a clearer understanding of its world-wide mission, and by creating a stronger Baptist identity throughout Europe. Dr John MacNeill, the Alliance President, said in 1930: 'The World Alliance would have fully justified its existence if only for the sense of brotherhood it has created and fostered among European Baptists.'

However, more trouble was to come. In the religious sphere the established national churches interpreted Baptist evangelism as illegal proselytism and pressurized governments to restrict it. Many pastors and church members suffered persecution and imprisonment. In Russia atheistic communism waged a continuous ideological battle against all forms of religion. In the political sphere the menace of rearmament and the rise of harsh dictatorships led the nations once again to the brink of war. In Germany there was the growth of National Socialism and the rise to power of Adolf Hitler. Benito Mussolini established his Fascist regime in Italy. Russian Communism clearly had imperialistic ambitions and was soon to embark on its conquest of Eastern and Central Europe. In Spain General Franco's revolt brought a reign of military terror and air blitzes, as well as launching a period of religious persecution for all evangelicals. In the summer of 1937 Dr G. W. Truett, the Baptist World Alliance President, and Dr Rushbrooke held another series of ten regional conferences in Europe, to strengthen Baptist fellowship in face of the mounting tensions and to generate spiritual confidence. The Second World War broke out in 1939, leading to six years of vast destruction, death and suffering. The continent was soon in total chaos. Military battles raged on and on with many casualties: air blitzes with saturation fire bombing destroyed major cities, causing unprecedented deaths among civilians and creating thousands of wandering refugees. Christian churches lost buildings, people, leaders and equipment to such an extent that it would take years to recover from the loss. Baptists were among the many who in various countries suffered at the hands of the German Gestapo, and then had to face the iron control of their Communist 'deliverers'.[8]

A NEW BEGINNING

As soon as the war ended Dr Rushbrooke visited Denmark and other parts of Northern Europe to offer the Alliance's support and friendship, and to begin the task of restoring broken relationships. When the war had been in progress for only a year, he had challenged Baptists wherever he could to prepare for peace. There would be many barriers to cross, and in the name of Christ they had to be crossed. Future peace and the unity of the Baptist, as well as the general human, family could only be secured if justice, co-operation and a willingness to make a new start together could be accepted by governments, churches and individuals.[9] In 1943 he persuaded the Alliance Executive to allow him to appoint an Emergency Relief Committee that would prepare plans for Baptist relief and reconstruction in the war-devastated lands once the conflict was ended.

He also urged the Alliance to hold a World Baptist Congress in Europe at the earliest opportunity. The Danish Baptist Union invited them to hold it in Copenhagen; the date was fixed for the summer of 1947. Uppermost in his mind was the creation of a European Baptist organization to unite Baptists in one reconciled body, caring for one another, learning from one another, and working together for the evangelization of their continent.

Unfortunately, he did not live to see his dream become reality. On 1 February 1947, the day before the annual Baptist World Alliance Sunday, he died of a stroke. Like Moses of old he had led his people to the edge of the promised land but could not enter it with them. Dr W. O. Lewis, who was appointed to succeed him, became his Joshua to bring the dream to fulfilment.[10]

The 1947 Congress in Copenhagen was an important landmark in European Baptist history, for it set in motion the process which led to the founding of the European Baptist Federation. The first step was to call a meeting in London for European leaders on 13-17 August 1948. The agenda included such major issues as religious freedom, post-war relief, theological education and evangelism. Two highly significant announcements were made during the proceedings. The first informed delegates that the Southern Baptist Convention of the USA had decided to donate $200,000 to establish a Baptist Theological Seminary in Rüschlikon, near Zürich, Switzerland. The second revealed the intention of the Baptist World Alliance women's group to form a European Baptist Women's Union. Both decisions were to have far-reaching effects for good in Europe for years to come, as later chapters will show. At this point in the story the primary item of interest is the recommendation which the meeting wholeheartedly approved. It stated:

> That the Baptists of Europe be encouraged to plan for a closer fellowship between the various national bodies, and that European members of the Executive Committee of the BWA and representatives of the co-operating mission boards and the Secretaries of the BWA constitute a planning committee to form a European Baptist Committee on Co-operation to further Baptist work in Europe.

A Committee of Seven was appointed to prepare the ground and to serve until the European Baptist Committee on Co-operation was established. The seven people named were the Revds Henry Cook (Great Britain), Jacob Meister (Germany), Manfredi Ronchi (Italy), Henri Vincent (France), Emil Pfister (Switzerland), A. A. Hardenberg (Holland) and the Revd Dr Bredahl Petersen (Denmark). Dr W. O. Lewis, as an Associate Secretary of the Alliance, was an *ex officio* member of the committee and was to serve as its convenor.

An outline plan of co-operation, submitted at the London meeting, expressed the hope that the new arrangements would make it possible to give advice on missionary work undertaken by various Baptist bodies in and out of Europe, and to promote evangelism, Sunday School work, work among women and young people, and other similar activities. The Baptist World Alliance Committee on Evangelism underlined this hope in a letter a day or two later, stating that the supreme aim must be to win people for Christ, to plant new churches, and to strengthen existing Baptist work through fostering fellowship and evangelism. Soon after the conference Henry Cook sent to all European Baptist Unions a circular letter giving details of the Committee of Seven and a copy of the provisional plan, asking them to study it and send their comments to the London office of the BWA by 1 February 1949.

Some interesting issues were raised in the letters of response. Samuel Vila of Spain asked what would be the position of Missions not related to the Alliance but active in Spanish Baptist Churches. Alfons Sundquist, on behalf of the Swedish-speaking Baptist Union of Finland, pledged their full support but warned that they were a very small group and would not be able to offer much. E. Pfister of the Swiss Union suggested the inclusion of a Confession of Faith for member unions to accept. However, the Swiss Baptists did not insist on this but acknowledged that it was a matter for each local church to decide. Positive support was given by the Unions in Denmark, Norway, Sweden, Germany, Holland, France, Italy, Switzerland and Great Britain. Encouraged by this support, the Committee of Seven met again on 8 October 1949 in the new seminary at Rüschlikon. Representatives of the Mission Boards of the American Northern and Southern Baptist Conventions, who were already working in Europe, shared their discussions. They drew up a draft constitution for distribution to as many Unions as could be reached, with an invitation to appoint representatives to a Council meeting in Paris in the following year. At that meeting the constitution would be formally adopted and what was now to be called the European Baptist Federation would be established.

The original constitution was as follows:

Preamble
The suggestion to form a European Baptist committee on co-operation arose out of the work of the Baptist World Alliance and directly from recommendations made during meetings held under its auspices in London in August, 1948.

I. Name
The European Baptist committee on co-operation shall henceforth be known as the "European Baptist Federation".

It is not a super-union with powers above the national **Baptist Unions**, but a federation for co-operation between the various European Baptist Unions. The Federation fully respects the independence of national Unions and of local churches. The Federation welcomes the participation of the various missionary societies, board and committees regularly working in Europe.

II. Purpose

The purpose of the Federation is: (1) to promote fellowship among Baptist in Europe; (2) to stimulate and co-ordinate evangelism in Europe; (3) to provide a board of consultation and planning for Baptist mission work in Europe; (4) to stimulate and co-ordinate where desirable the missionary work of European Baptists outside Europe.

III. Membership

The members of the European Baptist Federation shall be those European Unions of Baptist churches which are members of the Baptist World Alliance. The Federation shall work through (a) a General Council, and (b) an Executive Committee.

The **General Council** shall consist of: (1) One representative from each Baptist Union in Europe belonging to the Baptist World Alliance chosen by the Union or its committees; (2) one representative from each Baptist missionary society or board or committee working regularly in Europe; (3) the Associate General Secretary of the Baptist World Alliance; (4) the president and secretary of the European Baptist Women's Union and the European Baptist Youth organisation as well as similar officers of such auxiliary organisations as the General Council shall from time to time approve; (5) the Executive Committee of the Baptist World Alliance shall be asked to nominate five of its European members to serve on the General Council of the European Baptist Federation.

The **Executive Committee** shall have authority to carry on the work of the Federation between meetings of the General Council, and shall consist of seven members appointed by the General Council from its members.

IV. Ways and Means

The Federation shall seek to achieve its purpose by such means as the following: (1) General conferences of all the Baptist Unions of Europe; (2) regional conferences; (3) international training courses and fellowship meetings; (4) the exchange of ministers, evangelists, theological teachers, students and other leaders in various church activities.

V. Alteration of the Constitution
  This Constitution can only be altered at a meeting of the General Council, called after the proposed alteration has been referred to member Unions, and then only by a two-thirds majority of those present and voting.

  In addition to agreeing the Constitution, the committee decided to prepare a report for the Eighth Baptist World Congress in Cleveland, USA in 1950. They wanted Dr W. O. Lewis to become the Secretary/Treasurer of the Federation as part of his work as BWA Associate Secretary. Although the Alliance was housed in a new office in Washington instead of London, they requested that the London office be retained as his base. They also indicated their wish to nominate for election Dr Bredahl Petersen (Denmark) as the Federation's President and the Revd Henry Cook (England) as the Vice-president, with the presidency normally being for two years. Finally they arranged the first meeting of the Council in Paris (20-21 October 1950), and the first European Conference in Copenhagen (early August 1951).

THE EUROPEAN BAPTIST FEDERATION IS BORN

It was with eager anticipation that delegates gathered at 48 Rue de Lille, Paris on Friday, 20 October 1950 for an highly significant event in modern Baptist history.[11] Dr Lewis outlined the steps which had led to the formation of the EBF, starting from the first all-European Baptist conference in Berlin in 1908. He presented the Constitution for adoption and then declared the European Baptist Federation duly formed. The first decision was to accept the proposed nominations for the Federation's officers. Dr Petersen took the chair and guided the meeting through a number of necessary decisions. An Executive Committee was appointed, comprising the Revds Henri Vincent (France), A. A. Hardenberg (Holland), Manfredi Ronchi (Italy) and Dr

Hans Luckey (Germany), together with the officers. Revised dates for future meetings were also agreed - the next Council to be in Hamburg, 2-6 August 1951, and the first all-European Conference in Copenhagen, 29 July - 3 August 1952.

On the second day of the Paris meetings delegates turned their attention to priorities for European Baptist work in the next few years. The choices they made quickly revealed the new impetus which the Federation could give. In a remarkable gesture of reconciliation, the meeting recommended that Baptists of Europe should unite to help rebuild the bombed Bohmkenstrasse Church in Hamburg as a memorial to Oncken. Another visionary idea was to aim to open work in key places where no Baptist churches existed. Strasbourg was to be a strategic centre as the headquarters of the Council of Europe. It was therefore agreed to ask the French and Swiss Baptists to seek someone with knowledge of French and German to pioneer work there. Once a church was established European and American Baptists would provide financial support for the first few years. In order to take new opportunities in Spain an appeal for help was sent to Hispanic Baptists in the USA. The urgent needs of the small Union of Finnish-speaking Baptists in Finland were referred to the Scandinavian Baptist Council. There was general agreement that the Federation should appeal for aid for the completion of the new Theological School in Oslo. The minutes also reported that for the first time the needs of Baptists in Eastern Europe were mentioned.

All these choices were living expressions of the spirit of unity which was growing again after the tragic separations of war. Boundaries were being crossed in the name of Christ whose saving work included breaking down walls of partition between the nations. Out of this experience came an urge to pray. An Annual Day of Prayer for Europe was initiated for the last Sunday in October, the Sunday nearest to the day when the Federation was formed. Henry Cook undertook to maintain contact between meetings by producing a regular news bulletin for the member Unions. There would be no shortage of news to share, for these were days of new beginnings. Several other initiatives in addition to the birth of the EBF carried the promise of future growth. The Theological Seminary in Rüschlikon established under the presidency of Dr Josef Nordenhaug already had its first group of students in residence. The Federation President, Dr Bredahl Petersen, spoke positively about the partnership between the EBF and the Seminary in coming years. Many saw Rüschlikon as an ideal centre for conferences and courses for women, men, young people, lay leaders, preachers and pastors.

When Newton Marshall published his booklet, *Europe - the Desire of the Christ*, in 1907 he said that Europe was as important to Christ then as ever. He shared with his readers the vision of centres of civilization becoming centres for Christ - Rome, Paris, Berlin, St Petersburg and Madrid. To the Berlin Conference of 1908 he sent this challenge:

> Our call is to work by whatever means are possible that Europe may be reclaimed for our Master.

The rest of this book will attempt to explore the ways in which through the first fifty years of the European Baptist Federation our Baptist people have tried to be faithful to that calling.

CHAPTER NOTES

CHAPTER ONE   The Beginning

1   Their names were the Revd H. Novotny (Prague), the Revd M. Larsen (Copenhagen), Pasteur R.Saillens (Paris), Herr J. G. Lehmann (Germany), the Revd B. Roeles (Netherlands), Mr G. White (England), Pastor Ohrn (Norway), Baron Uixkiull (Russia), Signor Paschetto (Italy) and the Revd K. O. Broady (Sweden).

2   Sadly Newton Marshall died from typhoid in 1914 at the age of forty-two. He had become highly respected and was expected to play a significant role in British and European Baptist affairs.

3   J. H. Rushbrooke, 'Baptists in Continental Europe', *Baptist Quarterly,* 1, pp.197-9.

4   This point was developed in an article by Dr Erik Rudén, European Secretary of the BWA, in *The Watchman Examiner,* 14 March 1963, p.208.

5   Newton H. Marshall, *Europe - the Desire of the Christ,* Kingsgate Press, 1907, p.12.

6   The report of the London Conference was published by the Kingsgate Press - *Baptist Work in Europe.* See also Bernard Green, *Tomorrow's Man: A biography of J. H. Rushbrooke,* Baptist Historical Society, 1997, pp.80-84.

7   The three exceptions were Albania, Greece and Turkey.

8   A quantity of letters and documents giving personal details exists in the Angus Library, Regent's Park College, Oxford.

9   See Bernard Green, op.cit., p.183.

10   W. O. Lewis had served for some years in Europe as a representative of the American Baptist Foreign Missionary Society.

11   The official record of this meeting is in the first minute book of the Federation, pp. 2-9. It includes a list of all who were present and the greetings received from around the world. The founding Unions were Denmark, Finland, France, Germany, Great Britain and Ireland, Holland, Italy, Norway, Portugal, Spain, Sweden and Switzerland.

THE EARLY YEARS

When Winston Churchill chaired the Congress of Europe in The Hague in May 1948 he said with almost prophetic fervour:

> We must proclaim the mission and design of a United Europe whose moral conception will win the respect and gratitude of mankind, and whose physical strength will be such that none will dare molest her tranquil sway. I hope to see a Europe where men and women of every country will think of being European as of belonging to their native land, and wherever they go in this wide domain will truly feel "Here I am at home".

He did not suggest that this would be easy; but his words expressed a noble idealism which was appropriate for a continent ravaged by two horrendous wars within the space of thirty-one years.

Through the lens of political realism the European scene looked very different. Many thousands of people were not at home there. The Nazis had uprooted many by their forced migrations. Stalin had mercilessly deported vast populations in his policy of Russian expansion. The massive destruction of towns and cities in Germany and its occupied countries, first by invading enemies and then by the victorious onslaught of the Russian and Western Allied forces, created swelling tides of refugees and displaced persons.

After the war political rivalry between East and West grew intense. Several major issues became divisive: for example, the future of Germany and the general division of Europe. Russia viewed with understandable alarm the prospect of a strong and rehabilitated Germany. The Western powers saw a re-established but well-controlled Germany as a necessary defence against possible Russian encroachment westwards. The generous Marshall Aid Plan of the USA increased American influence in European affairs, and led eventually to the formation of the North Atlantic Treaty Organization (NATO). In response to this Russia imposed a strong control over the countries which embraced Communism in Central and Eastern Europe. This led to a rival power bloc of the so-called Warsaw Pact Countries. Germany, as an occupied country, was to feel the impact of this growing East-West confrontation. In 1949 the German nation was divided into two totally separate states - East Germany, which was under Russian control, became the German Democratic Republic within the Warsaw Pact; West Germany, under the control of the Western Allies, became the Federal German Republic within NATO. The city of Berlin, originally divided into four zones which were controlled by the British, French, Americans and Russians, was within the East German territory and therefore always under political threat. This polarization between East and West led inescapably to the so-called Cold War which was to last for almost forty years.[1]

This was the climate in which the European Baptist Federation grew up and came of age. One could not describe it as a helpful environment, but the challenge of it produced courageous spiritual determination among Baptists in both East and West. As the Apostle Paul once testified,[2] and as the history of the Christian Church often confirms, these adverse circumstances turned out for the furtherance of the Gospel.

Early in the twentieth century when the Baptist World Alliance was born and Europe became a major focus for its work, J. H. Rushbrooke began to speak and write with enthusiasm about the importance of European Baptists in the world church. With an optimism similar to Winston Churchill's he longed for the day when European Baptists would be linked inseparably together, whatever the political climate, and he committed himself to Europe as an essential part of home and family with these words:

We belong with these; we are closer to them than to any other.[3]

This spirit of idealism marked the early days of the European Baptist Federation but, just as we have noted in the political realm, there were strong tensions and hesitations. Could former enemies be trusted? How could war victims express love for those who took part in inflicting their sufferings? Were all representatives at united Baptist gatherings genuine brothers and sisters in Christ, or were some under-cover agents for their national governments? Some were heard to say: 'Yes, we will meet with them, but we are not prepared to pray with them.' Others confessed their inability to be in a meeting with Baptists from one-time enemy nations and not feel animosity against them.

In telling or hearing the story of the EBF, such inner struggles need to be understood. Only then can we recognize the triumphs of God's amazing grace which helped so many Baptist Christians to cross the boundaries separating them, and to discover together the truth expressed in a hymn frequently used in international Christian gatherings:

> In Christ there is no east or west,
> in him no south or north,
> but one great fellowship of love
> throughout the whole wide earth.[4]

THE HAMBURG COUNCIL 1951

The next meeting of the Federation's Council was on 2-4 August 1951 in Hamburg. Delegates could not escape the impact of the war damage suffered by the German Baptists. Seventy-four church buildings, including the Hamburg Theological Seminary, had been totally destroyed; a further one hundred and ninety were seriously damaged. Over fifty pastors were killed and eleven were missing, believed dead. Although this news saddened members of the Council, there was also a sense of joy that they were able to hold the meetings in the rebuilt seminary. Much of the building work had been undertaken by young men now released from war, and only too willing to devote their enthusiasm to raising again the buildings in which they would train for their future ministry.[5] Appropriately, theological education and ministerial training had a high profile in the Council agenda, through reports not only from Hamburg, but also from the various Baptist colleges and seminaries in Denmark, Rüschlikon, Italy, Spain and

Great Britain. As had been discovered after the 1914-18 war, the establishment and progress of the network of training schools throughout the European Baptist family was crucial if the spiritual needs and opportunities of the post-war situation were to be adequately met.

Reports from member Unions of the Federation told of steady recovery from the tragedies of war, and bore clear witness to the value of growing co-operation. Speeches of support and commitment within the wider family of the Baptist World Alliance were made by Dr E. A. Bell (the American Baptist Foreign Missionary Society), Dr J. D. Franks (Foreign Mission Board of the Southern Baptist Convention), Mr H. Streuber (BWA Relief Committee) and the Revd H. V. Larcombe (Continental Committee of the Baptist Union of Great Britain and Ireland). There is also considerable documentary evidence of generous help being given by the Scandinavian Baptists and by the smaller Unions along the western coasts of Europe, who had themselves been victims of the war. One notable example of this had been seen at the World Baptist Congress in Copenhagen in 1947. Many delegates came poorly clothed and emaciated by war-time hunger. Clothes and food collected by Scandinavians were brought forward with the offering at one of the opening rallies. They were dedicated to God in the name of Jesus; needy delegates were invited to help themselves after the meeting. One German delegate almost choked with tears, whereupon a Danish delegate put his arms around him, a moving symbol of reconciliation in Christ. An equally remarkable gesture was made by Danish Baptists who travelled to the border to meet German delegates with clothing, so that they could feel more presentable on arrival at the Congress.[6] Dr W. O Lewis was now able to report on the many urgent relief projects in Germany, especially among the displaced multitudes. Dr F. Townley Lord, the BWA President, described all this activity as the linking of both sides in the war into 'an alliance of loving service in the name of the Lord.'[7] More crossed boundaries!

But there were still more to cross. The Council was delighted to hear a letter read from the Polish Baptists, with the personal signatures of twenty-seven leaders. Though unable to attend the Council, they wished their fellow Baptists to know of their desire to be one with them. Despite many efforts to make contact with Russian Baptists and clear the way for them to come to Hamburg, none were able to be there and no message was received. But there was a ray of hope on the horizon. A Quaker delegation had recently visited Russia and returned to Britain with information about 3,000 Baptist churches, 400,000 members and maybe as many as three million adherents. Baptist leaders there had asked them to convey greetings to British Baptists, expressing their eagerness to form living links with them. When this news reached the Council there was a spontaneous move to make it a matter for urgent prayer. If such links could be formed there was a strong hope that fellowship in Christ would cross even the most resistant ideological boundaries.

Two strategic issues arising from the Paris Council in 1950 were taken a stage further. Progress was being made for establishing a church in Strasbourg, but now the vision of planting churches in key centres had also put Brussels, Greece and Iceland on the agenda. Meanwhile reports of investigations about overseas missionary work surprised delegates by the wide range being undertaken by individual Unions and shared by several. The question of possible co-ordination was raised. It was agreed to begin discussions about forming a European Baptist Missionary Society.

Looking ahead, the Council approved arrangements for the first EBF Conference (what we now know as the First European Baptist Congress). It was to be in Copenhagen, 29 July to 3 August 1952. The theme would be: 'Baptists and the Evangelisation of Europe'. In order to make it as comprehensive an event as possible, meetings of the Council, the European Baptist Women's Union, the Young People's Committee and sessions for both ministers and laymen were to be arranged.

In September 1951 a special message was sent to all European Baptists in the name of the Hamburg Council. It spoke of encouraging reports, close fellowship and plans for greater co-operation. Preliminary details were given about the forthcoming Congress. Many difficulties emphasized the need to undertake 'a great crusade for the salvation of Europe from its suffering, despair and sin'. This would call for 'unswerving loyalty to our Baptist testimony', claiming for every man and woman freedom of conscience and the right to a rich and fuller life. The message ended with the note of optimism which had been stirred at Hamburg. It urged Baptists everywhere to see the present time as a God-given opportunity: 'An hour of destiny for Europe'.

Henry Cook caught this spirit in an article he wrote for the *Baptist Times*. He reported that Baptists now existed in every European country except Albania. Many were isolated and their churches small; association with them was of crucial importance. He stressed how much this underlined the value of the European Baptist Federation and how vital it made a good attendance at the Copenhagen Congress. He went on to pose an interesting question: '*What if the Iron Curtain lifts?*' Invitations had already gone out to all Eastern European Baptist groups. If, in the providence of God, the curtain lifted, Baptists from Russia, Poland, Czechoslovakia, Romania and Bulgaria would be free to attend. So, in faith, two plans for the programme were being prepared, to allow for either contingency.[8]

THE FIRST EUROPEAN BAPTIST CONGRESS 1952

Expectations were high when the Congress assembled in Copenhagen on 29 July 1952. Early in the programme Dr W. O. Lewis spoke on 'Our Unity'. He referred to common beliefs held without a binding credal statement. Baptists had always feared that to be required to accept and recite a creed was no guarantee of unity; in fact, it could be divisive. He went on to describe what many would see as the heart of the Federation's life then and now. Common life and witness make Baptists one. When they meet to pray and sing, a true spirit of togetherness is felt. When they work together differences melt away. Therefore, it is vital to stay together, and to do their utmost to heal already existing divisions and differences of conviction. He voiced his own conviction that being together was possibly the most important aspect of meetings of Council, Congress or other conferences, especially for the smaller Unions. But he also warned that no-one must simply be content with meeting; action must follow.

The presidential address was delivered by Dr Bredahl Petersen, on the Congress theme, 'Baptists and the Evangelisation of Europe'. He asserted that neither 'Statechurchism' nor 'Sacramentalism' had succeeded in bringing the Gospel to the people of Europe. In the midst of rampant materialism and militant atheism the European Baptist Federation had a unique task, and the opportunity to exercise freedom. It existed to promote fellowship which respected freedom of conscience and interpretation. He issued a challenge to those with the necessary skills to explore the potential of a European Baptist Radio.

Although invitations had been sent to Baptists in Poland, Russia, Czechoslovakia and the Balkan States, none came. But greetings were received, and that in itself was a significant sign of intention and hope for coming years. The officers of the Federation also hoped that their invitations would assure their Eastern colleagues that they were seen as partners in Christ's mission to the continent.

There was a full programme with many participants - Swedish, German and Danish choirs, a Danish band, the Hamburg youth choir, the European Women's Union, and representatives of the German tent missions which were proving such a fruitful means of evangelism. On one evening the women met in Kristuskirken (the 1st Baptist Church in Copenhagen), the men in Købnerkirken (the 2nd Baptist Church), Sunday School Teachers in Fredskirken (the 3rd Baptist Church), and the young people in Gerbrandskolen. In those four gatherings twenty-five different speakers and leaders took part in two and a half hours! During the closing Festival Service Dr Henry Cook was inducted as President for the next two years, Dr Manfredi Ronchi of Italy was appointed Vice-president, and Dr W. O Lewis received an illuminated address to mark his 75th birthday and his twenty-five years of service to European Baptists.

Questions are frequently asked about the value of such large and often exhausting assemblies. Does anything of lasting worth result from them? Answers vary considerably, but without doubt there are always personal testimonies of life-long friendships formed, of lessons learned with transforming effects, and of inspiring moments which are interpreted as the work of the Holy Spirit. At Copenhagen a young minister was just beginning his work as the assistant to Dr Bredahl Petersen in the Købnerkirken. He was asked to be responsible for the Congress Office, where he made many contacts with Baptist leaders from all over Europe. He had already been to the Pastors' Conference held at Rüschlikon prior to the Congress and it had deeply impressed him. Seeds were sown that were to grow in a remarkable way. His name was Knud Wümpelmann. He became General Secretary of the Danish Baptist Union in 1964; this made him a member of the EBF Council and introduced him to the biennial conferences of European General Secretaries held at that period. In 1978-9 he was elected President of the Federation. In 1980 he succeeded Dr Gerhard Claas as General Secretary of the EBF until 1988. Then in the 1990s he assumed the presidency of the Baptist World Alliance for five years. He has given outstanding service to the European and world Baptist family. Now in retirement, he gladly acknowledges the immense influence of the European Baptist Federation and the Copenhagen Congress in his early, formative years.

Finance has always seemed to be difficult for the Federation. At the first Council in Hamburg budgetary arrangements were made with the BWA, but within the year only one Union contributed a mere £25.00! Although the EBF was a regional section of the Alliance it was crucial that it take steps towards becoming self-financing. This was made clear at the business session of the Congress. The Alliance cleared the deficit, but they provided no balance to carry forward. Post-war conditions were far from favourable, for very small income was likely to come from the severely restricted currencies of countries in the Communist bloc.

ROME 1953

When the Council next assembled in Rome in September 1953 the financial situation was much stronger. This reflected firm growth in the Federation's work and was evident in the matters before the Council. With joy members were able to welcome a delegation from Yugoslavia for the first time since the war. Another first event was to hold simultaneous meetings of the independent Youth and Women's organizations in the same venue as the Council, and to welcome their representatives to give reports and plan future liaison with the Federation. During the summer a conference of Baptist editors and publishers had taken place at the Rüschlikon Seminary. As a result a recommendation was tabled at Council that a European Baptist Press Service be set up to provide regular news and communication facilities. Members agreed that consultations should take place with the Baptist World Alliance so that specific proposals could be brought to a future meeting. In the meantime an earlier decision to issue a news-sheet was acted on. This would incorporate one page each from the Youth Committee and the European Baptist Women's Union. Whether the BWA was uneasy about the financial implications is difficult to judge: but the matter of a Press Service was left on the table for several years. Instead a new Alliance publication, *The Baptist World*, to be published bi-monthly, was commended. Churches and Unions were also encouraged to read the British *Baptist Times,* which usually gave good coverage to European issues.

Ever since the First World War, German Baptists had wished to return to their missionary work in the French Cameroons, but it was impossible because of the French Government's opposition. A plan was now devised to allow Dutch, Belgian, Austrian, Swiss, German, French and other Baptists to work there together. France was willing to accept German missionaries in that context. We have already discovered the surprise felt during the Hamburg Council at the amount of overseas missionary work being done by European Baptists. Discussion of the Cameroons situation now led to the appointment of a committee to explore the possibility of forming a European Baptist Missionary Society to be responsible for the work in the Cameroons and elsewhere. Henri Vincent, Henry Cook, W. O. Lewis and Herbert Mascher were selected for this task and were charged to bring their findings to the next year's Council. When Council met in Munich in

September 1954 the committee submitted a constitution for such a missionary body, and a special meeting was held at the close of the Council's proceedings to take the necessary steps to establish the European Baptist Missionary Society (EBMS).

Persistent attempts were being made to achieve more contact with Eastern European Baptists. Many restrictions hindered progress, but Dr W. O. Lewis was able to report that he had met with four Russian Baptist pastors during a recent visit to Stockholm. He believed the time was right to send a letter from the Council to the Russian Baptist leaders in Moscow. A draft was presented and approved. This followed a useful exchange of letters in 1951-2 between British and Russian Baptists, in which a proposal had been made for a two-way visit of representatives. However, patience was still required; it was to be another two years before any positive response was received.

Meanwhile in Czechoslovakia four pastors had been arrested and imprisoned on charges of espionage and speaking against the State. Allegations were made about the receipt of finance and gifts from representatives and organizations in hostile western countries; the names of Baptist World Alliance people were publicly quoted. On 29 June a Prague news agency announced that the prisoners had confessed to following instructions from the BWA to carry out spying and sabotage since the close of the war in 1945. It was clear that the Communist authorities had little or no understanding of Baptist organizations. Dr W. O Lewis wrote an article[9] clarifying what the Alliance was, and how its work had been essentially in relief of human need after both world wars. He also explained Baptist patterns of assistance in ministerial training and church building. He categorically affirmed that no information that could endanger Czechoslovakia had ever been sent to or from the Baptist World Alliance.

At one stage a Christmas card carried the news that sixty-one members of the lst Baptist Church in Prague had been arrested. Details were widely reported in the European press and an article was printed in the Russian newspaper, *Pravda*. Members of the Rome Council were informed of approaches made on their behalf to the Czech embassies in Britain and America. The Right Revd G. A. K. Bell, the

Anglican Bishop of Chichester, in his capacity as chairman of the World Council of Churches Executive Committee, had taken up the issue with the Czech Foreign Minister. The WCC had also made a direct approach to the President of the Republic, in order to vouch for the integrity of the Baptist World Alliance (and, therefore, the European Baptist Federation). In a letter to the EBF Council the BWA President, Dr Townley Lord, requested special prayer for the Baptists of Czechoslovakia, at the same time pointing out that 'no curtain can hinder the power of prayer'.

Over the coming years this became an important element in the work of the Federation - to support the persecuted, to act as their advocates, and to champion religious liberty. A later chapter will examine the matter in more detail.[10]

At Rome another Baptist Union joined the Federation - the Baptist Union of Austria. Roman Catholic political domination had prevented the formation of a Baptist church in Austria until 1869. Growth was small until after the two world wars, when moving populations and refugees included Baptists from other lands. They helped to establish enough Baptist churches for a Union to be created in 1953. There were strong links with the German Baptists and the North American Baptist General Conference. Their application for membership probably owed much to the influence of Dr W. O. Lewis, who had been in contact with their leaders for the past four years. He had encouraged them to form a Baptist Relief Committee in Austria, into which he could transfer relief supplies from world Baptists for distribution among displaced people. Another significant factor was the presence among them of pastors and youth workers trained at the Hamburg Youth Training School and Theological Seminary. Here again is evidence of the creative role increasingly being played by the European Baptist Federation, as it drew Baptists together in partnership and mutual help.

NEW OPPORTUNITIES

Towards the end of 1953 a construction project to provide several new buildings at the Rüschlikon Seminary was completed. This considerably increased the facilities available for courses and conferences. Immediately the opportunity was taken to plan a summer programme which included a Men's Conference on 'Religion and Life', a Conference for pastors on 'The Church', and a third for Baptist Theological Teachers. The lists of speakers comprised a wide selection of gifted people from many nations, from both Baptist and ecumenical bodies, and from denominational seminaries, the Swedish Parliament and several universities. This in itself was a crossing of boundaries. It also illustrates the value of a uniting body such as the Federation in being able to bring together for all its members a collection of speakers whom most individual Baptist Unions could not afford. It is no surprise to learn that many European Baptists were beginning to think of Rüschlikon's potential as a Baptist centre for a much wider purpose than a theological seminary.

An even more exciting prospect opened up in early May 1954. A letter from the Russian Baptists to Dr Townley Lord invited him to pay a visit to the Soviet Union with Dr Lewis and one other. The letter was signed by J. I. Zhidkov and A. V. Karev, President and Secretary of the All-Union Council of Evangelical Christians-Baptists (AUCECB), and was the long awaited response to the British Baptists' suggestion of a two-way visit. The letter stated:

> We are deeply convinced that your coming to the Soviet Union and our personal fellowship with you will bring to you and to us the greatest blessings, and serve to the closer union of our Russian Baptist Union with the Baptist World Alliance, as well as to the strengthening of the bonds of friendship between our people and the English nation.

Dr E. A. Payne, General Secretary of the Baptist Union of Great Britain and Ireland, was chosen as the third person. He had been one of the signatories to the British letter in 1952, but clearly the three men would be going as representatives of both the BWA and the EBF.

Their visit was made in June 1954. Before they went Dr Payne suggested that 'fellowship across the barriers of language, race and ideology is not easily achieved.' Was this an expression of personal apprehension? If it was, the welcome they received soon dispelled it. They spent four days in Moscow, six touring to Baptist communities in the Ukraine, two more in Moscow and one in Leningrad. Everywhere they went they received an ecstatic welcome from crowded congregations in what were obviously live and thriving churches. The programme included a meeting with the AUCECB Council as well as an interview with the Government Minister in charge of religious affairs. In Moscow they were present at a service of believers' baptism when twenty-one young people confessed their faith in Christ. They returned with an honest account of the legal restrictions and difficulties being faced by our Baptist people there. They also saw evidence of the strong, faithful witness being borne in a far from easy context.[11]

One surprise was to discover that the Russian Baptists had no contacts with the Baptists of Poland, Czechoslovakia, Romania and Hungary. There were still boundaries to cross to create fellowship throughout Eastern Europe, but an important start had been made. Any sign of a positive response to this visit and a suggestion for a return visit was eagerly awaited. Within a few weeks a request was received from Moscow for information about the European Baptist Federation, including a copy of the Constitution.

THE MUNICH COUNCIL 1954

A significant part of the care programme for displaced people in Germany was undertaken by the German Baptist Deaconesses. Their mother-house was the Bethel Deaconess House in Berlin, under the management of Dr Jacob Meister, which had been founded in 1887. They were already using centres at Bethany, Hamburg and Seekirchen, near Saltzburg, Austria, when in 1951 Dr Lewis shared negotiations with them to obtain and open another property in Maria Ward Strasse, Munich, as a part of the Baptist World Alliance's post-war relief programme. The property was purchased in the name of the Bethel Deaconess House and was to be known as the Bethel Baptist Rest

Home. The Deaconesses agreed to care for elderly people in need who belonged to one of three groups: displaced persons, ethnic Germans (Volkedeutsche) and refugees from East Germany. The Alliance undertook to bear the expenses. The legal agreement, signed in Berlin-Dahlem on 25 June 1952, between the Alliance Relief Committee and the Bethel Deaconess House,[12] stated that once the building was no longer needed for this purpose it would be available for the Bethel Deaconesses to use in any way they chose.

This was an imaginative and compassionate venture which the European Baptist Federation acknowledged by holding its Council meetings in the House on 15-16 September 1954. Special provision was made for Council members to share a service of worship with the Sisters and residents, in which believers from across many different boundaries were able to rejoice in their common faith and love in Jesus Christ. It was a telling symbol of the unity which the European Baptist Federation and Baptist World Alliance have always existed to make possible.

The Council meetings continued with the sense of optimism which such an event generated. The ambitious proposals at earlier meetings for planting new churches in strategic European centres were already beginning to take shape. A property had been bought for a church in Brussels. The congregation now had a pastor, and considerable help was being offered by missionaries from other countries who were doing language study in the city prior to service in the Belgian Congo. It was also reported that the French Baptist Federation had founded a church in Strasbourg. Another church had started in Metz, on the River Moselle in Eastern France, with financial aid from the British Baptist Continental Committee. The prospect of developing a centre for Baptist summer camps and international youth events became a distinct possibility when the Austrian Baptists announced that they had purchased a suitable country house in two acres of land. Urged on by Dr Bredahl Petersen, the Council agreed to explore the feasibility of the Federation entering into partnership with the Austrian Union for such a project.

There was still more encouragement when Dr Lewis told the story of the visit to the Soviet Union which he had made with Drs Townley Lord and E. A. Payne. Sustained prayer had been offered all over Europe and the world for a long time, eagerly desiring details of Baptist life in the Communist world and contact with Christian brothers and sisters there. 'O Lord, how long?' must often have been the cry in east and west; but now there was hope of a breakthrough. Patience had to last a little longer; but by the time the 50th anniversary of the Baptist World Alliance was celebrated in the World Congress in London in the summer of 1955, a return visit was paid by a delegation of Russian Baptists. Despite the threats and fears on both sides of the Iron Curtain, an important network of East/West Baptist and ecumenical relations was built over the coming years. This was to be a major factor in the story of the European Baptist Federation.

Life was far from easy for Christians in some of the Warsaw Pact countries. The saga of the imprisoned Czech pastors continued. One in fact had died in captivity. Although in principle the State Constitution guaranteed freedom of conscience and allowed both private and public profession of religious faith, in practice the State conducted a policy of opposition to the churches. The Society for the Propagation of Political and Scientific Knowledge organized many political rallies and voluntary service projects on Sundays. Political correctness required attendance at these and therefore openly discouraged church attendance. Yet church attendances grew! A similar pattern could be found in Bulgaria; latest news told of four pastors and one layman in prison there.

Changes were about to take place in the EBF. Dr Manfredi Ronchi was elected President for the next two years and Dr Hans Luckey of Germany became Vice-president. W. O Lewis was re-elected Secretary-Treasurer, but his time for retirement was approaching. Council approved the content of a letter to be sent to the General Secretary of the Baptist World Alliance, urging the need for an Associate Secretary to serve in Europe after Dr Lewis's retirement. So much good had been achieved in the first five years of the Federation's life. It was vital that this be continued and that the new opportunities beginning to arise be used to the full.

In that spirit European Baptists looked forward to the World Congress in London in the next year. Plans were begun for ministers who attended the Congress to stay for a while in Europe to take part in evangelistic missions. Also, in order to encourage wide participation in the Congress the usual round of EBF meetings would not be held. 1955 was to be another important landmark in European Baptist history, and to that we shall now turn in the next chapter.

CHAPTER NOTES

CHAPTER TWO   The Early Years

1   Material in this section owes much to my reading of relevant chapters in the following books: Norman Davies, *Europe: A history,* OUP (Oxford & New York), 1996 and *The Oxford Illustrated History of Modern Europe,* edited by T. C. W. Blanning, OUP (Oxford & New York), 1996.

2   Philippians 1.12.

3   J. H. Rushbrooke, *The Baptist Movement in the Continent of Europe,* 1923, p.4.

4   Written by John Oxenham (1852-1941).

5   A moving account of a personal visit to Germany at this time is given by Irwin Barnes in his book, *Truth is Immortal,* Carey Kingsgate Press, 1955, pp.101-104.

6   These two examples were drawn from *Baptists of the World 1950-1970: Recollections and Reflections by various world Baptist leaders,* a BWA publication dedicated to the memory of Josef Nordenhaug (General Secretary of the Alliance 1960-69) and printed by the Southern Baptist Radio and Television Commission 1970, pp.35 & 71.

7   *Baptist Times,* 16 August 1951, p.2.

8   Ibid., 15 November 1951, p.9.

9   Ibid., 3 September 1953, p.7.

10   See Chapter 9, pp.218-224.

11   A comprehensive report of their visit was sent to all members of the BWA Executive. International secular and religious media gave wide coverage, including three special articles in the *Baptist Times*, 8, 15 & 22 July 1954.

12   A free translation of the Agreement, dated 23 July 1951, is among BWA (European) documents in the Angus Library, Regent's Park College, Oxford.

3

CONSOLIDATION AND GROWTH

The Baptist World Alliance Ninth Congress held in London 16-22 July 1955 had a distinctly European flavour. The President was the Revd Dr F. Townley Lord, minister of the Bloomsbury Central Baptist Church, London. Among the vice-presidents of the Baptist World Alliance were two noted European leaders, the Revds Dr Manfredi Ronchi (Italy) and Dr Gunnar Westin (Sweden). A quick glance through the official report of the Congress shows that at least thirty-one Europeans participated in the programme, giving addresses, leading worship, offering prayer, making reports and in other ways. They came from north, south, east and west, clear evidence of the widening influence of the European Baptist Federation and its steadily increasing contribution to world Baptist life. Dr Arnold T. Ohrn, General Secretary of the BWA, himself a European, wrote in a Foreword to the report that the Congress theme, 'Jesus Christ, the same yesterday, today, and for ever', was intended to focus the thought of delegates not on Baptist organization and achievements but on Christ.[1]

TRIUMPHS OF GRACE

Our Christian conviction is that past, present and future are to be seen in the light of Christ's eternal love and lordship. Two moments in the Congress programme illustrated this. To use the phrase of a hymn sung several times during the week, they were 'triumphs of his grace'.

The first occurred in the opening session when the Archbishop of Canterbury, as President of the British Council of Churches, welcomed all the international visitors to Britain. He expressed his particular pleasure at being able to welcome the Revds Jakob Zhidkov and Nikolai Levindanto as representatives of the first delegation of Russian Baptists to attend an Alliance Congress since 1928. They had been his guests at Lambeth Palace during the previous week. Initially, the BWA

Administration Committee had been hesitant about inviting the Archbishop to the Congress, but he had played a key role in enabling the Russians to be there by negotiating that these two respected Baptist leaders be included in an ecumenical visit to the British Council of Churches with four others from the Russian Orthodox Church and two from the Lutheran Church. In this way it was possible to obtain visas for several other Russian Baptists to share in the Congress, including the Revd Alexander Karev and Miss Klaudia Tyrtova from Moscow, and the Revd Eugeny Raevski from Siberia. Several times during the Congress those present expressed their enthusiastic, almost rapturous welcome, clearly overjoyed that another boundary had been crossed and that the way was now open for closer co-operation with Baptist brothers and sisters in the east. The links forged then have not been broken since.

Alexander Karev, who was the General Secretary of the Russian Baptist Union,[2] is reported to have given a powerful message on 'Christ and the Church'. Preaching in a directly biblical manner which he said would be commonly recognized as the Russian way of preaching, he received a loud and long ovation at the conclusion of his address. Jakob Zhidkov also gave an informative account of the life, worship and growth of Baptists in the USSR, including an urgent appeal for support for world peace and disarmament. In years to come such deep spirituality and practical sense of Christian world mission were to be a constant challenge within the European Baptist Federation.[3]

The second significant moment in the programme was when Eberhard Schröder, head of the Kassel Baptist Publishing House, introduced three hundred German delegates, some of whom were from the Russian occupied zone. In a humorous, yet also sombre comment, he explained that the Iron Curtain was so strong that it was easier to travel from Germany to London or the USA than to go from West Germany to East Germany! Then, in heartfelt gratitude, he added: 'We receive active help through the Baptist family, and I take this chance of again thanking you for your forgiveness and love. As Baptists we are one in our faith, hope and love.' What finer justification could one find for such events which manifest the power of Christ to turn enemies into friends?

The Congress closed with a vast public rally in the Highbury Stadium, home of the Arsenal Football Club. What came to be called the Coronation Address was delivered by Dr Billy Graham on the theme: 'Crown Him Lord of All'. He struck a high note of optimism, yet his words were not facile or without challenge. The call to crown Jesus was made not only in the light of his triumphs but also with awareness of disappointments and difficulties still to be overcome. News from Spain spoke of a deplorable situation. Protestant churches were compulsorily closed, renting of other buildings was prohibited, and private house meetings often led to prosecutions, fines and imprisonment. Roman Catholic supremacy, using the full force of the civil powers, prevented Protestant marriages and shut the door to employment for many Protestant believers. Again, the euphoria of the welcome to the Russians could not mask the anxious disappointment about the absence of other Baptists from Poland, Czechoslovakia, Hungary, Romania and Bulgaria. Some were still in prison, including the Czech leader, Dr Henry Prochazka who was serving a twelve-years prison sentence. Seven years earlier, during a visit of BWA leaders to Prague, he had prophesied to Dr C. Oscar Johnson of the USA that they might not meet again, because visits either way would not be allowed. He even advised that it would be unwise to write to each other, lest it be misrepresented by the State authorities. While waiting for further triumphs of God's grace in breaking down barriers, there was much need for patience, discretion and courage.

No international gathering of Baptists could meet in those days, or often since, without reference to religious freedom. In many places believers were struggling to obtain it; in others they were learning how to keep and use it. Within the London Congress a conference on the issue was addressed by the Revd Professor Gunnar Westin of Uppsala University, Sweden.[4]

TIMES OF CHANGE

In the second half of the 1950s considerable changes took place in the European Baptist Federation. First, there were changes of personnel. Dr W. O. Lewis retired in 1956 after nine years of devoted leadership as the BWA Associate Secretary for Europe. He had been called to fill the gap caused by the sudden death of Dr J. H. Rushbrooke. This laid upon him responsibility for the large post-war programme of relief and reconstruction, the rehabilitation of German Baptists, and the renewal of relationships so much at risk after the Second World War and subsequently in the East/West divide. With consummate skill and pastoral sensitivity he won respect from all sides and, on his retirement, was greatly missed. Henry Cook was invited to serve as part-time Acting Secretary of the Federation, pending a new appointment by the BWA. A year later, another of the Federation's founding fathers, Dr Bredahl Petersen, departed for a new post in the USA. He had made a considerable contribution to the Federation in its first decade.[5] A new generation of leaders was to emerge in the next few years. One of them was Dr Hans Luckey who succeeded Dr Manfredi Ronchi as President. These changes led to important new policies which both consolidated and expanded European Baptist work.

Three more Baptist Unions became members of the EBF. Hungary and Romania joined in 1956. Both groups were spiritually flourishing and brought eager evangelistic zeal to the wider Baptist family. But they also brought problems. In Hungary a popular reaction against Communism had emerged; public protests called for greater freedom and a more open economic policy. The Russian Red Army, supported by tanks and other armoured vehicles, invaded the country in 1956 to crush the revolt and restore political control, despite widespread international condemnation. Hungarian Baptists needed the support and encouragement of their fellow Baptists; indeed, it was for such eventualities that the Federation existed. Romanian Baptists had endured hardship for the faith for years. The subtle pressures inflicted on them by the alliance of the Orthodox Church and the Government made them an urgent focus for prayer and practical support for years to come. Meanwhile Russian Baptists maintained the contact made in 1955 and were received into membership at the meeting of the EBF Council in West Berlin in July 1958. The Portuguese Baptist Convention was also enquiring about membership.

The Hungarian and Romanian Unions were automatically admitted to membership by virtue of their being members already of the BWA. This procedure was not widely acceptable. During the Council at Langesund, Norway in August 1956 proposals were made for definite applications for membership, to be dependent on meeting agreed qualifications. Another issue raised was the abandonment of the Vice-president's automatic succession to the Presidency of the Federation. Although that practice has generally been retained over the years, it was decided that Council must be free to make or accept other nominations. What may appear to have been a procedural matter was more likely to have expressed a spiritual conviction about the Holy Spirit's guidance. One must acknowledge that this was more true to Baptist principles. At Langesund Dr Hans Luckey of Germany became President and Dr Erik Rudén of Sweden Vice-president. Another change was to elect three representatives of the EBF to serve on the committee of the European Baptist Missionary Society.

When the Federation was first formed an Executive Committee was established, comprising the Officers plus representatives from Germany, France, the Netherlands and Italy. Subsequently the number of representatives was reduced to three who were changed every two years. In 1952 they came from France, Germany and Sweden; in 1954 from Denmark, France and Sweden; and in 1956 from Holland, Denmark and Yugoslavia. The clear intention was to ensure wider involvement in Federation affairs and a continual infusion of new people and ideas.

The Dutch Union had initiated the discussion which resulted in discontinuing the practice of automatic membership of the EBF through membership of the BWA. They also expressed their concern about the autonomy of the Federation, particularly in connection with the appointment of a new General Secretary. They argued that, although the Baptist World Alliance must rightly be the appointing body for their Associate Secretary for Europe, there should be proper consultation with the EBF corporately instead of with private individuals, because whoever was appointed would also be the Federation's General Secretary/Treasurer. A right to make or agree a nomination should therefore be given to the EBF. This led to prolonged debate about the future of the Federation. A special committee, chaired by Dr Ernest A. Payne, was elected to review the constitution.

The delay in selecting a new Secretary to replace Dr Lewis and the lack of official consultation led to further tension in 1957. A letter from the Executive to the BWA urged the importance of this matter. In the following year disagreement about the autonomy of the Youth Committee and questions about future relations between the EBF and the BWA, with special reference to where decision making should take place, underlined the necessity of consensus about constitutional procedures.

THE SECOND EUROPEAN CONGRESS

The Langesund Council began to plan for the next European Baptist Congress to be held 26-31 July 1958. Their aim was to hold it at venues in both East and West Berlin. This reflected the general attitude of German Baptists in the two sectors to the false division imposed on them by the East German Government. The Secretary of State for Religious Affairs insisted that the Congress must be held in one zone or the other. So the EBF Council settled for the West. State impositions of this sort carried little weight with East German Baptists. Of course, they had to be obeyed, but ways of getting round them were regularly found. For years, when the BWA and EBF arranged conferences, committees and assemblies at which German Baptists from both regions were present, special joint meetings took place within the programme. These made it possible to maintain close contact and exchange experience. Political segregation could not stifle their Christian love and concern for one another; spiritually the boundaries were meaningless.

The theme and spirit of the Congress were strikingly positive despite the tensions of the Cold War and the harassment and pressure which many Baptists suffered. Fifty years after the first Conference in Berlin in 1908, when those present were predominantly from the West, Eastern delegates at this Congress far outnumbered those from the West. This was to be a feature of the Federation's life in coming years. It caused questions and differences of opinion about theology, biblical interpretation, culture, moral standards, worship and ministry. The dominance of Western leadership had to come to terms with the more diverse nature of Baptist fellowship. Such a transition was not easy but it was certainly beneficial.

Berlin's Deutschlandhalle was a magnificent venue for the main meetings. A large banner in German, Russian and English proclaimed the Congress theme: 'Christ our Hope - Europe our Responsibility'. At the opening ceremony a welcome was expressed by Dr Martin Niemöller, the former U-boat commander who had become President of the German Evangelical Church and of the Social Committee of Christian Churches in Germany. He said that the Church was only free when it was not on the defensive, when it was not anxious about its own life but 'God-trusting and missionary in spirit.'

A special meeting was arranged for the East Berlin representatives on the EBF Council with the members of the Executive Committee and various officers and leaders of the Baptist World Alliance who were present. Two East German Government officials were also invited; the Secretary of State for Religious Affairs and the Vice-president of the People's Council. Appreciative comments were made about the good relations between the German Democratic Republic and the Free Churches. In a vote of thanks at the close of the meeting Dr Theodore Adams pointedly remarked: 'Our people have struggled in the past for freedom. Baptists are pioneers in that struggle. By freedom we mean liberty to believe according to conscience, and liberty not to believe; that the man who believes and the man who does not believe shall have equal rights before the State, and the State shall not compel men's consciences.'

A four-point declaration was issued from the Congress. It expressed gratitude that for the first time since the war Baptists from East and West had been able to have greater contact. Delegates from many nations had shared their common faith that Christ alone was their hope, and he alone could redeem the world and set up the kingdom of peace and righteousness for all humanity. They also promised to pray for the leaders of the nations in their search for peace, that they would not use the technical achievements of the modern age to create even more horrible weapons of war. Finally, they affirmed their commitment to European evangelization.[6]

Summing up the value of the Congress Dr Arnold T. Ohrn asserted that the most important thing about it was that it had taken place. Many from East Germany and Eastern Europe had met with fellow believers from the West. They had been made newly aware that in hard days they were not walking alone. The thoughts, prayers and practical help of Christian colleagues were a vital expression of unity in Christ, and an essential part of the important role of the European Baptist Federation.

THE NEW SECRETARY

At the Executive Committee and Council held prior to the Congress at the Deaconess Mutterhaus, Bethel, Berlin-Dahlem and the Charlottenburg Baptist Church, Berlin, Dr Ohrn announced that the BWA Nominating Committee wished to submit the name of Dr Erik Rudén, General Secretary of the Baptist Union of Sweden, as the new Associate Secretary for Europe. He expected this to be endorsed by the Alliance Executive at Rüschlikon immediately after the Congress. Although his announcement aroused much debate once again about appointment procedures, there was fortunately unanimous support for the nomination. However, there was a strange development later in the Council when the EBF Nominations Committee report was presented by Dr Ernest Payne. After welcoming the nomination of Erik Rudén and expressing the hope that he would accept, they made the following four recommendations:

1. That Erik Rudén should be invited to become Secretary of the EBF from the time of his taking up the post of BWA Associate Secretary until the next meeting of Council.
2. That Henry Cook continue as Acting Secretary until Erik Rudén becomes Secretary
3. That Dr Rudén be elected EBF President in succession to Dr Hans Luckey until such time as he becomes Secretary.
4. That Brother Huizinga be elected Vice-president and, if and when Rudén becomes Secretary, Acting President of the EBF.

This was an unusually convoluted set of proposals. In view of the earlier debate one can only assume that the committee intended to make it crystal clear that the EBF claimed the right to choose its own Secretary. It should therefore be consulted by the BWA over the appointment of the Alliance's Association Secretary for Europe, who would normally hold the dual post. For the moment they had made their point. But this issue caused tensions on a number of future occasions. The balance between autonomy and inter-dependence among Baptists is sometimes a precarious one!

These difficulties should not be allowed to overshadow the outstanding service given by Dr Rudén from 1959 to 1965 and the widespread popularity he won. The Revd Ronald Goulding of England, who was President in Erik Rudén's early days as General Secretary, described him as the main architect of the growth of the Federation during the 1960s. His tireless travelling among the Baptists of north, south, east and west, together with his skilled fluency in three or four languages, enabled him to communicate widely. Consequently, he secured ready support for his many proposals for expanding the Federation's influence. Two other factors were of undoubted assistance to him. One, to which Ronald Goulding drew attention, was that a generation of gifted and courageous Baptist leaders of various nationalities survived the war and maintained their faith. Despite their political diversity they related well to one another and thus became useful partners in the new Secretary's many endeavours. The second factor was the presence and influence of the International Baptist Theological

Seminary (IBTS) at Rüschlikon. Those who studied there from all parts of Europe formed the next generation of leaders and enjoyed a camaraderie akin to what the New Testament calls fellowship (*koinonia*). This led to a natural spirit of Christian unity and trust.[7]

The proposals about Secretaryship and Presidency took effect in the autumn of 1959. A special Federation meeting was held at Baptist Church House, London for the official installation of Dr Rudén and to say 'thank you' to Dr Henry Cook. Speakers included Dr Ernest A. Payne and Dr Arnold T. Ohrn, and greetings were given by Dr Josef Nordenhaug on behalf of the Rüschlikon Seminary, Dr Edwin Bell for the American Baptist Foreign Missionary Society and Dr G. W. Sadler for the Southern Baptist Convention. The new Secretary brought substantial experience to his work. He was trained at the Baptist Theological Seminary in Stockholm and undertook further studies at Stockholm University. He then became pastor of a small church before becoming the youth pastor of the Uppsala Baptist Church. In 1938 he was elected as Associate Secretary of the Baptist Union of Sweden, and was promoted to the Union's General Secretaryship in 1940, a post he held until this new appointment. Initially he opened an EBF office in Stockholm, but at the request of the BWA he moved with his wife, Kerstin, and their family to London, where the Alliance's office in Baptist Church House was reopened.

His vision and enthusiasm gave European Baptist life a new vitality. Just before he came into office he visited the Soviet Union to establish contact with Russian Baptists and to gain awareness of their current situation. His first annual report to the Council in Vienna in September 1960 was full of interest. He spoke of his many visits to different countries, and particularly about the struggle for religious liberty in Spain where there was a new burst of church closures. Changes in law now made new church planning, public evangelism and religious publishing by Baptists illegal. Despite such problems he was eager to persuade the Federation and its member Unions to move on from the post-war programme of relief and reconstruction to a new dimension in which evangelism, theological training and Christian education had primary significance.

There was a noticeable change in the style of leadership, which was reflected in the minutes and reports of that period. They were longer and more detailed, and, therefore, provide a fuller picture of what took place. In the course of his first report he analysed the features of specific areas of European Baptist work, and conveniently suggested thinking in terms of seven regions:

1. North Europe - Norway, Sweden, Denmark and Finland.
2. North-East Europe - Poland, Czechoslovakia and USSR.
3. Southern Europe - Portugal, Spain and Italy.
4. South-East Europe - Yugoslavia, Bulgaria, Romania and Hungary.
5. France, Netherlands and Belgium.
6. The British Isles.
7. German-speaking nations - Austria, Germany and Switzerland. [8]

He hoped that a quarterly magazine about to be launched, *The European Baptist,* would keep Baptists in these regions informed about one another and so reinforce and enlarge their fellowship. By 1961 he reported to the Executive Committee that he had already visited nineteen of the twenty-three member Unions. He had also conferred with government officials in Spain, Poland, Yugoslavia, Czechoslovakia and East Germany.

The minutes of successive Executive and Council meetings contained a steady flow of policy decisions which indicated a willing response to his positive leadership. In Belgium, for example, the small company of Baptists were affiliated to the French Baptists. They now developed a closer co-operation with the EBF. A Belgian Committee was created, made up of the Belgian leaders and representatives of the Federation, the American Baptist Foreign Missionary Society and the Foreign Mission Board of the Southern Baptist Convention. This proved to be a partnership which gave much needed support and encouragement in a minority situation where lack of recognition and public ostracism were often experienced. In due course there were also particular demands to be met because of the growth of Dutch, Flemish, German and Polish language churches in Belgium. An earlier suggestion from Dr J. D. Hughey to form a European Baptist Men's Movement now moved forward, when a Men's Committee was launched with Mr Cyril Petch of London as its secretary. But strict limits were set to its activities, probably to prevent it from developing an independent life of its own. It could only work with the Rüschlikon Seminary in organizing Men's Conferences, until the EBF gave it new guidelines.

Another innovation was introduced by Dr Hughey which was to have far-reaching consequences for good. After a long delay, progress was at last made with the idea of a Press Service. No doubt this became possible in the context of the new spirit of advance aroused by Dr Rudén. A second conference of Baptist writers and publishers had been convened at Rüschlikon. From it emerged a proposal that the Faculty of the Seminary should explore possible partnership with the ABFMS to establish a European Baptist Press Service (EBPS) at Rüschlikon, fully supported by the EBF and BWA. The Foreign Mission Board of the Southern Baptist Convention offered to second one of its trained journalists, Dr John A. Moore, as the first Director. They would also equip an office, and pay his salary and travelling expenses. The EBF undertook to meet the costs of a part-time secretary, postages, paper and other operational costs. This package was placed before the Federation Council in 1960 and received wholehearted backing. Thus began a service which has been of exceptional value to the Baptist family for almost forty years, and still functions effectively from the Federation's office in Hamburg. Its purpose was not primarily promotional, but to gather and distribute Baptist news and matters of general interest to its readers. When a report of its first year's activities was given to the Executive meeting in Brussels in September 1961, special attention had to be given to overcoming a confusion which had arisen between the Baptist agency (EBPS) and the Ecumenical Press Service (EPS) operating from the World Council of Churches in Geneva. Production was rising and mailing lists continually growing.

Other exciting innovations prepared the way for future progress. Erik Rudén had requested the International Baptist Seminary to try to build a library of visual aids to be made available on free loan to churches and national Baptist Unions. At first the aim would be to create a collection of film strips; then additional facilities would include slides, motion films, records and tapes, with an overall catalogue to be circulated throughout the Federation. Closely linked with this initiative was a positive response to the challenge given several years ago to explore the possibility of having a European Baptist radio station at Rüschlikon. The new President of the Seminary, Dr Hughey, had already arranged a radio and television conference. As a result of it steps were being taken to identify the opportunities all over Europe and to equip a studio for the preparation of programmes.

In August 1962 at the Baptist Seminary in Stabekk, Norway, Dr Rudén informed the EBF Council that at a Foundation Meeting of the Alumni Fellowship of the IBTS there had been a lively discussion about issuing a scholarly journal in English of Baptist history and theology. This would obviously assist in the creation of a stronger Baptist identity, as well as encouraging future scholars and producing Baptist apologetics. No continental Baptists possessed such a journal; ordinary Baptist papers were not suitable for scholarly writings. A recommendation to the EBF Council urged the Federation or Seminary to be responsible for taking the matter further. The General Secretary was asked to investigate such journals among world Baptists and to enquire about the feasibility of co-operating with the *Baptist Quarterly,* the journal of the British Baptist Historical Society.

It is interesting to note in many of these new ventures a close liaison between Dr Rudén and Dr Hughey, and the way in which Rüschlikon was becoming a strategic centre of European Baptist life.

A LIVELY, GROWING FELLOWSHIP

By the early 1960s the EBF had become a lively and growing fellowship. Much of its work was thriving. It was clearly succeeding in building Baptists together in one family across many boundaries.

Mutual support and co-operative action were no longer just future ideals but contemporary reality.

Limits of space will not allow the whole story to be told in detail, but in brief summary we may note that the European Baptist Women's Union was well established and busily active throughout the continent. An important consultation took place early in 1962 with leaders of the BWA Women's Department during their visit to Sweden. Two people who made a substantial contribution to future work in Europe now joined the EBWU Committee - Mrs Kerstin Rudén, the General Secretary's wife, and Miss Dorothy Finch, of the Women's Department of the Baptist Union of Great Britain and Ireland. Youth work was also thriving. Members of the Youth Committee visited ten countries in two years. Young people were exchanging visits from country to country, and a highly successful All-European Summer Camp had been held. The Hamburg Seminary had hosted a Baptist Students' conference, while at Rüschlikon youth leaders from many Unions had got together.

Within eight years of its formation the European Baptist Missionary Society was being supported by at least nine Unions and had twenty-five missionaries serving abroad. A major new concern was how to combat the growing influence of Islam. New churches had been built and opened in Paris, Warsaw and Serbia. Good progress was reported from the church in Strasbourg where a young pastor had recently settled. Dr Rudén had entered into negotiations with the Czech Government and was planning an important conference for Eastern European Baptists in Prague in 1963. Similarly, he had met State officials in Spain to secure the reopening of closed churches and, in addition, had made a major breakthrough by obtaining permission to hold a conference in Barcelona for Baptists from Latin countries in the south of Europe. Approximately two hundred delegates were expected from Portugal, Italy, France and Spain. There have been times over the years when Baptists in Southern Europe have felt somewhat marginalized. Rudén was wise enough to recognize that the needs of Eastern Europe must not be allowed to be so much the centre of attention that the needs of these other countries were ignored.

Of course, this book would present a distorted picture if it did not also record failures and disagreements. There were a number of these during the late 1950s and early 1960s. Hubmaier House, the new centre in St Gilgen, Austria, faced management and financial problems which led people to ask if it was being used for the purpose intended and was fulfilling the conditions under which it was held in trust. A deaconess from Bethel was sent to take over the running of the house. The EBF appointed a special committee to take charge of the affairs of the centre. By 1961, to everybody's surprise, the centre was closed and sold. The committee was asked to consider ways of using the sale proceeds and report its findings to the EBF Council.

During a BWA Executive meeting at Rüschlikon immediately after the 1958 European Congress the EBF Executive was called together to discuss the formation of an Alliance Bible Study and Membership Training Committee. Two Europeans were invited to serve on it - the Revds Helmut Pohl of Germany and Stuart Arnold of England. There appears to have been some unease about the proposals, because it is reported that the EBF insisted on the closest possible relationship with the Federation. A month later a clue to this unease was given when the chairman of the new committee, Dr G. S. Dobbins of the Southern Baptist Convention announced that he had unilaterally prepared a five-years course from 1960 to 1965. The EBF complained about the lack of consultation and would not promise to use the course. In their view some Unions would already be committed to other programmes.

A few years later this sensitivity about American influence [or was it dominance?] in Europe raised its head again. Sven Ohm of Sweden, in his capacity as Secretary of the Youth Committee, had written to suggest that European Baptists should co-operate with the Judson Press by distributing an American devotional magazine, *The Secret Place*. The Press had already dispatched 1,000 copies for distribution, in the hope that this could become a joint enterprise. The Executive refused to support this proposal. They argued that several English language devotional magazines already existed in Europe and it was not appropriate to make one of them a specifically Baptist enterprise.

Another area of work which caused occasional tension and hesitation was ecumenical relations. In the summer of 1960 the Federation was invited to send representatives to an Ecumenical Conference at Nyborg, Denmark. After soundings had been taken with the BWA it was agreed to recommend that, since the EBF was not a church, invitations should in future be sent to national Baptist Unions. This was a rather confusing response; did it imply that Baptist ecclesiology looked upon a Union as a church? Or would Unions be expected to discover the mind of local churches? This illustrates a difficulty which Baptists have always felt when trying to express and act upon their understanding of church alongside the different concepts of other denominations. In order not to give a totally negative reply, a message was conveyed that, while invitations should be addressed to the Unions, the Federation would appreciate being able to send an observer to Nyborg.

THINK CONTINENTAL!

It is appropriate to end this chapter with some important comments made by Dr Rudén in a report he presented to the EBF Executive in Lisbon 9-11 June 1963.[9] He spoke of the new Europe emerging from the ruins of war years. Therefore it was important to 'think continental'. The continent was still divided, but the Christian Church was breaking through the barriers. More than 50% of European Baptists were in Eastern Europe. This fact was both an opportunity and a special responsibility.

He went on to list some significant issues which were relevant in planning future work: for example, the widespread population upheaval, the many small churches with limited resources and so unable to be self-sufficient, and the number of students who were travelling from country to country for their studies. In his view, co-operative evangelism was essential, and therefore the ecumenical question had to be faced. Also in the world of the Cold War the peace question could not be avoided. He concluded by stressing the urgent need for trained Baptist theologians able to make their contribution to the debates about Communism and Christianity, society and social justice, peace and righteousness, religious liberty, and the task and status of the Church in the various modern expressions of the State.

These incisive comments need to be kept in mind as we move on in the next two chapters to consider, first, life for Baptist Christians behind the Iron Curtain, and then, the developing work of the European Baptist Federation in all parts of Europe.

CHAPTER NOTES

CHAPTER THREE   Consolidation and Growth

1 *Report of the Baptist World Alliance Ninth Congress (London 1955)*, pp.5f.

2   Known as the All-Union Council of Evangelical Christians-Baptists. It was formed by a merger of the Baptists and Evangelical Christians in 1944. A year later Russian Pentecostals and the Baptists and Evangelical Christians of the Baltic countries also joined it.

3   A copy of an informative document about Russian Baptist life, written by Alexander Karev and given to BWA leaders during the Congress, is in the BWA (Europe) Box File 1 in the Angus Library, Regent's Park College, Oxford.

4   *Report of the Baptist World Alliance Ninth Congress (London 1955)*, pp.321-326.

5 He had helped to draw up the original constitution, served as the first President, chaired the 1st Congress in Copenhagen and assisted with the planning of the 2nd Congress in Berlin.

6 Reports of the Congress are to be found in the *Baptist Times*, 24 & 31 July, and 7 August 1958.

7 Ronald Goulding made these comments in 1997 during an interview with Thornton Elwyn of the British Baptist Historical Society.

8   EBF Minutes, book 1, p.75.

9 The text of the report is in an appendix to the Minutes of this Executive meeting,

4

BEHIND THE IRON CURTAIN

The words 'Iron Curtain' describe the boundary fixed between East and West Europe to maintain total separation, and to block observation and contact between communist Russia with its satellite nations and the countries of Western Europe. Its origin can be traced to 1948 when Russia, under the leadership of Josif Stalin, responded to what it saw as the threat of the North Atlantic Treaty Organization (NATO), formed by the USA and the nations of Western Europe. Through the Warsaw Pact Russia created its own military alliance between the Union of Soviet Socialist Republics (USSR) and the other socialist nations in Central and South-eastern Europe. For more than forty years the Iron Curtain was a major symbol of the so-called Cold War which existed between East and West, with the USA and USSR being the two major world powers vying with one another for supremacy.

The practical implications of this separation were considerable. Geographically, travel between East and West was seriously limited. Visas were difficult to obtain; communication by any means was strictly monitored. Espionage was rife, with the result that all visitors were kept under close surveillance. Economically, difficulties were caused by currency restrictions, trade sanctions and import controls. Military expenditure escalated beyond reason as both sides developed more and more advanced weaponry. They soon had each other targeted by numerous inter-continental missiles, which increased the enemy mentality and stimulated fears of a nuclear holocaust. Rockets and satellites were blasted into space to provide greater spying ability and to develop early-warning devices for defence against nuclear annihilation. Accusations and counter-accusations, propaganda and misinformation sped back and forth around the world, inevitably keeping international tension and suspicion high. This was the environment in which the Christian churches tried to do their work and maintain relationships with one

another. To say it was not easy is an understatement, for strong
political and ideological barriers existed on both sides of the Iron
Curtain.

Within the Soviet Union and other eastern countries scientific
atheism was a prevailing philosophy. Although the State constitution
provided for religious liberty, it also specifically encouraged anti-
religious propaganda. There was a rigid separation between State and
Church. The churches were not permitted to undertake social work or
any form of Christian education for children and young people. These
were the prerogative of the State; the Church must not interfere. Yet
the State did not hesitate to interfere in those realms which were
essentially the prerogative of the Church! Consequently, Christians
faced much irritating restriction and harassment. Discrimination
against them was common in almost every sphere of life. Church
buildings were arbitrarily closed, confiscated and commandeered for
secular purposes. Christian literature was not permitted, or was
severely limited, and Christians had no access to the media either to
proclaim their faith or to defend themselves against false accusations.
Prisons and labour camps housed hundreds of religious prisoners at
various periods. Believers could even be sentenced to years of harsh
treatment in mental institutions.

Within the communist world there were many different countries,
cultures, laws and consequent attitudes to religion. Some States were
consistently harsh; others were at times quite enlightened and
tolerant. In some situations ethnic and nationalist prejudices
prevailed. In some a desire to express independence of the Soviet
Union meant that the authorities did not always follow a rigid party
line. This book is not intended to relate the full story of Baptists in
every country. It is essentially about the life and work of the
European Baptist Federation in partnership with the various national
Baptist Unions. What follows in this chapter is bound to be selective
and incomplete. Hopefully, it will be an adequate, general survey of
EBF involvement in the joys and sorrows of Eastern European
Baptists, offering aid in times of need, acting as advocates in
situations of hostility and suffering, providing resources and

encouragement in places of opportunity, and sharing many occasions of worship, celebration, conference and close fellowship - all normal activities of the universal Church of Christ.[1]

Let no one imagine that this was one-way traffic. Those of us who travelled east for various Baptist or ecumenical events never failed to be deeply moved by the devotion and persevering courage of the Christian brothers and sisters we met. We have been humbled by their deep spirituality. This was evident in their eagerness to hear the Word of God, and by the remarkable evangelistic progress they made even when the freedom and abundant resources enjoyed in the West were not available. The European Baptist Federation has benefited greatly from the contribution of visionary leaders, gifted preachers, faithful committee members and the many Christian insights they brought into our common life from behind the Iron Curtain.

A SERIOUS SPLIT

In the Soviet Union the 1929 law on religious associations imposed considerable limits on the churches. Over the years more and more regulations were introduced, until it became normal for local and national Councils of Religious Affairs to exercise control over Baptist life. They could supervise the appointment of pastors and leaders, demand information about new members, examine church finances, restrict or prevent the ministry of visiting preachers, enforce rules against the religious education of the young and require the registration of church buildings. In such a context persecution was common. There was no lack of opportunity for the authorities to close churches or imprison church leaders and members, often without trial. The State denied that this was religious persecution by insisting that those who were punished were guilty of breaking the law. From the 1930s, under the policies of 'Stalinization', a vast and frightening network of secret police, show trials and prison camps, bore down heavily on all who could be suspected of anything less than whole-hearted submission to State authority. Christians who questioned what they felt to be unjust laws could be accused of opposition to the State. Religious work was often condemned as parasitism which contributed nothing to the life of the nation. Spreading the gospel, writing Christian literature, and associating with Christian bodies in the West could easily be interpreted as slander, treason, or disseminating ideas harmful to the State.

In 1948 the All-Union Council of Evangelical Christians-Baptists drew up a new Statute which set out details of their organization. It contained general regulations for worship and ministry to be observed by local churches. It also explained procedures for appointments, decision-making and leadership. There were probably two motives at work in producing this document and circulating it to all churches. The first was to make sure that the various groups which had merged to form the Union recognized where authority rested and would accept the Statute as the basis of unity. The second was to express as clearly as possible how to live within the framework of the law and so retain their right to exist and practise their religion. An important tool in maintaining unity, and in encouraging churches in the many ups and downs of life in a socialist society, was the regular publication of the journal *Bratskii Vestnik* (Brotherly Messenger), first launched in 1945. It contained photographs of Baptist people and events, news of the churches, scripts of sermons, commentary on key passages of scripture, and the text of special documents. It became a valuable means of communicating with the churches and of spreading news of Soviet Baptist life to others within the Baptist World Alliance and the European Baptist Federation.

The Second World War had brought considerable respite for the churches. Stalin entered into a Concordat with them which allowed them to worship and considerably reduced the hostility which they had experienced in his earlier years. They responded with patriotic loyalty throughout the war and, afterwards, were ready to support the Russian cry for world peace. The wise leadership of their respected President, Jakob Zhidkov, and General Secretary, Alexander Karev, enabled them to seize the opportunity to grow and consolidate their work. In the early 1950s they could report many new churches and baptisms, as well as the hope that they would soon have greater liberty to produce Christian literature, bibles and hymnbooks. As we saw in the previous chapter, contact with world Baptists was restored and in 1958 the AUCECB became a member of the EBF.

This respite was short-lived. When Stalin died in 1953 Nikita Kruschev came to power. At first, hopes were raised by his deliberate policy of de-Stalinization, but by the end of the decade he made a violent onslaught on religion, once again creating a situation in which every conceivable restriction and prohibition was ruthlessly enforced.

The next action of the AUCECB led to a serious split among Baptists. In 1960 they issued new Statutes to all their churches, accepting the limitations imposed by the laws, and instructing their member churches to lessen, or even discontinue, evangelical and evangelistic practices which would in normal circumstances be a vital part of the churches' life. At the same time a Letter of Instruction was sent to the Senior Presbyters[2], making it clear that they were responsible for ensuring that the new Statutes were enforced. There is little doubt that they were compelled by the State to take this action. Kruschev must have hoped that it would radically weaken and undermine the life of the churches, which were becoming far too strong for his liking. But there may have been another factor at work, prompting the question - how far did the AUCECB leaders consider it wise to persuade their churches to live within the restrictions imposed by law? How to survive in a hostile society has often been a searching question for Christians. Should they reject the demands of the State, claiming the authority of Scripture which says: 'We must obey God rather than men'? Or should they attempt to live, as far as conscience would allow, within the nation's laws, also claiming scriptural injunctions such as: 'Render to Caesar the things that are Caesar's, and to God the things that are God's' and 'The powers that be are ordained of God....'?[3] One way invariably led to suffering and martyrdom; the other to continuing existence and limited freedom, but with opportunity to find new ways of witness.

Both points of view existed among Soviet Baptists. Consequently, there was an immediate outcry against the new Statutes. For some time there had been rumblings of discontent about the stance of the leaders of the AUCECB. They were accused of betraying Baptist principles and compromising the gospel. In yielding to government pressure they were seen to be violating a proper separation between State and Church. The opposition soon formed themselves into a separate body known as the *Initsiativniki*, meaning 'Pure' or 'Reform Baptists'. Their leaders included A. Prokofiev, G. Kryuchkov and Georgi Vins, who called on the AUCECB to withdraw the new Statutes. Claiming to be the true Union, they declared Zhidkov, Karev and the other board members of the AUCECB excommunicated. Openly flouting the law, they held many protest meetings and circulated illegal letters (*Samizdat*), threatening to excommunicate all those who continued to obey the All-Union Council.

The Soviet government's reaction was immediate and ruthless. Within a short time a large number of the *Initsiativniki* leaders and members were arrested, tortured and imprisoned, and many of them died. A Council of Prisoners' Relatives was formed, with Mrs Lidia Vins, the mother of Georgi, playing a leading role. This body was eventually renamed the Council of Churches of Evangelical Christian-Baptists (CCECB), otherwise known as Reform Baptists. Throughout the 1960s and 1970s the two Baptist bodies maintained their separate existence, and all attempts to reconcile them failed.[4]

This situation created difficulty for the European Baptist Federation. Clearly they had to maintain fellowship with the AUCECB, supporting them in their work, sharing their problems, taking up their cause when necessary, and doing nothing that would endanger their improving relationship with the Communist authorities. They were eager to visit Baptists in the Soviet Union, as they did other members of the Federation. They also did all within their power to hold EBF events in the East and to use the gifts of Baptist leaders from the various socialist countries in committees and conferences. Whenever there was cause to speak out against abuses of human rights and religious freedom, they were careful to use proper channels, preferring quiet, patient diplomacy rather than loud, public protest. What, then, should be their attitude to the CCECB, and especially to its bitter persecution and suffering? Care had to be taken to safeguard the standing of the EBF with the government and to avoid any action which would have serious repercussions for the AUCECB. Yet the CCECB were fellow-Christians suffering intensely for obedience to their conscience and being denied the liberty for which world Baptists had always striven.

The dilemma faced by the Federation was intensified by international reactions to the situation. Widespread protest on behalf of the Reform Baptists led to their being described as the 'true church', while those who tried to be law-abiding citizens, and thus gained freedoms and avoided sufferings which the others endured, were caricatured as the 'false church'. This led to comparisons between the 'official' churches and the 'underground' churches, the former being condemned as infiltrated by the KGB, the latter being praised as a pure and therefore persecuted minority. It was never as simple as that. In his book about Baptists in the USSR, *Out of Great Tribulation,* Dr E. A. Payne urged the need for deep sympathy towards the leaders of both the AUCECB and the *Initsiativniki*. He continued:

> Those who keep within harsh laws, but find ways of circumventing their more restrictive features, have often to face decisions as perplexing and agonising as those who decide to break the laws and take the consequences. Bitterness and schism between those who differ on these issues are much to be deplored. Both parties honour the pioneers of an earlier day and invoke their example. Both parties long for a time of greater freedom and opportunity. [5]

Unfortunately, the Reform Baptist leadership did not trust the EBF and BWA because of their association with the AUCECB. Despite this there is undeniable evidence that both bodies faithfully encouraged prayer for all who were suffering in the Soviet Union. They consulted regularly about the possibilities of reconciliation, and did not hesitate to communicate to Soviet ambassadors and government leaders their concern about violations of human rights. In September 1970 the EBF

Council which met in Glasgow asked Knud Wümpelmann, the General Secretary of the Baptist Union of Denmark, to visit the Soviet Union informally to try to make contact with the Reform Baptists. In January of the following year he was invited by the All-Union Council to pay another visit to discuss with them the current religious situation. Such attempts to bridge the gaps between the two parties in the dispute were never easy. The Alliance and the Federation were not prepared to allow the numerous protests and accusations to gate-crash into the agendas of their committees and congresses. Sometimes they were obliged to foil devious attempts to secure a public hearing. But they sat down with representatives of either side whenever it was necessary, and often raised the sufferings of prisoners and their families with ambassadors and governments, with the United Nations and through ecumenical bodies like the World Council of Churches and the Conference of European Churches. They never ceased to pursue the possibility of reconciliation and to pray for all concerned.

THE DECADE OF THE 1960s

The previous chapter told the story of the first four years of Erik Rudén's secretaryship. He and Ronald Goulding formed a good partnership as Secretary and President during 1960 and 1961, when they were both conveniently living in London. Initially Dr Rudén visited most of the member Unions and then asked his colleague to undertake a number of visits in Eastern Europe while he himself concentrated on contacts with Spain, Portugal and Italy. This enabled him to draw the three south European groups into closer links with the EBF and to negotiate the reopening of closed churches in Spain. When he ended his service as General Secretary of the Federation in July 1965, the appointment of Ronald Goulding as his successor was a highly suitable and popular choice, especially in Eastern Europe.

At his first Executive in Stockholm in September a report about Baptist work in East Germany must have encouraged him. The Union consisted of 220 churches with 26,000 members. Dr Rudén's visit had shown publicly and politically that they belonged to a large international family and were not to be despised as a small and insignificant sect. This helped them to establish good relations with the State authorities, which were further enhanced by the excellent work being done in the Deaconess Home for the mentally retarded. They had an active and successful seminary at Buckow, growing youth work and a programme of church building. In all these spheres of work they looked upon the BWA and EBF as a crucial lifeline. This news prompted the European Baptist Theological Teachers' Conference to accept an invitation to hold their first annual conference in Eastern Europe at Buckow in 1967.

When the Federation Council met at Haven Green Baptist Church, London in August 1966 Ronald Goulding presented a report of his first year's work. He had visited eleven Baptist Unions, including Poland and the USSR in the East. Attempts to visit Hungary and Romania were thwarted by failure to obtain visas. He gave Council members a review of the religious freedom situation, explaining the wide variations that existed. In Romania and Bulgaria the communist regimes were severe; but in Poland, Yugoslavia, the USSR, Hungary, Czechoslovakia and East Germany a measure of leniency was allowing the churches to make progress. For example, the Polish nation had celebrated 1,000 years of Christianity in their country. Baptists had shared in the celebrations, using them as an opportunity for evangelism and education. Meanwhile, East Germany had become the only communist country to permit religious broadcasting. Services from all the churches, including the Baptists, were featured every Sunday. In Yugoslavia the building of a new seminary at Novi Sad, with a sanctuary and living accommodation, was going ahead. The EBF, the Southern Baptist Convention and the American Baptist Foreign Missionary Society had agreed to share the cost. Baptists there had received a great boost when the national President of Liberia, Dr William Tolbert, who was also the President of the Baptist World Alliance, made a state visit to the country. He took the opportunity to speak publicly in support of Baptists and drew attention to the new seminary building project.

It is worth pausing here to note that religious life in Yugoslavia was generally more free than in the majority of Eastern European countries. After the Second World War General Tito became the President of the new People's Republic. Although he was an unashamed communist, he refused to accept the dominance of the Soviet Union, and from 1948 they became a totally independent nation. Soon afterwards his government adopted a policy of non-alignment, which in due course brought them into close contact with Pandit Nehru of India in forming an international non-alignment bloc. In practical terms this led to freedom of travel both in and out of the country, as well as open trade with other nations. Tourist trade flourished, the currency was always stronger than those within the Warsaw Pact countries, and the Christian churches were blessed with a more congenial situation than many of their fellow believers experienced elsewhere in the East.

An innovation which Ronald Goulding introduced for approval at the London Council was to hold a conference at Rüschlikon in March 1967 for Presidents and Secretaries of the member Unions with the Federation Executive Committee. The agenda would include a review of the Federation's constitution and committees, future developments, the Conference of European Churches (CEC), finance, and the possibility of simultaneous evangelism throughout Europe. One of his hopes was that Baptist leaders from all parts of Europe would grow together in fellowship and mutual support. No decisions would be made, but a report and recommendations would be referred to the Executive for consideration.

In September 1967 an historic meeting of the Executive was held at the Novi Sad Seminary. It was the first time that such a meeting had taken place in Eastern Europe, and it was chaired by the Revd Michael Zhidkov of the Moscow Baptist Church, who was the first Eastern European to become President of the EBF.[6] This was the first occasion too when so many Eastern European leaders were able to meet together. The list of those present included notable names like Dr. Josip Horak (President, Baptist Union of Yugoslavia), the Revd Janos Laczkovski (President, Baptist Union of Hungary), the Revd J.

Tzunea (Secretary, Baptist Union of Romania) and the Revd Alexander Karev (Secretary of the AUCECB). In a report of the Presidents' and Secretaries' conference Ronald Goulding was able to inform delegates that, despite the Cold War tensions, this had been the largest gathering of national Baptist leaders ever recorded in Europe.

J. Tzunea brought to the Executive an invitation from the Romanian Baptist Union, with Government permission, for Dr Rudolf Thaut and the General Secretary, with Jérémie Hodoroaba as interpreter, to visit Romania as soon as possible. The Government was eager to discuss complaints about alleged discrimination against Baptists and refusals to grant permits for Baptist representatives to attend BWA and EBF events. The visit gave opportunity to meet both Government and Orthodox Church representatives, and there was an immediate sign of hope when two Romanian Baptists attended the Baptist World Alliance Executive meeting in Liberia.

In the following year Michael Zhidkov completed his two years as President. Before handing over to Dr Thaut at the Council held in the Hamburg Seminary, he expressed the genuine concern felt within the AUCECB about the sufferings of the *Initsiativniki*. Was this a way of saying that although it was not wise for the All-Union Council to intervene publicly on their behalf, they wished it to be known that any action the EBF felt able to take would have their sympathetic support? Such questions are difficult to answer. Unfortunately, many accusations were made around the world, casting unfair blame on the AUCECB for the position they took. The wise words of Dr E. A Payne were most appropriate:

> How far is it right to try to intervene in the affairs of another country, to break its laws and regulations oneself and to encourage others to do so? Does agitation and protest from outside help or hinder developments towards a more tolerant and free society? Is our own witness and organization so healthy and successful that we can pass judgment or offer advice to others? These are difficult questions to answer. They should certainly not be answered hastily and without counting the cost to others besides ourselves.[7]

Michael Zhidkov not only expressed genuine concern but also confirmed the sadness caused by the serious division among Baptists. He indicated that some of the dissidents were now returning and being welcomed back into the family. Desire for reconciliation was firmly on the agenda.

At the same Council meeting news was given of progress being made in different parts of Eastern Europe. Financial aid projects were approved for new churches in Koszalin and Bialystock in Poland, and for help with the buildings of the Pec Mission Station in Yugoslavia, near to the Albanian border. Romanian Baptists were growing to such an extent that they had appealed for help towards six new 2,000 seater churches. The Federation decided to seek support for these from the Foreign Mission Board of the Southern Baptist Convention and the American Baptist Foreign Missionary Society. Further aid was promised for church building work at Neszemely and Gyor in Hungary.

Following the promising discussions by Ronald Goulding and Rudolf Thaut with the Romanian Government and Orthodox Church, one of the West German representatives, Gerhard Claas, met the Romanian Minister of Cults and Baptist Union officers to sort out difficulties about the Romanian Mission Committee. The committee had been set up some time earlier in Paris to assist Jérémie Hodoroaba in his broadcasting and bible work. He was broadcasting several services per week in the Romanian language via Trans World Radio, with the support of the EBF. There were representatives of the Federation on the committee, but it was an independent body. No Romanian Baptists were able to travel and participate in its deliberations. The Government and Baptist Union were now insisting that it become an official EBF committee, with Romanian Baptists represented on it. Gerhard Claas proposed that it be named the EBF Romanian Committee and be similar to the existing Belgian and Austrian Committees. Its membership should consist of representatives from Germany, France, the EBF, the Southern Baptist Convention, the ABFMS and the European Baptist Convention, plus two from the Baptist Union of

Romania and Jérémie Hodoroaba. This was approved by the Minister of Cults and the Baptist Union officers, and subsequently by the original Paris Committee. Gerhard Claas and André Thobois of the French Baptist Federation were to represent the EBF.

It would be easy to assume that because of the various signs of hope and progress during the 1960s the tide had turned for the churches. That would be a false assumption. Many Christian believers still suffered for their faith and churches generally were subject to close control. Restrictive laws could be enforced at any time according to the whims and unpredictable policy changes of both national and local officials. Any attempt to step outside the party line laid down from Moscow met with instant punishment, as events in Czechoslovakia in the second half of the decade showed.

When Alexander Dubcek took over from Novotny as State President in Czechoslovakia early in 1968 there was a popular hope for significant reform. For several years the Protestant churches had been giving a strong lead towards freedom and human rights, encouraged primarily by the Evangelical Church of the Czech Brethren and the influential theologian, Josef Hromadka. He was a leading figure in the Protestant world and in the Prague Peace Conference: a convinced Communist, but never a party member, he believed that a way could be found for the Christian Church to be integrated into a socialist society. While some Baptists and other evangelical Christians were unsure about him, they were as eager as many other groups, such as writers, artists, and musicians, to press for relaxation of the State's control of their activities. The so-called 'Prague Spring' which came with the promise of Dubcek's liberalizing policy, led to a new optimism not only in the churches, but also in many areas of society. This was a situation which the Soviet Union could not tolerate. On 21 August their armed forces invaded Czechoslovakia and crushed the 'uprising' mercilessly. Inevitably, the churches once again felt the full force of repression. For years to come Baptists were to experience many restraints and difficulties.

At the EBF Council in Hamburg in September, Ronald Goulding expressed his fear that the invasion had put the clock back ten years. Its immediate result was that Polish, Romanian, Yugoslavian, Hungarian, USSR and Czechoslovak Baptists were not permitted to send representatives to the Council. A main topic of discussion was, of course, the urgent need for prayerful and sympathetic support of the churches in Czechoslovakia, and for discernment of ways of helping them.

THE 1970s

The 1960s had shown that in the socialist countries of Eastern Europe there was an unpredictable ambivalence between keeping pressure on the churches and showing a more favourable face to the world by allowing them a measure of freedom. For Baptists this led to periods of more religious activity and growth, only to be followed by renewed opposition which brought frustrating setbacks. These ups and downs are clearly illustrated in the records of the European Baptist Federation.

Bulgarian Baptists, for example, faced difficulties for years. They were a small minority group in a predominantly Orthodox country, and were subject to continual denunciation by the Orthodox Church and oppression by the State. Their relationships with other Baptists were forcibly limited, leaving them isolated and deprived of the benefits of fellowship within the EBF. In September 1970 Ronald Goulding told the Council in Glasgow that relationships with Bulgarian Baptists had been restored. Yet by the time of the Fifth European Baptist Congress in Zurich in 1973, the situation was reversed again. No Bulgarian representatives were allowed to attend, despite numerous invitations and a direct appeal to the Government. Member Unions of the Federation were urged to approach the Bulgarian ambassadors in their countries, apparently to no avail, for the Bulgarians continued to be absent from European and international Baptist events, even when they were held in a socialist country.

A similar pattern of success and setback was also experienced in Romania. The fruitful negotiations about the radio ministry of Jérémie Hodoroaba and the formation of the EBF Romanian Committee in 1969 had given new hope. But in 1972 the Romanian authorities suddenly withdrew their approval. They insisted that no Romanian Baptists could serve on the committee, and that it was not to be an official EBF committee. So it once again became an independent body operating from Paris, although the two Federation representatives continued to serve on it. In the providence of God this was not to prevent the ministry of Jérémie Hodoroaba. By 1978 he was broadcasting the gospel to Romanian people in Europe via TWR, Monte Carlo and Bonaire. Nine weekly short-wave programmes were being transmitted into Eastern Europe and the Middle East. As many as three million Romanian believers in Bessarabia, now part of the Soviet Union, used his programmes as their main spiritual resource. Romanians in Hungary, Yugoslavia and Czechoslovakia were also receiving them. But his main audiences were in Romania itself; messages of appreciation were even coming from Orthodox believers and priests. In addition to religious broadcasting, he was publishing numerous books including thousands of Romanian hymnbooks, children's Christian educational material and translations of Billy Graham's *World Aflame.*

In the non-aligned Yugoslavia considerable progress had been made by the Baptist Union churches. However, in 1973 the EBF received news that the First Baptist Church building in Belgrade had been demolished by the authorities for new road developments. No alternative site had been offered to the church and the suggested compensation was far from adequate. Members of the congregation were still worshipping amid the debris. The EBF Council in Zurich in the July of that year agreed to make a direct approach to the Yugoslav Government. Baptist Unions in the West were asked to make supportive appeals through the relevant embassies. The Council also promised that when a satisfactory solution was achieved the building of a new church would be the first priority in the Federation's European Aid programme.

The Revd Andrew MacRae, of the Baptist Union of Scotland, was the Federation President in 1970 and 1971. He had played a major role for some years in the Evangelism and Education Committee. Their agenda always had to take account of the fact that direct, public evangelism was not legally possible in the East. Yet, during his presidency, a special Pastors' Conference was held in Prague. To his delight many Eastern Europeans attended it; indirectly there was a strong evangelistic content to it. When he looked back on his two years in office he spoke of this conference as one of the most memorable events. He also told of encouraging advance among Baptists in the USSR and of the excellent prospects for their future under the leadership of Alexei Bichkov who had been appointed General Secretary on the death of Alexander Karev.

In July 1973 Alexei Bichkov raised questions at the Executive in Zurich concerning reports in world Baptist journals about the actions and sufferings of those he called 'dissident Baptists'. He reaffirmed the AUCECB's eagerness to be reconciled, but suggested that the published articles did nothing but harm. Committee members reminded him of the widespread public and media interest in these issues, which made it impossible for the Baptist press to remain silent. Many Baptist church members regularly offered prayers, raised money and supported efforts to send bibles and Christian literature to the 'underground' churches. While organizations like the European Baptist Federation and the Baptist World Alliance consistently avoided being drawn into actions and statements which would be harmful to the AUCECB churches, they could not ignore the desperate needs of persecuted Christians or ignore flagrant abuses of human rights. Their dilemma remained as large as ever. Dr Claus Meister eased the tension by proposing a consultation between AUCECB representatives, Executive members and Baptist journalists during the period of the current Council and Congress.

A. Bichkov was elected Vice-president of the Federation in 1975 and became President in the following year. In his first year as President, when the Executive was held in Moscow, he presented an important paper on an International Religious Conference of Peace Advocates. This was sent to all Unions as a basis for study. He had also arranged for a delegation of the Executive and Dr David Russell of Great Britain to meet Mr Titov of the USSR Council on Religion, to be followed by a press conference.

Later in the same year the Council met in Budapest, the capital of Hungary. Ronald Goulding had been called to head up a new Division of Evangelism and Education at the Baptist World Alliance offices in Washington. His successor as General Secretary was Gerhard Claas, the General Secretary of the West German Baptist Union since 1967. Prior to that he had been pastor of the Düsseldorf Baptist Church (1953-58), Youth Secretary of the Baptist Union (1958-64), and pastor of the Johann Oncken Baptist Church, Hamburg (1964-67). He had trained at the Hamburg and Rüschlikon Seminaries, having been one of the first group of students when Rüschlikon was opened in 1949. When he was talking with colleagues after his election, he was so emotionally stirred that he wept at the thought that, in a continent where there were still strong feelings about the events of war, the Baptist family was willing to accept and trust him, a German! In such moments, the power of God's grace to cross boundaries which divide is manifestly clear. Gerhard Claas quickly showed that he was worthy of such trust.

During that Council in Budapest, Alexei Bichkov accompanied Ronald Goulding and Gerhard Claas on a special visit to the Ministry of Religious Affairs in Budapest. Such meetings were now becoming more common. They helped considerably in building relationships of trust, and made it possible for the Federation to convey to the authorities concerns about issues of religious freedom and human rights and allay fears that Baptists were in some way a threat to the State.

When Alexei Bichkov completed his presidency at the Council in Santa Severa, Italy in September 1977 he expressed appreciation of the maturity with which the EBF dealt with urgent matters. He drew attention to three significant emphases which he had noted in the Federation's work: preaching the Gospel in the modern world, training and education for believers, and the growing social responsibility being developed among European Baptists in issues of peace and international co-operation. He also underlined the importance of the Helsinki Final Act for normalizing the political climate in Europe. This was sound Christian statesmanship, clearly intended to impress people and rulers in both West and East. The Council responded by approving two resolutions: one calling for an end to nuclear weapon testing and the arms race, and the other welcoming the ten principles of the Final Act of the Helsinki Agreement.[8]

The new General Secretary immediately expressed concern about issues of religious liberty and human rights. In his first year he intervened with State officials on behalf of Romanian Baptists. Although he only remained in office for just over three years, he became well-known and respected by communist officials in many countries. For example, in 1978, he paid an important visit with Denton Lotz to Bulgaria, where Baptists had a hard time with the authorities for many years, and greatly appreciated the advocacy and support of the EBF.

A number of other events and developments in this decade merit attention. In 1977 a catastrophic earthquake struck Romania. The Baptist Seminary in Bucharest was so badly damaged that it needed considerable rebuilding. Ten Baptist churches were either destroyed or damaged. A public hospital in Craiova suffered the loss of essential equipment. The EBF launched an immediate aid operation. In addition to gifts for needy families, it was decided at the Vienna Council in 1978 to allocate substantial money towards the reconstruction of the Seminary. Clinical equipment to the value of DM 250,000 for the hospital in Craiova was obtained through the Baptist Albertinen Hospital in Germany and the German Missions Trade Agency. A year later further assistance was given in partnership with the ecumenical agency, Inter-Church Aid, to provide heating and amplification equipment for some of the churches. Baptist President Mara expressed thanks on behalf of the Romanian Government and the Baptist Union. He hoped that the Union would soon be able to host the Federation Council in Romania; this would show their gratitude and make some amends for their inability because of currency restrictions to contribute to EBF funds.

In the early 1970s Dr Denton Lotz of the ABFMS in Valley Forge, USA, was appointed to serve in Europe, with special responsibility for Switzerland, Germany, Austria and Eastern Europe. In September 1978 he introduced to the EBF Council a scheme for a Summer Institute for Theological Education (SITE). He proposed a summer study programme at the Rüschlikon Seminary for four weeks each year, to be supplemented by a correspondence course for students to work on at home. His aim was to provide educational resources for Eastern European pastors and students in coming years. A mini-library would be needed for each person on the course, to provide access to theological and biblical literature not available otherwise. The Council wholeheartedly approved the proposals and appointed Denton Lotz as SITE Director. In less than six months he had received many applications for the first course. When the Council assembled in Brighton, England in June 1979, he was able to report that thirty had attended it, a good proportion of them being from the East. Twenty had enrolled for the three year correspondence course leading to the SITE Certificate of Theology. Course materials were being supplied by the Baptist Union of Great Britain and Ireland and the Southern Baptist Convention Seminary Extension Program (Nashville).[9]

A similar project had also been initiated by the Scandinavian Baptist Unions. Their original hope in the 1960s was to establish a Nordic Free Church Lay Academy in Sweden, closely linked to the EBF and supplementing the work of the International Baptist Theological Seminary in Rüschlikon. Discussions between Erik Rudén, Dr Gordon Lahrson, the American Baptist Churches (ABC) European representative, Knud Wümpelmann of Denmark, and Kaare Lauving of Norway, together with the Swedish Free Church Educational Organization, led to the conclusion that a permanent centre was not feasible. Instead, they decided to form a Lay Conference Committee as a joint venture between the Scandinavian Baptist Unions and the ABC. Their plan was threefold:

- to arrange short, concentrated training courses for lay people, in order to equip them for local church leadership;
- to arrange conferences of general interest about important issues of contemporary church life;
- to create opportunities for Christians of various professions in Northern and Eastern Europe to discuss the challenges they met in church and society.

The European Baptist Federation was involved from the outset and received regular reports to its Council or Executive. The General Secretary or another appointed representative of the Federation usually acted in a consultative capacity. From 1970 onwards annual conferences were held in one of the Scandinavian countries; then in 1974 and 1979 the venue was the East German Baptist retreat centre, Martin Luther King Haus, in Schmiedeberg. The response from Eastern European Baptist Unions increased year by year, due no doubt to the non-aligned status of the Scandinavian countries in Cold War years.[10]

David Lagergren, who became General Secretary of the Swedish Baptist Union in 1972, once commented that their Union was able to exchange visits with all the Eastern Unions during the 1970s and received almost annual invitations to the Soviet Union. He attributed this to the fact of Sweden's neutrality. While such inter-Union visits contributed much to the growth of Christian fellowship, he sensed that there was also a weakness within them. The contacts were chiefly at leadership level; for ordinary church members this probably meant very little. Maybe this was an added reason for persevering with international conferences, training courses, youth camps and congresses, whether they were organized by the EBF, BWA or various ecumenical agencies. While not wishing to detract from their educational and spiritual value, it could be argued that their greatest benefit was in the meetings and friendships of believers from East and West.

There was noticeable determination on both sides of the Iron Curtain to finance such visits for those unable to pay for them. In 1979 General Secretary, Gerhard Claas, wrote to all western members of the EBF Council, appealing for gifts to establish a scholarship fund to assist at least one hundred eastern delegates to attend the next European Baptist Congress in Brighton, later in the year. The Baptist Union of Great Britain and Ireland promised to host them; the scholarships would cover their Congress fees and provide them with pocket money. The European Baptist Women's Union, who had a fine record of generosity to all sorts of needs and projects throughout the Federation, promised to make sure that one woman delegate from every Union could attend the Congress at Brighton. Another way for contributions to be made was for the East Germans to pay air fares for the Scandinavians for the Nordic Lay Conferences held in the east, and for the USSR Baptists to cover flights for European delegates to the BWA Council meetings in Manila. Those who benefited could then donate the equivalent of their fares to either EBF or BWA funds. Barriers could be crossed when legal ways of getting round currency restrictions were used for the Lord's sake!

Early in 1979 an important Seminar-Consultation took place in Moscow, attended by about forty leaders of the Baptist Unions in nine socialist countries. Knud Wümpelmann (EBF President), Gerhard Claas (General Secretary) and John Wilkes (Director of the European Baptist Press Service), with their wives, were invited to share in it. In an introductory speech Gerhard Claas commented that since two-thirds of the EBF membership lived in socialist countries, the seminar was a special opportunity to consider the contribution of Baptists to the Federation's common work and to the life of each nation. Any show of nationalism was inappropriate; what was needed was a strengthening of friendship and fraternal co-operation. Speeches by Y. K. Dukhonchenko (USSR) and J. Laczkovszki (Hungary) stressed the role of the Christian Church in the quest for lasting peace, disarmament and justice. Other addresses were delivered by A. I. Mitzkevich (USSR) on the contribution of Evangelical Christians-Baptists to the forthcoming EBF Congress in Britain (1979) and the

BWA Congress in Canada (1980), Knud Wümpelmann on the EBF and the Charismatic Movement, Gerhard Claas on the special contribution of Baptists in socialist countries to the life and ministry of Baptist communities, and Alexei Bichkov on the Social Ministry of Evangelical Christians in the Soviet Union. Fraternal greetings were conveyed by Stanislav Svec (Czechoslovakia - CSSR) , Rolf Damman (GDR), Michel Stankiewicz (Poland) and J. Laczkovszki (Hungary). During the discussion Gerhard Claas proposed that each Union should set aside monthly a time for prayer for peace. Two years earlier he had addressed a World Conference of Religious Workers for Lasting Peace which was held in Moscow.

Alexei Bichkov's address was probably one of the most significant. He dealt at length with the changed position of the Church in socialist society, brought about by the new attitude of government and population to the churches. He attributed this to their patriotism during World War Two, their attempts to live as model citizens, and their commitment to the search for peace. In particular he compared the vertical emphasis of the faith of Russian Baptists with the horizontal priorities among many western Baptists. The importance of this address was in his honest attempt to interpret the new Church/State relationship that was steadily being formed. In the West there was a tendency among some evangelicals to be critical and suspicious about this, assuming that to be truly Christian required believers to be totally anti-communist. Future developments in the East were to show that it was not as simple as that. The overall theme of the Moscow Consultation was 'The Service of the Church in the Modern World'. This implied that the Church must find a *modus vivendi* in a multiracial, multicultural and multipolitical humanity. It must also learn to respect those who are one with them in the faith of Christ but different from them in their understanding of their mission in the world. One of the fundamental tasks of the EBF has always been to cultivate such an expression of unity, mutual respect and support.

An earlier example of this issue arose in 1973 when a split occurred among Romanian Baptists. Josif Ton, a teacher on the staff of the Bucharest Baptist Seminary, publicly declared that the Government had acted illegally against the churches and the Baptist Union had betrayed its Christian heritage by submitting to State demands. He published his views in a document entitled 'The Present Day Situation of the Baptist Church in Romania', which was smuggled abroad and widely disseminated. The inevitable tensions this created led to a split in the denomination and caused difficulties for the EBF and BWA who tried to mediate between the Government and the two parties in the Baptist Union. On 13 December 1973 a crucial meeting was held at the Department of Cults in Bucharest at which were present Dr Ronald Goulding (Associate Secretary of the BWA), Dr David Russell (General Secretary of the Baptist Union of Great Britain and Ireland), N. Covaci and J. Tzunea (President and General Secretary of the Baptist Union of Romania), Dr D. Dogaru and Mr Nemciu (President and Vice-president of the Department of Cults), with an interpreter and one other. Dr Dogaru described the situation from the Government's point of view, and the Baptist representatives had opportunity to speak for Josif Ton and their understanding of his document. They were able not only to secure a promise that he could continue teaching in the Seminary but also to discuss the questions which he had raised in his document. They were careful to dissociate themselves from some of the methods of independent Christian groups around the world, and made clear the Federation's and Alliance's commitment to just and honest negotiations with any State on a proper legal basis.[11]

More and more Baptists asserted their independence, and adulation of Josif Ton's 'heroic' stand by many groups in the West led to State repression, which in turn led to many trials and imprisonments. Ton himself was the victim of considerable police harassment. In 1974 he published a second document, 'The Christian in Socialism', which he described to an English friend as a Christian manifesto to the socialist society. Again, this was disseminated world-wide; he also sent a copy to the head of the State. This intensified the problems; it also left many in Romania, the EBF and the BWA uncertain where he actually stood. On several occasions Gerhard Claas and others from the EBF or BWA sought to reconcile the warring factions, without much success. Eventually the Department of Cults insisted that the Baptist Union must firmly settle the matter. When Ton issued a third document - 'Evangelical Believers and Human Rights in Romania' - eight of his colleagues were dismissed from the Union. He seems to have safeguarded himself by agreeing that in future he would make his protests internally rather than publicly. Ambiguity about his motives continued, but it must be admitted that he had put his finger on crucial issues which, as we shall see, socialist governments in one country after another had to face with Baptists and other churches by the late 1980s.[12]

INTO THE 1980s

The new decade was one of the most formative periods for the members of the European Baptist Federation behind the Iron Curtain. Despite the remarkable progress made in the 1960s and 1970s, the difficulties faced by churches and believers in most socialist countries were still immense. For many the personal costs was heavy. There was always uncertainty about future freedom. Even when official policy became more moderate, the laws weighted against religion remained on the statute books and could be applied at any time according to the whims and moods of local and national authorities. Political fears and ambitions continued to determine government policies at home and abroad. One Russian Baptist pastor put their position in perspective in the 1970s with this comment: 'The only time we can be sure of is today. We may not be free tomorrow. So we use today to the utmost and leave our future in God's hands.'

As the story of the 1980s unfolds one can begin to see the dawn of a new day approaching. What eventually took place was a testimony to the patient endurance and unshaken faith of countless Eastern European Christians. In their view it was also confirmation of the promise of Jesus to build his church on the rock of faith in him, so that the powers of evil could not prevail against it.[13]

1980 began with two key EBF events in Eastern Europe. In February the Executive met in the Romanian capital, Bucharest; but it was planned as more than a routine meeting. Linked with it was a four-day programme of visits to the Romanian, Hungarian and German language Baptist churches. A delegation of nineteen people was divided into small groups in order to visit as many places as possible. Gerhard Claas wrote in his report to the EBF Council several months afterwards:

> This visit was an unforgettable experience for all participants. The overwhelming hospitality, the participation in dynamic church services, absolutely packed with people, the intensive testimony of many church members, the quality of the musical performances and many more experiences were so encouraging and inspiring.

For many generations Romanian Baptists had suffered grievously at the hands of the State and the Orthodox Church. Yet they were experiencing phenomenal growth with 10,000 baptisms a year.[14]

The second key event was the meeting of the Federation Executive and Council at Paris in April. Denton Lotz introduced a proposal for the formation of a Books and Translations Committee. Its purpose would be to integrate and co-operate with the SITE mini-library scheme, the Baptist translation and book centre in Vienna, and EUROLIT, the joint project of the Baptist Union of Great Britain and Ireland (BUGBI) and an ecumenical organization known as FEED THE MINDS (FTM). EUROLIT had been created by Dr David Russell (General Secretary of BUGBI) and the Revd Alec Gilmore (a Baptist in FTM), with the needs for Christian literature in Eastern Europe in mind, and had already been introduced to the Executive meeting in Bucharest. Each of the three bodies would retain its own leadership and funding, but the Books and Translations Committee would link them all in a complementary programme. It would be a separate, specialist committee because the Evangelism and Education Committee was too general in its brief and was already over-committed.

The Executive approved the proposal for recommendation to the Council, adding a suggested make-up for the new committee. The whole scheme met with the warm support of the Council. It was an imaginative development which had far-reaching influence throughout Europe for years to come. Its story will be dealt with in more detail in a later chapter. Interestingly, a member of the Council expressed the hope in open discussion that there would be two-way traffic, so that Alexander Karev's books might be made known in the West.

The delegates in Paris received with pleasure the news that Michael Zhidkov had been appointed a chaplain at the forthcoming Moscow Olympic Games. This was surely a sign that opportunities for Christian witness were being won by genuine efforts to be loyal to State and to Christ. The Council agreed to donate a communion set for him to use.

The Council also approved the nomination of Knud Wümpelmann as General Secretary in succession to Gerhard Claas, who was about to become General Secretary of the Baptist World Alliance, subject to confirmation of his election at the Alliance Congress in the summer at Toronto. The EBF office would then be moved to Copenhagen. Another change in personnel was necessary because Denton Lotz was returning to the USA; Ronald Goulding was asked to serve as interim director of SITE. The Summer Institute had become one of the most successful EBF enterprises. Sixty students were already registered for the current year.

The next meeting of the Council was at the German Baptist Family Centre in Dorfweil in the autumn of 1981. In his first report Knud Wümpelmann drew attention to three major international conferences which had taken place in the past year:

1. In May/June 1980 the Conference of European Churches (CEC) met in Madrid to consider 'Confidence Building' as part of the post-Helsinki consultation process. Because of the Soviet Union's involvement in war in Afghanistan and NATO's placement of middle-range missiles in Europe, the political emphasis had changed from disarmament to *détente*. This conference issued a strong call to churches to support confidence building measures.
2. In September 1980 there was a World Parliament for Peoples of Peace in Sofia, Bulgaria, arranged by the World Peace Council.

3. In April 1981 the AUCECB called together its Senior Presbyters and representatives from the other socialist countries, to discuss with six BWA leaders the theme 'Confidence Building and Choosing Life'. Afterwards, they issued an appeal to all fellow-believers in Europe, USA and the rest of the world for constant prayer and supportive action for peace.

Such topics were to feature frequently in reports, discussions and resolutions in the coming years. The new General Secretary brought to his tasks strong personal commitment in these directions. He was obviously aware that the Christian Church had been given a mission and message of reconciliation, and since this was a vital part of the original aims of the Federation, he ensured that it was not neglected. The current political climate also gave it high priority.

Dr David Russell, reflecting on his presidential visits to every Eastern European country except Albania, spoke of four factors needing the Federation's attention. One was the need for a firm stand for peace in response to the massive build-up of the arms race. Another was a willingness to take up urgent human rights issues in accordance with the principles of the Helsinki Final Act. A third was to plan more visits in the East to break down boundaries which hindered faith and resource sharing. Such planning, he urged, should be jointly undertaken to avoid the common tendency for the West to impose their choices on the East without genuine consultation. Finally, he pressed the case for more good theological literature for use across the whole range of church life, building on the work of SITE, the Books and Translations Committee and EUROLIT. His remarks must have sounded like music to Eastern European ears!

The Dorfweil Council heard Dr Thorwald Lorenzen, a member of the Faculty of the Ruschlikon Seminary, deliver an outstanding paper on 'The Bible and Human Rights'. He emphasized the special role of the Christian Church in responding to such issues of human concern, not simply in humanitarian terms, but out of the context of faith in Jesus Christ. Year by year, EBF committees and councils were having to deal with problems of member Unions which confirmed the relevance of his message. For example, the European Baptist Theological

Teachers' Conference (EBTTC) reported to the Council in Denia, Spain in 1982 that Romanian Baptists were once again in crisis, because the government refused to allow sufficient admissions of students to the Bucharest Seminary for ministerial training. Urgent negotiations on their behalf were necessary. In the following year, the Baptist Church in Georgi Dimitros Street, Varna, Bulgaria was scheduled by the State authorities for demolition, without proper consultation with the church. This aroused international Baptist protest, which strengthened the hands of the Bulgarian Baptist Union, led by the Revd Theo Angelov in partnership with the EBF. But the authorities proved intractable; it was only after a prolonged saga of negotiations and prayer that a satisfactory solution was achieved in the 1990s, but that will come later in the story.

Clearly, what was taking place in Eastern Europe by the 1980s was the meeting of spiritual and political forces which were struggling for the soul of a continent and its member nations. The Communist leaders were trying to come to terms with the inescapable fact that, however they had endeavoured to eradicate religion from their culture, it had grown stronger, and they would be wiser to be in dialogue and *détente* with it. This not only gave the churches new opportunities; it also opened up in church and nation searching questions about the role of the church within a socialist society. Eyes of faith claimed to see God at work in this process. Biblical teaching about the divine Spirit struggling with the principalities and powers in high places seemed remarkably relevant. Within the space of a few years an unbelievable transformation was to take place. God was preparing his people for a new Europe, and the European Baptist Federation was to be at work in one of the most significant periods of the twentieth century.

During an Executive meeting in Spain in 1982, David Russell expressed his concern for Albania, which was the only sizeable European country where the EBF had no contact. He requested that this should be made a matter for prayer and that reliable information should be collected. The Revd Jan Auke Brandsma from the Netherlands undertook to deal with this and present a report to the Council in 1983. He gave a paper entitled 'Religious Life in Albania' at the Council in Sodertälje, Sweden on 30 September 1983. Albania had declared itself a People's Republic after the Second World War, and immediately began to denounce all forms of religion, confiscate church property, and imprison, torture or even execute religious leaders. In 1967 it declared itself the first atheistic state. All religious institutions were outlawed; within a few months more than 2,000 churches and mosques were seized. But the Christian faith had not been exterminated. Jan Auke Brandsma was able to report that, even after four decades of severe repression, there was evidence of Christian believers, both young and elderly, worshipping secretly in small groups and holding prayer meetings in their houses. They were mainly Roman Catholic and Orthodox. He had not been able to obtain any information about the existence of evangelicals, but he was convinced that prayer for the situation in Albania should be faithfully offered. President Enver Hoxha was advanced in age and there were signs of internal political unrest. Who could tell what might happen at the time of his death? Such a question should alert the EBF to the need not only to pray but to be ready to act in support of Christians in the country. Seven months later Dr Russell raised the matter again, urging the importance of prayer and open ears. Just over a year later, in 1985, President Hoxha died. Restrictions began to be lifted and doors long shut were opened. Soon the EBF was to have a unique opportunity to be involved with various world mission organizations, working in partnership with Albanian evangelical believers.

In the remainder of the 1980s and the last decade of the century a new chapter in Eastern European church history would be written, which confirmed what has been the unceasing faith of the Christian gospel through the centuries - that God is always crossing the boundaries to work out his purposes of love. Despite much opposition the Word of God is not bound.

CHAPTER NOTES

CHAPTER FOUR   Behind The Iron Curtain

1 Relevant books giving more details include Walter Sawatsky, *Soviet Evangelicals since World War II*, Herald Press (Canada & USA), 1981; Trevor Beeson, *Discretion and Valour,* revised edition, Fount Paperbacks (UK) and Fortress Press (USA), 1982; E. A. Payne, *Out of Great Tribulation,* Baptist Union of Great Britain & Ireland, 1974. Also various articles by D. S. Russell have been published in the *Baptist Quarterly.*

2 Regional superintendents with oversight of churches and pastors.

3 Acts 5.29; Matthew 22.21; Romans 13.1.

4 In addition to the books listed, see M.Bourdeaux, *Religious Ferment in Russia,* Macmillan, 1968 and *Faith on Trial in Russia,* Hodder & Stoughton, 1971

5 E. A. Payne, op.cit., p.56.

6 Michael was the son of the beloved Jakob Zhidkov who had celebrated his 80th birthday in 1966. He was trained at Spurgeon's College, London.

7 E. A. Payne, op.cit., p.56.

8 See chapter 9 for more about peace and human rights issues.

9 Fuller details about SITE and associated projects will appear in chapter 8.

10 See *Building Bridges,* personal conclusions concerning the activities of the Lay Conference Committee 1970-1996, by Sven Svenson, Stockholm, 1996. English translation by Ragni Lantz.

11 A copy of Ronald Goulding's full report of this meeting is in the Angus Library, Regent's Park College, Oxford.

12 A useful commentary on these events can be found in a reprint from the *Journal of Church and State* (Vol.21, No.3, 1979) of an article by Alan Scarfe (Professor of Eastern European Church History, Institute of Slavic Studies, and Executive Secretary, Society of the Study of Religion under Communism, Wheaton, Illinois, USA), entitled 'A Call for Truth: An Appraisal of Rumanian Baptist Church-State Relationships'.

13 Matthew 16.18.

14 Denton Lotz, 'Baptist Witness in Eastern Europe', *Baptist Quarterly,* 28, pp.73-5.

5

NORTH, SOUTH, EAST AND WEST

Early in his time as General Secretary of the European Baptist Federation, Ronald Goulding stated in a report to the Council:

> I believe that beyond any question of doubt the EBF has more than justified its existence over these past years and has now become an indispensable part of the work among Baptists in Europe.[1]

He recalled that there had originally been doubts about the need for such a body, and fears that it might take to itself too much power. Such reactions had been groundless. The number of issues requiring more than local or national consideration had led to encouraging growth in the Federation. Some matters which proved too difficult for individuals, churches, committees or unions had been resolved by appeal to the wider fellowship. He paid warm tribute to the enterprising leadership of his predecessor, Dr Erik Rudén, who had won the trust and support of the member Unions. His own view was that a primary achievement of the EBF was in becoming a 'bringing together agency'.

Almost twenty years later when the 7th European Baptist Congress was held in Hamburg, a public resolution was passed welcoming the political attempts being made to 'develop co-operation and enhance mutual understanding in Europe, as indicated in the final document endorsed by Foreign Ministers at the European Security Review Council in Madrid, September 1983.' The resolution went on to urge a freer interchange of citizens and a wider dissemination of information, so that closer union might grow between the nations. In a preamble to the resolution it was noted that the EBF already contained within its membership Baptists from north, south, east and west, despite the political and economic divisions of the continent. As a practical step to increase such bringing together beyond the boundaries local Baptist churches were encouraged to enter into twinning links with other Baptist churches in other lands. The Executive and Council of the Federation were invited to facilitate such links.

This expression of a Baptist desire to make a positive contribution to the healing of a divided Europe did far more than echo the earlier comment of Ronald Goulding. It also embodied the vision of Jesus, expressed in his promise that many would come from the east and west, the north and south, and sit down together at the same banqueting table in the Kingdom of God.[2] Such a spiritual concept has profound significance for the life and work of the Christian Church; it provides the theme of this chapter in which we explore the growth of the EBF throughout the whole of Europe and even beyond.

STRUCTURED FOR MISSION AND SERVICE

When Ronald Goulding made the comments with which this chapter began, he also recommended a thorough review of all the Federation's committees and commissions. He wished to avoid allowing the EBF to settle in a rut; he was eager too that it should equip itself and its member Unions for the future. The review was undertaken initially by the Secretaries' Conference which met annually from 1967 to 1969, and again in 1971. Its report was referred to the Executive for recommendations to be presented to the Council at Novi Sad in August 1972.

In the late 1950s a Bible Study and Membership Training Committee had been established. Very little about it occurs in the minutes until 1963, when it appears as the Bible Study and Membership Commission. Its work had expanded to provide courses on bible study, Baptist history and principles, Baptist missions around the world and Christian education.[3] A purposeful sectional meeting took place at the 3rd European Baptist Congress in Amsterdam, when plans were announced for an All Europe Conference to be held at Rüschlikon in 1967 for those engaged in children's, youth and adult education, with the theme 'The Bible in Education Today'. This was full of promise which was never realized. By 1972 the Commission had changed course again. It had become the European Baptist Christian Education Committee, aiming to provide Christian education materials for the Unions, but this was thwarted by wide variations of language, cultures, theology and structures, and by the stringent financial limitations within the Federation. Regional conferences were attempted, but failed to secure the right participants; feeding ideas through the Unions did not happen. This must have been a frustrating experience and it probably came as no surprise when the review report indicated that the committee had ceased to exist. The retiring President of the EBF, Andrew MacRae, stated in his presidential report that the poor quality of Christian education in many churches and Sunday Schools was an urgent problem. He was therefore asked by the Council to explore future possibilities. A year later the Executive approved his recommendation that the European members of the Baptist World Alliance Commission on Christian Education should form the initial membership of a new EBF committee. Its main brief would be to co-ordinate the agendas of the two groups. The following were appointed: Andrew MacRae (chairman), Gerhard Claas, Josef Nagy, Sven Ohm, Karl Heinz Walter and Michael Zhidkov.

Another result of the review was that henceforth the Youth Committee and the Men's Committee would be appointed by the EBF Council, although they would remain free to elect their own officers. They were to be answerable to the Federation and must justify their budgetary requests. An Evangelism Committee had begun when many evangelistic efforts in different countries needed co-ordination by the sharing of personnel, resources and experiences. More recently it had formed close links with the BWA programme 'World Mission of Reconciliation in Jesus Christ', with the intention of encouraging churches to carry it out in Europe. A Radio Committee grew out of the launching of the studio in Rüschlikon and had developed an helpful role in organizing conferences on broadcasting in Eastern Europe, offering practical help to Baptist broadcasters. The European Baptist Women's Union was acknowledged as an autonomous body which had been founded a year earlier than the EBF. It faithfully worked in many ways within the EBF, but provided its own budget, elected its own officers and committees, and also made and directed its own programmes. Later in this chapter a brief account of its contribution to European Baptist life will be given.

One other matter of considerable importance was included in the report of the review; namely, finance. Because of currency restrictions in the East and limited resources in the smaller Unions, there was always difficulty in meeting budgetary requirements. Ronald Goulding appealed for greater financial support in order that the committees and programmes of the Federation might function more effectively.

Having spent so much time on structures, the Council unfortunately soon had to deal with the issue again, because their parent body, the Baptist World Alliance, was busy with its own process of reorganization. Dr Carl Tiller of the USA attended the 1974 EBF Council at Stabbek, Norway, to convey the result of the Alliance's discussions about their Regional Fellowships. Three new ones had been established - the North-American Baptist Fellowship, the Caribbean Baptist Fellowship and the Asian Baptist Fellowship - and all of them were in the process of preparing a constitution to submit to the BWA. Although the EBF was the pioneer Regional Fellowship and had already existed for twenty-four years, the Alliance had decided that they too must submit a constitution for approval if they wished to remain in membership. Other conditions were laid down with this requirement. They would have to share in financing the regional office. Their General Secretary would have to accept responsibility for Baptists in Africa and the Middle East. Future General Secretaries would be appointed by the BWA Council after consultation with the EBF. Alliance Commissions must have parallel bodies in the Federation, although the EBF would be free to have additional ones if they wished.

One can imagine that these requirements caused lively discussion and not a little questioning. When the Alliance had undergone a previous review of its role and structures in the early 1960s, Dr Arnold Ohrn, the BWA General Secretary at the time, asked the Russian Baptist leader, Jakob Zhidkov, for his opinion. His reply was forthright! 'A cat only licks itself when it has nothing better to do; a Society only bothers about its constitution when it feels free from more urgent tasks.' For the Russian Baptists there were at least two more urgent needs to consider - evangelism and world peace. No such gems of wisdom were reported from the 1974 discussions. Council unanimously passed the following recommendation from its Executive:

> That the Council of the European Baptist Federation recognises the need for the continuation of the European Baptist Federation as a specifically European entity and resolves that its constitution and organisational status should be submitted for the approval of the Baptist World Alliance as required to meet the terms of the Baptist World Alliance constitution.

Was this merely submissive compliance? Or was there a strong hint of independence in the phrase 'a specifically European entity'?

Dr Claus Meister, the current EBF President, then presented a report of the Executive's discussions on the previous day about the priorities of organizational reform and outlined the main principles to be written into the constitution and bye-laws:

- The Council to meet annually.
- Each Union/Convention to have its General Secretary or President as its voting delegate, plus a second representative.
- Six lay members (men, women and youth) to be elected by Council, and the Men's Committee then to cease.
- A revised make-up of the Council and Executive, and the latter to be given more significance by meeting every six months.
- The following Departments and Committees to be created: Relief and Fellowship Aid; Finance and Administration; (both directly responsible to the Executive); Evangelism and Education (elected by the Council); and later, Communications was added.

Two hesitations were expressed in debate. Alexei Bichkov felt that African Baptists should be encouraged to form their own Regional Fellowship as soon as possible, to ease the excessive load of the General

Secretary, but especially to help them aim for self-determination. Rolf Damman hoped that the true value of the EBF would not be lost in organization.

The general principles outlined by Dr Meister were agreed. Drafts of the new Constitution and Bye-laws would be sent to Unions in readiness for final approval at the 1975 Executive and Council in Bilthoven, Holland. Dr Robert S. Denny, the BWA General Secretary, was present at Bilthoven to speak about the newly approved Alliance Constitution, and to consult with the EBF about a successor to Ronald Goulding, who would be leaving in a year to take up a new appointment as Director of the BWA Division of Evangelism and Education. The person in mind was Gerhard Claas. He would have to give a year's notice to the German Baptist Union and could begin as the new General Secretary on 1 October 1976. This would give time to move the office from London to a continental site. Mrs Barbara Askew, who had served as Ronald Goulding's secretary for several years, was asked to maintain the London office as long as necessary on a day-to-day basis.

After careful consideration of the Unions' responses, the draft Constitution and Bye-law changes were amended and approved. The nomination of Gerhard Claas, the office proposals and the necessary budgetary provisions for the new structures were also accepted. Generous financial help was promised by the American Baptist Churches and the European Baptist Convention. In due course the office was moved to the site of the Albertinenhaus deaconess home and hospital in Hamburg. The London office closed on 30 September 1976. It had existed within Baptist Church House since 1906, and a plaque commemorating this was to be put there by the Alliance.

When the Council held its meetings in Vienna in September 1978, Knud Wümpelmann as President stressed how important it was for the Federation to remain sufficiently flexible to accept change and adjust its structures to actual needs. At the same time Gerhard Claas added that he and Ronald Goulding had recently attended the first African Baptist Conference in Nairobi, Kenya. A committee had been formed to prepare a Constitution with the aim of inaugurating an

African Baptist Fellowship by May 1979. That goal however was delayed until 1982.

Structures again became a major issue in the late 1980s, but we will leave the subject here for the time being and move on to matters of mission and service which merit attention.

MIGRANTS AND MUSLIMS

As early as 1962 the plight of numerous migrants around Europe led the EBF to explore how the churches could alleviate their needs. Unions were asked to supply information about the situation in their own country. Some form of commendation to other Unions of Baptists on the move was also suggested. At the Executive in Lisbon in June 1963 a comprehensive report on mission work among migrants was submitted by the Revd Irwin J. Barnes of Britain, following a recently convened consultation. He singled out two specific tasks: to locate and identify migrants, and to meet their material and spiritual needs.

For immediate action the report suggested that the EBF office should prepare a list of sources for bibles and Christian literature in the necessary languages. In partnership with the German Baptist Publishing House in Kassel tapes and tracts might be produced. A commendation form for use by pastors would be needed in the Spanish, Portuguese, Italian and German languages, preferably with some form of certificate to indicate good standing in home churches. It might be possible to include some vacation work among migrants for Rüschlikon students.

There were also some creative ideas for long-term planning. Consideration should be given to possible practical resources and personnel from national Unions to be used in missionary work in areas where compatriots had settled. Provisional plans were proposed for an EBF conference; but Irwin Barnes urged the desirability of ecumenical partnership, wherever possible. A Baptist conference on 'Our Task among the Migrants of Europe' was held at Duisburg 10-12 October 1964. Those present identified some crucial aspects of the work, such as problems for the churches, efforts already being made, the relation between evangelism and social work, family care, the difference between evangelism and proselytism, migrants' reactions, and co-operation with local churches, international and interdenominational agencies. An outcome was the formation of an EBF Migration Committee. Dr Thaut presented its first report to the Executive in September 1965, including a request for a Directory of Western European Baptist Churches and a printed list of bibles, tracts and books in the languages mentioned earlier plus Greek and Turkish. By 1967 Arabic had been added. Wolfgang Mueller took over the chairmanship from Dr Thaut.

As expected, work among migrants soon became ecumenical. The Commission of the Churches for the European Community (CCEC) had been formed in 1962, with an Ecumenical Centre in Brussels. It met twice a year and was intended for evangelism and pastoral care among the staff of the European Community(EC). By 1973 it was recognized as a body able to monitor EC policies and comment on them from a Christian point of view. Two highly relevant items on their agenda were 'The Community and the Third World' and 'The Community and the Migrant Workers'. In 1974 the Baptist Union of Great Britain and Ireland, through its Secretary for Social Affairs, the Revd Donald Black, asked the EBF to consider becoming involved with CCEC. He also requested an opportunity to report on the Commission during the coming year. This was referred to the Executive but seems to have led to no specific action, probably because of the difficulties felt by those from Eastern Europe.

Meanwhile, the Federation was by no means uninvolved in the migrant issue. In 1970 Kerstin Rudén reported to the Glasgow Council that the EBWU had made generous financial gifts to various national Baptist initiatives among migrant workers and gypsies. In 1976 the EBF Relief and Aid grants included one for work among Yugoslav immigrants in West Berlin. In 1978 similar help was given to three special projects:

- for the Portuguese Baptists' programme for the resettlement of refugees returning from the civil war in Angola;

- for the West German Baptists' ministry among 7,000 German-speaking emigrants from the Soviet Union;
- for mission among guest workers from Spain (mostly Catholic) and Turkey (mostly Islamic).

A year later Gerhard Claas recommended to the Council that a gift be made to Ivan Adolf, an immigrant from the USSR, who had applied for aid via the West German Baptist Union, to enable him to serve in the resettlement camp in Una-Massen. During the 6th European Congress which followed that Council meeting, delegates wholeheartedly passed a resolution expressing their disquiet at the plight of the dispossessed and homeless peoples of the world. Sometimes people doubt the value of such resolutions and question to whom they are addressed. In this context it can be reasonably argued that to discuss such a topic is in itself an educational process. Experience shows that it often strengthens the resolve for Christian action and quickens much intercessory prayer in local churches.

A remarkable story was told at the EBF Council meetings in Sodertälje, Sweden in 1983, when there was discussion about aid for a small church in Portugal. Two years previously the church had thirty-one members; now there were sixty-two. Fifteen more candidates were ready for baptism, thirteen house bible classes were operating, and as many as a hundred converts had responded to their evangelism. In addition to starting a new congregation in a nearby town they had also secured a site for an old people's home and an orphanage. The original members of this church had all been *Returnados* from Angola and Mozambique, drawn together by the Portuguese Baptist ministry among guest workers mentioned earlier.

A significant change of direction in work among migrants occurred in the 1980s. General Secretary Knud Wümpelmann told the Council in Denia, Spain in 1982 that there were approximately twenty-four million Muslims in Europe. Over eighteen million had deep roots in the Asiatic regions of Eastern Europe, where Islam held sway. But five and a half million were in Western Europe, having come as 'guest workers' in the 1960s and 1970s. They had settled permanently with their families in many places, creating a totally new social and religious situation for themselves and for the Christian churches. For example, there were two million Muslims in France, but only one million Protestants. Knud Wümpelmann spoke of 'the challenge on our doorstep'. He also recalled the biblical imperative to welcome and care for 'the stranger within your gates'.[4] In the autumn of 1982 a Muslim Awareness Conference, initiated by Dr J. D. Hughey, was held in Dorfweil with valuable input made by Bill Wagner, Isam Ballenger and Dr Hughey.[5] Four stated purposes were to awaken awareness of the Muslim presence, religion and social conditions, to examine the extent of Christian ministry among them, to share information about literature, and to help Baptists promote local Christian mission among them. Members of the conference confessed their sense of shame at their ignorance and inactivity. They called one another to prayer and loving outreach, and resolved to seek help and advice through study and contact with a number of Middle East institutions in Beirut. During the next three years a special Mission to Muslims Committee, under the chairmanship of Bill Wagner, was busily active. It reported to the Council in Glasgow in 1986 that it had access to a large number of books, pamphlets and courses in Arabic and Turkish and was in contact with existing projects in Yugoslavia, France, Germany, England and Belgium. During 1985 aid had been given to meet the extra demand for an excellent book on Islam by the Yugoslav Baptists. An approach had also been made to the European Baptist Theological Teachers' Conference to look at the question of Islamic studies in Baptist seminaries. A second conference was held in Belgium in 1987. When the Council met in Dorfweil in 1988 a moving appeal for prayer was made by the committee on the basis of Leviticus 19:33-34. They recommended that churches with Muslims in their area should take seriously the education of members.

EVANGELISM AND AID

An Evangelism Committee started modestly in the mid 1960s to plan occasional conferences and encourage people to share their faith. In

1971-2 they pursued the BWA programme in Europe, 'World mission of Reconciliation in Christ'. In 1975 the EBF Council welcomed the formation of the new BWA Division of Evangelism and Education, with Ronald Goulding as its Director. They expressed their hope for a new awareness of the teaching mission of the Church, with adequate provision of leadership training, seminary involvement and basic guideline literature. To express its links with the BWA Division the Federation's committee was renamed the Evangelism and Education Committee, and in 1976 launched a five-year theme for the churches, 'New People for a New World through Christ'. Eager to stress that the main initiative must rest with local churches, they described their task as to be a resource centre not a programme planner. Before long they were so conscious of the great need for evangelism throughout Europe and the inadequacy of their efforts that they made an official request through their chairman, the Revd Andrew MacRae, for a Director in church growth and conference planning. They specifically named Dr Bill Wagner as their choice. There was also pressure from some quarters for an evangelist at large.

For a number of reasons the Executive and Council felt unable to accede to these requests. Financial constraints seriously limited staff appointments and the range of policies. Despite their disappointment the 'E & E Committee', as it was commonly known, laboured on and achieved much. But there were different understandings of mission within the Unions; and opportunities and freedoms varied greatly from East to West. Traditional national and majority churches in some countries were hostile to the evangelistic efforts of Baptists and other evangelicals, which led to legal restraints being applied on the grounds that they were guilty of proselytism. However, man-made boundaries could not exclude God. In north, south, east and west, many conversions and baptisms were being reported. New churches were being planted; extensions to church buildings were taking place. A new sense of the Spirit of God at work in many parts of Europe created a spirit of optimism. By the mid 1980s the Federation was able to establish a permanent Institute for Mission and Evangelism

(IME) which would far exceed what any part-time committee could achieve.

In the ninth chapter of this book a more thorough assessment of issues of Christian mission and service among Baptists will be given. So we pass on now from evangelism to a brief survey of the Federation's programme of Relief and Aid. Ever since the BWA's programmes of European relief and reconstruction, master-minded by Drs J. H. Rushbrooke and W. O. Lewis after the two World Wars, there has been an important place for such matters in both the Alliance and the Federation. There has been close co-operation between Baptist World Aid and the EBF Relief and Aid Committee. In most Executive and Council meetings proposals and requests for help were on the agenda. The following items form only a proportion of what has been achieved over the years, but they indicate the needs which arise and the opportunities which emerge. All of them can only be met by the shared compassion and willing partnership of the Federation's members. No attempt has been made to put them in chronological order.

When natural disasters occur immediate help is needed. Emergency funds were provided for stricken families after severe earthquakes in Romania in 1977 and Italy in 1980-81. Considerable help was given for the rebuilding or repair of church buildings in both countries, and for the almost total reconstruction of the Bucharest Baptist Seminary. The Romanian government insisted that the building work could not begin until all homeless families were rehoused. This meant a frustrating delay of eleven years. Baptist churches in Yugoslavia and the Liege area of Belgium were also assisted after earthquakes. Heavy flooding seriously disrupted life in the Christian charitable home known as 'Schmalkalden', in which the East German Baptists were involved. The Federation made a substantial contribution towards the restoration work.

Political unrest, economic pressures and industrial disasters have also made heavy demands on national Unions. Resources have been made available to safeguard adequate pensions for Italian pastors, to deliver food to the hungry in Poland, to enable care to be offered to refugees and displaced peoples in various countries, and to supply medicines, surgical equipment and sometimes medical treatment in other lands which was not available in the patient's own country. When the Chernobyl nuclear explosion occurred a vast programme of relief was needed. This included help with nursing and medical care, restoration and building work, holidays for children afflicted by radiation sickness and pollution, and much personal help and compassion for churches and families.

But aid has by no means been restricted to disaster situations. Innumerable needs have arisen through successful evangelism and church planting, through ministries of compassion, and through the development of conference centres, theological seminaries, new bible schools and denominational centres, especially more recently since the decline of Communism and the rise of independent, democratic states. The following are a few illustrations: a new church in Lille, another in Gottwaldov, Czechoslovakia, a children's home in Rome, the Cascais Baptist Centre in Portugal, extra buildings for the Baptist Theological Academy in Budapest, the newly developed Baptist Theological Seminary in Radosc, Poland, and much earlier, help towards the Baptist Centre in Denia, Spain. Over many years the EBF Books and Translations Committee, in partnership with other Christian agencies, organized the supply of bibles in various languages, biblical commentaries, theological books and mini-libraries for the benefit of pastors, teachers, leaders and members in Eastern European Baptist Unions. Generous gifts were received towards this from western unions and churches, and frequently from the European Baptist Women's Union. Special projects like the production of the Gospels in Braille for Russians received a number of EBF Relief and Aid grants.

In 1986 there was an extended discussion in the Executive at Glasgow to draw up more specific guidelines for European Baptist Aid. Three categories were identified:

- **Emergency Relief** - to provide food, shelter, medicine, blankets and more long-term projects for refugees and victims of disasters.

This aid was to given without regard to nationality, ethnic background, political views or religion.

- **Church Aid** - for Baptist Unions and Conventions only, towards church buildings and seminaries, courses and programmes like SITE, and the supply of literature, hymnbooks, bibles, and other necessary resources. An essential principle for this aid was that it must all be done within the framework of the different nations' laws.

- **Fraternal Aid** - to supply special medicines or medical treatment for Baptists in financial need, to provide pocket money at committees for members from currency restricted countries, to help those in need of convalescence, rest or rehabilitation to go to Casa Locarno, an ecumenical centre in the Mediterranean area.

A general principle was established to encourage co-operation with other aid agencies, Baptist or otherwise, in meeting what was essentially *human* need. Close liaison obviously needed to be maintained with Baptist World Aid.

This careful classification of European Baptist Aid turned out to be timely, for within a few years there were vast political upheavals in Eastern Europe which led to much economic instability and human need. The following chapters will unfold the story and reveal the heavy demands made upon Baptist compassion and generosity.

WOMEN AND YOUTH

Within the limits of space it is impossible to describe in detail the work of all the committees. Two have been selected here to illustrate how much has been achieved by such groups of people.

The first is the **European Baptist Women's Union** (EBWU). This was launched in 1948, a year before the Federation, in response to concerns expressed within the Baptist World Alliance about post-war planning in Europe. The prime movers were Mrs Ernest Brown (England), Mrs George Martin (USA) and Mrs Edgar Bates (Canada). Plans were made for an annual week of prayer in the first week of November, a news bulletin, and the exchange of Christmas gifts and greetings. The organization would be under the wing of the BWA Women's Committee. Their first report was given to the inaugural EBF Council at Hamburg in 1951 and they participated in the programme of the 1st European Baptist Congress in Copenhagen in the following year. By 1958 some of the EBWU committee were advocating closer ties with the Federation. They already presented reports to the Council and their president was an Executive member. They were now eager to have close links with the Rüschlikon Seminary and began to press for two women to be included in EBF delegations to Eastern Europe.

In the 1960s they fell into line with other Women's Unions which had been formed by making the first Monday of November their annual Day of Prayer. At this a love-offering would be made, half of it for the work of the BWA Women's Department, and the other half devoted to urgent needs and causes in Europe to be identified year by year. Successive presidents made outstanding contributions to Baptist life across national and political boundaries - Mrs Ruth Pepper (1955-62), Mrs Elizabeth Flügge (1962-67) and Miss Dorothy Finch (1967-70). Their secretary, Mrs Kerstin Rudén (1964-72), was also a frequent visitor. Between them they visited Baptist women in France, Italy, Portugal, Norway, Holland, Spain, Austria, Sweden, and Switzerland, as well as making pioneering journeys to small groups of Baptists in Israel, Lebanon and Jordan. Elizabeth Flügge attended the Prague Peace Council in 1964 as an EBF delegate. While she was there she took the opportunity to confer with the women of the First Baptist Church in Prague and to hold conversations with male Baptist leaders from Russia and Hungary. Several attempts to obtain visas for visits to Eastern European countries were abortive, as were invitations for women from those lands to attend the biennial European Baptist Women's conferences. At last Kerstin Rudén was able to make the first official EBWU visit to the Soviet Union in 1966; also Mrs Klaudia Pillipuk (née Tyrtova) from Moscow was able to become a member of the EBWU committee.

The value of these efforts can be seen in the list of causes supported from the Day of Prayer offerings in the 1960s: Romanian bibles, EBF migrant mission and care, an orphanage in Portugal, an elderly peoples' home in Spain, two new churches in Belgium, a kindergarten in Austria, and training for pastors' wives and the fiancées of theological students. Each year such generosity helped to build lasting relationships and provided opportunities for expanding the influence of the EBF. It made many Baptists aware of the larger family to which they belonged, giving encouragement and hope in difficult situations, and quickening their Christian mission. During the 1970s this was reflected in their support and prayer for new church building schemes in Czechoslovakia, Poland and East Berlin, youth centres in Italy and Hungary, a summer youth camp in Yugoslavia, a Baptist Evangelism Centre at Rocca de Papu in Italy, and the Portuguese Baptist orphanage in A Guas Santas Maia.

The EBWU devoted much attention to leadership training in their summer conferences and in the programmes connected with their international visits. Patient prayer and effort were rewarded when for the first time two women from the USSR attended the conference in Doorn, Holland in 1977. Two years later, at the 6th European Baptist Congress in Brighton, England, the thirtieth anniversary of the founding of the EBWU was celebrated. Thousands of Baptist women held hands to sing the theme-hymn of the Saturday afternoon rally, 'Blest be the tie that binds'. Mrs Nell Alexander of England spoke about four strands in the 'tie': their common faith, fellowship, purpose and love. Earlier Mrs Marie Mathis, President of the BWA Women's Department, emphasized togetherness in prayer. The final item was a dramatic presentation entitled 'Turning Point', which is still talked about as an unforgettable experience. It portrayed the beginnings of the EBWU by showing a group of European Baptist women at a meeting in Baptist Church House, London just after the Second World War. They found it hard to overcome the barriers and bitterness of war. So they said together, each in their own language, the words of John 3:16. That was the turning point; the barriers were broken down, and the fellowship formed that day had grown ever since and would not cease.

Another turning point was at the EBF Council in Santa Severa, Italy in 1987. The following important resolution was passed:

> This Council resolves to encourage further the member bodies of the EBF to take steps to enhance the role of women, in accordance with the spirit of the Gospel, in contributing to the leadership of local churches, regional and national bodies and the EBF.

This was not going to be an easy issue to resolve in view of the wide differences of church tradition and biblical interpretation among Baptists. In 1978 the Revd Birgit Karlsson of Sweden had been asked to address the Vienna Council on 'The Role of Women in the Church'. Mai Britt also attended an EBF conference on 'Men and Women in the Church' as an official delegate of the EBWU. In addition to being an ordained minister, Birgit Karlsson held significant leadership posts in the Baptist Seminary and the Baptist Union of Sweden, and during the 1980s was a prominent contributor to the life and work of the BWA and EBF. It was no surprise to those who knew her when she was approached to consider nomination for the Vice-presidency of the Federation. She faced a dilemma, for she realized that such an appointment might cause division; yet she felt that it was necessary for Baptists to face and live with their diversities. After much thought and prayer she accepted nomination and was elected without any significant reaction.

Difficulties surfaced when she was expected to succeed to the Presidency two years later. Eventually, the EBF leaders asked the BWA leaders to share in a dialogue in which those who opposed her election could express their views openly. It could not have been a pleasant experience. Emotional depths must have been painfully stirred, not only for Birgit Karlsson herself and those who were in favour of her appointment, but also for those who knew of her valuable service and had grown to love and respect her, yet felt obliged to be true to the tradition and convictions of their congregations and Unions by voting against her. After patiently listening to the debate for several hours, she asked if she might share her personal testimony of God's calling. This ended with the plea that the gathered company should advise her whether to let her nomination stand or to withdraw it. She was willing to withdraw it if by becoming President she caused division and harm to the EBF fellowship. Several weeks later she received strong encouragement from the EBF leaders to go forward. She did, and from 1993 to 1995 served as President with distinction. Afterwards she was eager to make it widely known that those who opposed her had asked for forgiveness for the pain they had caused her and invited her to their Union's annual conference. She readily responded to both requests and was overjoyed to be able to give a message of greetings at the conference.

The repercussions of this event have undoubtedly led to some heart-warming experiences for the leaders and members of the European Baptist Women's Union. When we reach the point in the EBF story that records the remarkable events of the 1990s in Eastern Europe, we shall discover how widely God has used the witness and service of Baptist women. There can be no doubt that the pioneering work of the EBWU for the past fifty years has opened many doors previously shut, and has been an invaluable expression among European Baptists of the abounding grace of God.[6]

The work of the **Youth Committee** may not have been so dramatic, but young people have an important place within our churches. Throughout Europe there are countless young people seeking answers to profound questions about their future in a rapidly changing continent. This gives youth ministry a high profile.

The committee had a chequered career in its early days. At first it was the BWA Youth Committee, but it needed to be rooted more firmly in Europe and so was attached to the EBF. In 1958 it ran into difficulty because Joel Sorenson, the chairman, and Günter Wieske, the secretary, were ill and unable to go on serving. There was unease about the committee's independent financial appeals which cut across general budgetary policy. EBF leadership also urged them to spread their projects to all parts of Europe and not just to the East. Fresh focus and publicity were secured through a new magazine, *Youth Contact*. Within a few years the work of the committee was making good progress. Committee members began to organize visits to youth projects in different countries. Young people and leaders enjoyed exchange visits. European youth camps, student conferences, youth workers' consultations and training sessions were held, and an international camp for Baptist young people was hosted in Amsterdam. These activities created a ground swell of support which resulted in the attendance of over 400 European representatives at the BWA 6th World Youth Conference in Beirut.

By the mid 1960s Sven Ohm of Sweden had become the committee secretary. He brought to the Executive in 1965 proposals for a youth centre and church in Salzburg, to be financed by the resources of the original St Gilgen appeal in Austria. This was agreed, but the Executive suggested that hostel accommodation should be included in the scheme so that it could serve as a Baptist Centre for European youth. Another promising development took place in connection with the Italian Baptist Village at Santa Severa, 60 km north of Rome. It was an ideal centre for the Youth Committee and other EBF groups to use, but urgent financial help was needed for restoration work and refurbishment. The EBF Council promised to support this appeal.

When Andrew MacRae completed his term as EBF President in 1972 he spoke appreciatively of the quality of youth leadership around Europe. Bearing in mind that the 1960s and 70s were the period of a radically changing culture among young people, this comment was highly significant. A succession of three gifted chairmen guided the affairs of the committee during the period: Peter Tongeman (England), Sven Lindström (Sweden) and Karl Heinz Walter (West Germany). Christian youth leadership was not easy in days when the so-called New Morality held sway. Pop culture and current attacks on religious beliefs, moral values, and all forms of authority, produced a permissive society which undermined much Christian work. This process created unease among some Eastern European Baptists about life-styles in the West and made them hesitant to expose their young people to Western influences. This was the context in which the annual European Baptist Youth Secretaries' Conferences began. For many years they tried to break down barriers which kept young Baptists apart. In 1972 a conference was held in the East for the first time at

Schmiedeberg (East Germany). The BWA Congress in Stockholm in 1975 included a special evening youth event, designed to let young Baptists experience Christian togetherness on a larger scale. A year earlier, as many as six hundred Europeans attended the Baptist World Youth Conference in Portland, Oregon, USA. This also broke new ground by introducing small group activities and becoming far more participatory. EBF youth work was thus playing a vital part in building unity and training future leaders.

It was at this time too that a review of the Federation's committees gave the Youth Committee higher profile by recommending that its members should in future be appointed by the Council. This gave their work a regular place on Council and Executive agendas and led to their having a representative on the Executive. Under the chairmanship of John Brandham, the Youth Committee was moving in some new directions. A good example of this occurred in 1976-77. They enthusiastically welcomed the Helsinki Conference reports, especially the Final Act. In particular, they welcomed Section 7 with its *Declaration on principles guiding relations between participating States* and Section 1(d) headed *Co-operation in humanitarian and other fields* A final paragraph specifically related these issues to religious faiths, institutions and organizations. After a thorough study of the documents, the Committee were eager to help young people in the churches understand and fulfil such aims. They were disappointed that there were so many hindrances to international contact between young people in the churches. As a practical step towards overcoming this they encouraged Baptist youth secretaries in the member Unions to attempt some official exchange programmes between East and West, North and South. In their view the work of the EBF and relations between national Baptist Unions were vital factors in achieving this. But one of their major frustrations was that in some European countries there were many young people in Baptist churches with no provision for organized youth work. They, therefore, laid before the Council a special resolution on the subject. When it was approved they sent copies to the General Secretaries of all member Unions.[7]

During the next decade a busy programme was maintained under a succession of enthusiastic leaders such as Lars Georg Sahlin, Jörg Swodoba, Asbjørn Bakkevoll, Paul Montacute and Uwe Kühne. Events included a conference in Sweden on 'The Church and Change' with special reference to mission among young people (1980); a youth secretaries' conference in East Germany (1981); an international youth leaders' conference near Nürnberg and an international camp in the Netherlands (1982); a European youth camp on the Isle of Wight (1983); and a youth camp and programme of youth participation in the 7th European Baptist Congress at Hamburg (1984).

But there were problems to be surmounted. Numbers supporting events began to decline, despite the fact that those present often expressed delight at the quality of organization, hospitality and liveliness. Some countries never replied to mail nor attended meetings, even when offered financial help for travel. Few representatives came from Eastern Europe. Feedback suggested that such topics as mission, social action and political responsibility were not popular. At a time when demonstrations throughout Europe were inducing thousands of young people to take up causes, church responses were often so small. There seemed to be little connection between simple, personal faith and the burning issues of the day. In an effort to counteract these problems an international Youth Ministry Exchange Programme was suggested. Draft proposals were presented by Uwe Kühne, setting out possible structures, identifying purposes and participants, assessing the financial implications, and indicating the respective responsibilities of the Federation, the Youth Committee, the member Unions and local churches. It was an ambitious scheme for which there would need to be much more consultation. The EBF felt unable to undertake any extra expenditure in view of the current state of its finances. Consent was granted for a modest pilot scheme to be attempted, involving the Netherlands, Norway, Sweden, Great Britain, Switzerland and West Germany.

However, a completely new set of circumstances was about to overtake Europe in ways that would radically change Baptist agendas. The Youth Committee, like the European Baptist Women's Union, was

to face significant challenges and opportunities in the 1990s. We shall
turn to these in due course.

CONGRESSES AND CELEBRATIONS

Since the formation of the EBF, European Baptists have had an
opportunity to meet together in a major Congress every five or six
years. The event has been held in a different part of the continent each
time, usually in a national capital or some other well-known city,
where travel and tourist facilities, hotels, and suitable meeting places
were readily available. A Programme Committee, specifically
appointed by the Federation for each Congress, organizes the schedule
of events which usually spreads over four or five days in July or
August. The host Baptist Union has major responsibility, in close
liaison with that committee, for carrying out the local arrangements.

We have already taken note of the 1st European Baptist Congress
held at Copenhagen in 1952, with the theme 'Baptists and the
Evangelisation of Europe'. The second took place six years later in
West Berlin, with the theme 'Christ our Hope - Europe our
Responsibility'. The largest number of Baptists to meet together since
the Second World War assembled from twenty-two countries. They
heard from Dr Josef Nordenhaugh a report of the impressive post-war
relief work undertaken by the BWA and EBF. Almost 9,000 displaced
people had been resettled outside Europe. Through the clothing centre
five million pounds weight of clothing had been distributed to families
in need in many countries. Dr Edwin Bell also gave a survey of
reconstruction country by country. Approximately 360 new church
buildings had been erected. The sense of unity in Christ dispelled any
tendency to perpetuate bitterness provoked by war or divisions caused
by differences of conviction.

The 3rd Congress was held in Amsterdam in 1964. The overall
theme was 'Jesus Christ - the Way, the Truth, the Life'. The first
event on Saturday afternoon, 15 August, was the official opening of
the John Smyth Memorial Baptist Church, three hundred and fifty-five

years after the Baptist pioneers, John Smyth, Thomas Helwys and their fellow believers were baptized there in 1609. Those present were thrilled by the special visit and powerful preaching of Dr Martin Luther King Jr, the Baptist pastor and civil rights campaigner from the USA. Ronald Goulding was able to report that since 1928 the number of Baptists in Europe had more than doubled. In the city where ecumenism had taken on more significance by the founding of the World Council of Churches there in 1948, it was appropriate that one of the public resolutions approved by the Congress called on Baptists to approach Christians of other denominations in a spirit of love and openness, and to use opportunities for fellowship and co-operation.

The next Congress in Vienna in 1969 dealt with the topic ' The People of God in the World of Turmoil'. There had been doubts about the wisdom of choosing this venue, but it turned out to be an excellent idea. It was an open door for many Eastern Europeans. The widest ever representation from the whole of Europe was achieved. The official report spoke of 'a huge ecumenical guest response', which ensured that the standing of Baptists as a minority group in Austria was considerably strengthened. One of the EBF leaders voiced the question many were feeling: 'Is not this a miracle?' On the opening night Swedish young people invited 300 young Czechs to a meal; they subsequently exchanged addresses, with a pledge of continuing friendship. This was publicly commended as an example to urge the many other young people present from sixteen countries to grow together through shared church holidays, work camps, service projects and similar activities. Linked with this emphasis on youth participation was the fact that most speakers were in their 30s and early 40s - a deliberate 'launching' of potential leaders for the future.

Michael Zhidkov from Moscow urged Baptists in the West not to talk constantly about what Russian Christians were not allowed to do. They should tell the story instead of what they could do and were doing - professing their faith, bringing up their children in the Spirit of Christ, uniting for worship, and faithfully preaching God's Word. No special evangelistic campaigns could take place; but there were many services in the churches every week, and funerals, weddings, birthdays and house-warmings were opportunities for witness. A gasp of wonder was heard among the delegates when he told them that an average of 5,000 new converts were being baptized each year! On the final Sunday two open-air rallies of 3,000 people took place, at which Dr Billy Graham gave stirring evangelistic messages. Many responded to his appeals. A public statement was issued from the Congress, with a plea for people throughout Europe to accept the ministry of reconciliation between themselves and God, and therefore with one another.

The theme of the 5th Congress in Zurich in 1973 was 'The Future of the Church and the Church of the Future'. There was an historic moment during the opening events in the Congress Hall. Greetings were brought on behalf of the Working Fellowship of the Christian Churches of Switzerland by Dr Johannes Vonderach, the Roman Catholic Bishop of Chur. Swiss Baptists had been among the founder members of the Fellowship, but it was rare in those days for a Roman Catholic to share Baptist events in Europe. Dr Claus Meister's presidential address affirmed what he described as the 'almost hilarious confidence' that 'God opens the future we shape'. He brought the Congress down to earth by this startlingly simple comment: 'The future begins on Monday as soon as you get home.' There were two new features in the programme. Each day news was communicated visually through an item described as 'Information in pictures'. On the Saturday evening young people from a number of countries led a Gospel Festival which Karl Heinz Walter of West Germany chaired.

In 1979 the 6th European Baptist Congress assembled in Brighton, England, to consider the theme 'So weak, and yet so strong'. The thirtieth anniversary of the European Baptist Women's Union was celebrated in a special afternoon rally attended by coach loads of women from many parts of Britain. The EBWU fulfilled a promise to pay for one female delegate from each Union to be at the Congress. They all stayed in the same Hall of Residence on the campus of Sussex University. This enabled them to enjoy an unforgettable week of fellowship, reminiscent of the experience portrayed in the dramatic presentation 'Turning Point', which we have already described earlier in this chapter.

Among the speakers at Brighton were Knud Wümpelmann (President), Milada Pohlova (Czechoslovakia), Thorwald Lorenzen (Rüschlikon), Michael Zhidkov and Glen Garfield Williams, a Baptist pastor who was the highly respected and trusted General Secretary of Conference of European Churches. Daily bible studies and discussion groups in different languages allowed much more general participation. At a Saturday rally the Christian pop-star, Cliff Richard, presented some contemporary style Christian songs and hymns. While this was received with acclamation by many people, there were those from Eastern Europe whose theological outlook and musical tradition caused them to be disturbed by such an approach in a Christian gathering. Among the public resolutions passed were two related to political happenings of importance for all Europeans. The first welcomed the signing of the Salt Two Agreement on arms control by the USSR President, Leonid Brezhnev and the USA President, Jimmy Carter. The second took note of the election of the European Economic Community Parliament, expressing the hope that it would be an instrument of service, peace and justice world-wide rather than seeking only economic power and security for its member states. Afterwards, Gerhard Claas paid tribute to Barbara Askew who had undertaken the double task of committee chairmanship and congress organizer due to unforeseen circumstances arising quite late in the preparations.

The German Baptists excelled in the planning of the 7th Congress in Hamburg in 1984. A new experience was for the programme to be predominantly in the German language with simultaneous translation facilities in six languages. Another useful innovation was to print in parallel German and English all programme literature and an illustrated book of reports and speakers' scripts published after the Congress. Daily bible study and discussion groups were also in different languages. The main theme was drawn from Jeremiah's advice to the Jewish exiles in Babylon - 'Seek the welfare of the city.'[8] On the first evening the traditional roll-call of the nations was

changed into a dramatic building of a large jigsaw puzzle to form a
pictorial background to the Congress platform. A delegate from each
country fixed a piece illustrating his/her own country. When the
picture was complete it graphically presented the Congress theme.
Contact with the city community was achieved through a television
service and two open air meetings. The civic authorities were also
invited to share in several events, which ensured good media coverage.

There were several tense moments, unknown to most delegates,
when representatives of dissident groups attempted to secure a place in
the programme to publicize controversial views on moral, political and
theological issues. The gracious and firm leadership of the President,
Dr David Lagergren of Sweden, and other EBF officers prevented this
by arranging long and difficult discussions behind the scenes. A tragic
drowning at the Youth Camp in Mölln of a young English Baptist,
Jonathan Graham, cast a shadow over the proceedings. Subsequently,
his parents inaugurated a memorial fund, which has ever since
provided grants to assist needy young people to attend similar youth
events.

By far the most moving moment in the Congress was when Pastor
Günter Hitzemann made a public confession of guilt on behalf of the
Baptist Union (Bund Evangelisch-Freikirchlicher Gemeinden) in the
Federal Republic of Germany for remaining silent and inactive during
the time of the Nazi regime. The statement was remarkable for its
sincere humility and the acknowledgement that, although most of them
belonged to a generation who experienced only a part or nothing of
that time, they felt implicated in the guilt of their nation and the shame
of their Union's failure to stand publicly with the Confessing Church
against what happened. The statement ended:

> We pray to God that we may learn from this part of our history, so
> that we may be more alert in regard to ideological temptations of our
> day.

At a later session David Russell (England) and Peter Barber (Scotland) made a response of thanks and forgiveness on behalf of the non-German participants. The key words of their message were:

> As we listened we became all the more aware that the burden of history lies heavily upon us, but at the same time that there is mercy and forgiveness through the Cross of Christ. As brothers and sisters in Christ we join our fellow German Baptists in their earnest prayers, knowing that we also stand in need of the mercy and grace of God.

Many non-Germans responded to the President's invitation to speak to a German person sitting nearby, to talk and pray together. Tears of both sorrow and joy flowed freely; friendships were born in that moment, and many letters of reconciliation in Christ were posted in the weeks following. Surely it was for such works of the Holy Spirit that the EBF came into existence. The Congress wholeheartedly passed a resolution which called for international peace and a freeze on the arms race, categorically stating that all forms of war, especially nuclear war, are an affront to God's purpose.[9]

Further Congresses come later in the story. We look now at two other celebrations which must not be overlooked here. September 1981 marked the twentieth anniversary of the European Baptist Press Service. When it was founded in Rüschlikon in 1961 its first director was a Southern Baptist Convention journalist, John Allen Moore. He served until 1965 and created a quality and style of service which quickly won support. He was followed by Mr Theo Sommerknap from 1965 to 1973. John M. Wilkes then operated part-time from Paris until 1976 when the EBPS became full-time again and returned to Rüschlikon, where he served until 1985. The next director was Stanley Crabb until 1996. He and his wife had served in various capacities as American missionaries since 1958. During Karl Heinz Walter's General Secretaryship the service was transferred to the EBF office in Hamburg, where Martha Skelton became the director after Stanley Crabb's retirement. Throughout the years the directors have made a valuable contribution to the life of the Federation. In addition to their journalism they have travelled far and wide to share fellowship with Baptists and often to bring a timely message of encouragement and support.

The Press Service has issued regular press releases to editors of European Baptist Union journals, Union-related radio and television religious broadcasters and other religious news agencies. European Baptist General Secretaries, EBF and BWA officers, various libraries and study centres, are on the mailing list. Reports and articles are prepared for inclusion in the European pages of *The Baptist World*. There is also a photo service. For research and documentation the Press Service supplies subject and personnel indexes which are available at their office and in the library of the International Baptist Theological Seminary. For many years the EBF has received generous support towards its work from the Southern Baptist Convention Foreign Mission Board. The Southern Baptist History Commission has completely microfilmed all the documents.

The other celebration was the thirtieth anniversary of the EBF, marked by a jubilee service during the Paris Council, 23 April 1980. Many French Baptists joined Council members for this service which was led by their President, the Revd André Thobois. One of the original seven founders, eighty-five year old Dr Henri Vincent, spoke on 'How it began', explaining how and why the Federation was formed.   Gerhard Claas followed him with 'How it developed', tracing achievements of the thirty years. David Russell dealt with 'Baptist Principles' with particular reference to the Baptist contribution as a minority church to church life and society in modern Europe. Stanislav Svec and Knud Wümpelmann were invited to say what the Federation had meant to them personally.

This was Gerhard Claas's last meeting as General Secretary, prior to leaving for Washington to become General Secretary of the Baptist World Alliance. In his final report to Council he reminded members of the Europe of thirty years ago 'bleeding from innumerable wounds'. He described how the EBF was used by God in a work of reconciliation and peace, in rebuilding and relief, and in co-operative mission. It had become a fellowship of faith, love and mutual trust. His closing words were:

> We deeply thank our Lord and God who has been blessing the work of the European Baptist Federation so richly and of whom we know and confess: 'He who began a good work in you will bring it to completion at the day of Jesus Christ.' (Phils 1.6)

AND SO MUCH MORE!

Many more pages could be filled with accounts of the multitudinous events and activities of the Federation. Some will be included later in the story, but here we must be content to mention briefly just a few of them. Two important co-operative committees were established in the 1960s. One was the Austrian Committee, made up of Baptist representatives from Austria, Germany, Sweden, Great Britain and the USA. Its purpose was to support the small number of Baptists in the predominantly Roman Catholic country of Austria, until they were able to join the EBF as an autonomous national Union.[10] The other committee was the Belgian Committee. In 1958 Belgian Baptists were the smallest fellowship in Europe and were unable to obtain any legal recognition from the government. They were made a Home Mission field of the EBF, and were aided and overseen by the special EBF committee until 1989, when they formed themselves into a newly structured Union within the Federation.[11] For many years Maurice Entwistle of the American Baptist Foreign Missionary Society gave excellent service as secretary of the Belgian Committee.

In 1965 the European Baptist Convention (EBC) sought membership of the EBF. It was a body of thirty-two English-speaking churches which mainly owed their origin to Southern Baptist work among American Forces personnel. Because of constitutional difficulties within the BWA and EBF full membership was not possible, but they were invited to have non-voting representatives at future Federation Councils and Congresses, and to encourage their churches to join the appropriate national Unions. The EBC has made a valuable contribution to Baptist work over the years. It was eventually able to become a member body, and one of their leaders, John Merritt, was called to the Presidency of the EBF in 1991-2.

Following the first appearance of Middle East representatives at the 1986 Council, changes to the Constitution and Bye-laws were approved to provide for membership of Middle East Baptist bodies. In due course the following were welcomed: the Lebanese Baptist Convention, the Jordan Baptist Convention, the Association of Baptist Churches in Israel, the Egypt Baptist Convention and the Syrian Baptist Convention.

Knud Wümpelmann once commented that God must be fond of varieties because he has created so many of them everywhere in nature. The same can be said of people and nations, of churches and denominations, and indeed of the European Baptist Federation. In chapters which have presented glimpses of EBF involvement with Baptist life and work behind the Iron Curtain, and have then stretched our horizons to see how far the Federation's work reaches in north, south, east and west, have we not really been discovering God at work? In order to be what the New Testament calls us to be - co-workers with him - we constantly need to cross boundaries of nation, language, politics, culture and theology, in order to reach Christian consensus. This is a crucial part of EBF life. There is no place for proud nationalism, nor for arrogant insistence on our own brand of theology. A true internationalism and Europeanization are needed, so that we can speak and act together whenever possible. This must be more than human détente or peaceful coexistence. We need to be a unique, united Christian family speaking with one voice and acting with one prophetic purpose, yet respecting and accepting the differences between us. Knud Wümpelmann believed he saw this happening in the EBF. He described it with a slogan borrowed from the Lutheran World Fellowship –
Reconciled Multiplicity!

CHAPTER NOTES

CHAPTER FIVE   North, South, East and West

1   From the Secretary's report at the EBF Council at Haven Green Baptist Church, London, August 1966.

2   See Luke 13.29; cf., Matthew 8.11.

3   Details of the courses are given in Appendix 5 of the annual report to the Amsterdam Council 1964.

4   e.g., Deuteronomy 5.14; 14.21; 24.14; 31.12.

5   Bill Wagner was a Southern Baptist Convention worker in Belgium, Isam Ballenger the SBC representative in Europe, and J. D. Hughey   from Rüschlikon Seminary.

6   To mark their 50th year the EBWU published two books in 1998:

Yona Pusey, *European Baptist Women's Union: our story, 1948-1998.*

Hilde Sayers, *The Transition from the Old to the New Europe.*

7   The full resolution is recorded in the minutes of the EBF Council held at Santa Severa, September 1977.

8   Jeremiah 29.7.

9   The text of the Apology, Response and Resolution can be found in the book of Documents printed after the Congress.

10   *EBF Prayer Calendar 1998*, statistics for the Baptist Union of Austria record 17 churches and 1,161 members. President: Horst Fischer.

11   Ibid., statistics for the Baptist Union of Belgium record 32 churches and 917 members. President: Samuel Verhaeghe.

6

THE CHANGING FACE OF
EASTERN EUROPE

After the Helsinki Conference on Security and Co-operation in Europe in the first half of the 1970s, human rights and freedom frequently appeared on international agendas. This led to more open debate in Eastern Europe and to the possibility of dissent. By the 1980s the nations of the world were more ready to hold summit meetings, and to explore such issues as a nuclear freeze and disarmament. Some of this was political posturing; in reality the arms race between the USSR and USA was escalating. However, a different climate of opinion was emerging. Opponents began to talk together, and within Eastern Europe the iron control once exercised by the Soviet Union seemed to be yielding to occasional tolerance. Attitudes towards the Christian Church were less rigid and hostile, even though speeches and documents continued to express the traditional hard line. Some would argue that the communist authorities were having to come to terms with the fact that their attempts to destroy religion were futile.

Then, in 1985, to quote the modern historian, Norman Davies, 'There appeared a new star in the East.' Mikhail Gorbachev became General Secretary of the Communist Party of the Soviet Union.[1] Leonid Brezhnev had died in 1982, after eighteen years in power. He was succeeded first by Yuri Andropov and then by Konstantin Chernyenko, each of whom ruled insignificantly for a very short time before succumbing to serious illness. Gorbachev was incredibly different from any leader the Soviet Union had ever known He soon engaged in successful arms talks with the American President Reagan, reaching unexpected agreements to reduce nuclear arms. One sentence in Norman Davies's history of Europe sets the scene for this chapter:

The Committee of Seven with Dr W.O. Lewis (BWA) at Rüschlikon, October 1949, when they drew up the original EBF constitution. (BT photo)

Baptist leaders from Eastern Europe at Novi Sad, 1967. Stanislav Svec, Michael Zhidkov, Janos Laczkovski, Joachim Tzunea, Adolf Lehotsky. (EBPS photo)

EBF Executive at Rüschlikon, 1971. José Goncalves, Claus Meister, Robert S. Denny (BWA), Ronald Goulding.

EBF Youth Secretaries meeting at Schmiedeberg, East Germany, 1973

Brighton Congress, England, 1979

Hamburg Congress, Germany, 1984

Knud Wümpelmann placing a document in the wall of the building of the Baptist Education Centre at Radosc, Poland, 1989. (EBPS photo)

Laszlo Gersenyi, Director of the new International Baptist Lay Academy, speaking at the dedication, July 1990. Assistant Director Errol Simmons is on the left. (EBPS photo)

John and Virginia Keith of Canada, pioneers of Baptist work in Albania, with Karl Heinz Walter, 1992.

EBF Council in Kishinev, 1993. Victor Loginov, Karl Heinz Walter, John Merritt, being welcomed by local Baptists.

EBF Council at Dorfweil, September 1994, with representatives of three new Unions being welcomed by Birgit Karlsson.

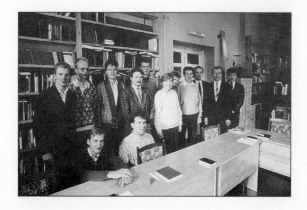

Students at the new Baptist Theological Seminary, Riga, Latvia, 1993

Groups of children from Chernobyl, having a meal with a family in Bremerhaven, Germany, and at a camp in Oskarshamn, Sweden. (EBPS photos)

(Below) Repairing a church in Moldova, with help from BR-E.

Visit to Patriarch Alexei in July 1997. *(From left)* Denton Lotz, Patriarch Alexei,Karl Heinz Walter, Pjotr Konovalchik.

Hungarian Romanian representatives at the EBWU fiftieth anniversary celebrations, Prague, 1998, with the President, Yona Pusey

The first 'pre-fabricated' church built by the EBF in1998, at Montana,
North Bulgaria.

Inside the building

(Above) The Baptist Theological Seminary, Rüschlikon
(Below) The International Baptist Theological Seminary, Prague

By the time of the Malta Summit in December 1989, Presidents Bush and Gorbachev felt free to announce that the Cold War had ended.[2]

The face of Eastern Europe and the whole of the East/West scenario were soon to be radically changed.

Bit by bit the Soviet Union relaxed its firm hold on the nations it had for so long controlled. Two magic words seized the world's headlines - *Glasnost* and *Perestroika* - the first meaning a new honesty in expressing convictions and raising questions previously forbidden, and the second indicating the wish for new structures for a new age. Both concepts were welcomed with alacrity. The liberation for which world Christians had prayed over many years started to become reality. In a way that he probably never imagined or intended, Gorbachev became a catalyst for changes which left the political map of Europe and the life of the Church miraculously different.

DAWN OF A NEW AGE

As early as 1986 the new spirit of openness in the Soviet Union showed in the press. Headlines and articles created public debate about religion. Writers could come into the open without fear. Novels, films and television documentaries raised religious questions and exposed past injustices. News began to filter out that condemned prisoners of conscience and Christian believers were being released. There was opposition from traditionalists and others in the Kremlin with vested interests. Gorbachev was adamant; in the new Russia he hoped to build, he must be able to give a positive answer to the West on issues of human rights. In their world travels he and his wife, Raisa, frequently met religious leaders and visited churches.

The 1,000[th] anniversary of the first Christian (Orthodox) baptisms in Russia was due to be celebrated in 1988. Gorbachev encouraged plans to make the celebrations a fitting acknowledgement of the part played by religion in the nation's history. He was reported to have admitted past errors in treatment of churches and believers, and to have expressed his conviction that Christians had an important part to play in the building of a new society. The Millennium celebrations were an outstanding success; they received international coverage, and major changes in religious laws were a direct outcome of them. Baptists eagerly shared in the events, using them as the opportunity to start public evangelism, distribution of religious papers and magazines, Sunday Schools and youth work, and, perhaps one of the most surprising outcomes, to accept the invitation to visit prisons and provide volunteers for pastoral care in hospitals. All this represented a U-turn which was described as 'nothing short of a miracle'.

In 1987, during a visit to Moscow, Knud Wümpelmann met Mr Konstantin Kharchev, Chairman of the Council for Religious Affairs. It was a very positive meeting, which even closed with prayers. *Glasnost* was much in evidence. Permission was granted to import 5,000 sets of the Barclay New Testament Commentary in Russian, with fifteen volumes in each set.[3] There was also a favourable response to the offer made by the BWA to present 100,000 bibles to the USSR as a contribution to the Millennium celebrations. At the 8th European Baptist Congress in Budapest in 1989, Alexei Bichkov was able to announce that he had been notified by the Council of Religious Affairs that the Seminary which Russian Baptists had long dreamed of establishing in Moscow could now go ahead, with facilities for a four-year course for up to fifty students. In the same year Baptists were allowed to hold a public Festival of Praise in the Bolshoi Theatre. A year later the AUCECB was free to hold a Congress at which they freely elected new leaders and approved a new charter. New attempts were made to initiate reconciliation talks with the Reform Baptists, but without much success. However, it was confirmed that all their imprisoned members and leaders had been released, and in 1993 the CCECB was also permitted to hold a free Congress and openly practise their faith. Regretfully, the old theological polarization between the two bodies remained. The CCECB has not joined the Baptist World Alliance or the European Baptist Federation.

New ideas which had long been simmering beneath the surface of communist society throughout the whole of Eastern Europe now erupted. In Czechoslovakia, for example, in November 1989, students took to the streets of Prague in public protest, calling for more significant changes in the life of their nation. Day after day support for them grew; their demonstrations were peaceful but strong. On Thursday, 17 November, armed units of the Ministry of the Interior brutally suppressed their protests. Many people were injured and at least one student was killed. At the 4th Baptist Church in Prague on the following Sunday, the congregation made an unprecedented response. They issued a public protest addressed to all Baptists in the world, asking them to intervene in whatever way possible, and to pray for those who initiated the protest, the perpetrators of violence and the innocent victims.

Three days later the Baptist Union leaders, meeting in Brno, sent a strong letter of protest to the Prime Minister and the State Presidium, signed by Dr Pavel Titera (President, Central Council of the Baptist Union) with Pavel Kondac, Richard Novak, Jan Pospisil and Vladimir Dvorak (representatives of the Czech and Slovak Councils of Baptists). They expressed unashamed support for the democratization of society and, therefore, responsible dialogue with those of different conviction. 'We are convinced', they said, ' that this harsh use of force against peaceful citizens, perhaps holding other opinions, is an abuse of human dignity and an attack on freedom of conscience and freedom of speech.' Strong stuff! But it was in the true spirit of *Glasnost*. They claimed that it was also in the best traditions of the Czech people, whose history included such names as John Hus, the fifteenth-century reformer, Peter Chelcicky, a founder of the Czech Brethren, and Johannes Comenius, the seventeenth-century educator honoured in Prague University. Above all, they grounded their protest in the gospel of Jesus Christ, bearer of new life and peace.[4]

A process had started which the authorities could not stop, and within a few weeks the government was toppled without more conflict. In 1990 democratic elections initiated a new age of freedom. This led to the separation of the two major national groupings of Czechs and Slovaks into independent republics in 1992. Two years later, by mutual consent, two separate Baptist Unions were formed and, in due course, both joined the European Baptist Federation.[5]

On 9 November 1989, just before the Czech uprising, the world was amazed and thrilled to watch on television the hated Berlin Wall being broken down, with no attempts by the East German guards to prevent it. People from East and West poured through the gaps, to greet one another, to celebrate the end of one era and the dawn of a new one. A few days afterwards, at the Charlottenburg Baptist Church, Bismarck Strasse, West Berlin, near to the Brandenburg Gate, the congregation was overjoyed to welcome a tide of East German Christians coming in to worship with them. A spontaneous and emotional outburst of love, joy and praise marked that never-to-be-forgotten service.[6]

The revolution which led to the downfall of the communist authorities in the German Democratic Republic was, of course, part of the strong tide of *Glasnost* flowing all over Eastern Europe. But it is important to recognize that many factors contributed to it. The faithful, persevering witness of the churches, despite much suffering, was undoubtedly one of them. Their attempt to remain part of the society in which they were placed, and their loyal citizenship, making them appreciative of what they saw as good socialist ideals, yet also critical of what was unjust and oppressive, gave them integrity among the people. When change became possible they were able to play a leading role. The Protestant churches in particular, including many Baptists, organized numerous public prayer meetings. They consulted with politicians, or with the general population, sometimes with both. They dealt with current issues in fearless, prophetic preaching, constantly urging the importance of peaceful revolution.

Jörg Swoboda, a lecturer at the East German Baptist Seminary in Buckow, edited a remarkable book in 1990, tracing the course of the revolution and the part the churches played in it.[7] Because it was written by people personally involved it bore the authenticity of eye-witnesses, including Baptists who played a significant part in the events. It also included extracts from prayers and sermons of those unforgettable days. Keith Clements, the General Secretary of the Conference of European Churches, described the book in a review of the English version for the *Baptist Quarterly* as 'compelling reading'.[8] In his view the author has made a valuable contribution to Baptist history by showing clearly how East German Baptists met danger with courage, to help achieve such radical political change. One of Jörg Swoboda's colleagues at Buckow, Christian Wolf, contributed an essay to the book reflecting on the relationship of Christian faith to contemporary society and events. Some years earlier, he had preached an outstanding sermon at the European Baptist Congress in Hamburg (1984) on 'Churches in Socialism'. He acknowledged then that it was not easy to adapt to such an environment, but Christians should accept the situation where they were and not flee from it. God called them to 'seek the welfare of the city', even when it was hostile to the church and undermined welfare for many people. Events now proved him right.

The East German government surrendered its power, and the political reunification of Germany gradually moved forward, though not without fears and tensions. However, the reunion of the two Baptist Unions was wholehearted and joyous. The first official East/West German Baptist meeting for thirty years was held in Berlin early in 1990. Within a few months both Unions had affirmed their desire to become one again, a step they took officially in the Spring of 1991.

Gorbachev's attempts to reform and reshape the Soviet Union started a chain reaction which left no country in Eastern Europe untouched. Poland's communist regime was driven by public protest and industrial strikes to confer with Lech Walesa and his Solidarity movement. In 1989, when free elections became inescapable, voters thoroughly ousted the government. Their land was no longer a satellite of the USSR. One of the first acts of the new government was to pass a law of religious freedom. Polish Baptists were a small group, but very active and forward-looking. They took the opportunities of new freedom to evangelize, plant churches, develop their own theological seminary, train leaders, open Christian schools and enter the broadcasting world. They found in freedom, as they had in Russian occupation, that the EBF was a strong ally in their needs. Similarly, the EBF found them a valuable member, ready to share their vision and gifts with others in the Baptist family. They were the first Eastern European Union in the post-communist age to make an annual contribution to Federation funds.

Hungary quickly followed suit when political negotiations led to the end of the communist republic and the establishment of a multi-party state with democratic elections. A liberalizing influence had been at work in the religious sphere for some time. With so much change taking place throughout Eastern Europe, the EBF took the bold decision to hold the 8th European Baptist Congress in Budapest in July 1989. It was the first Congress to be held in the East, and by one means or another a vast crowd of Eastern European Baptists were determined to be there. For many it was their 'first time out'- a sort of Baptist fiesta in which choirs and bands played a major part! It was by far the biggest crowd of Baptists ever to gather in Europe. Appropriately, the Congress theme was 'Come and see what God has done'. The President of the Hungarian Parliament caught the spirit of the occasion when he gave an official welcome to all the delegates, saying that the Baptist emphasis on individual faith and the responsibility of every church member to share in the government would be a key factor in the building of new nations and a new Europe. Speeches and discussions took place openly on such issues as human rights, torture, the death penalty, and China. EBF leaders encouraged everybody to look towards a united Europe, and to shape a strategy within the Federation for one mission to the whole continent.

The climax was an ecumenical rally addressed by Billy Graham in Hungary's largest sports stadium. Its capacity was 73,000; but an estimated 90,000 people came, and the proceedings were relayed to thousands who thronged the streets of the city. The railways even offered bargain fares to get such crowds there. Newspapers, radio and television gave the event maximum coverage for days. The most exciting testimony to the power of God to cross the boundaries which communism had erected was in the response of 17,000 people to Billy

Graham's evangelistic appeal. Some undoubtedly were brought to faith then; but a considerable number wished to testify that God had delivered them from bondage, and to use the opportunity to exercise their freedom publicly.

Political trouble had also been brewing in Romania in protest against President Ceaucescu's Stalinist style of dictatorship. Large crowds took to the streets in many cities, including Bucharest, Timisoara, Arad and Cluj, where there were strong groups of Baptists. Some of the Baptist leaders and preachers used the opportunity to preach and pray publicly, and to show their solidarity with the general populace in their demands   for justice and peace. Tragically, just before Christmas 1989, the protestors were attacked by armed forces in what turned out to be a violent and bloody revolution. An estimated 4,000 were killed, and many more injured. On behalf of the Baptist World Alliance, Dr Denton Lotz publicly deplored such violence against innocent people. He called on the State President and his government to recognize the 'new reality' of a Europe in which freedom of religion and conscience could be enjoyed by all. The European Baptist Federation immediately endorsed his challenge, backed by letters of protest from the Conference of European Churches, the World Lutheran Federation, the World Alliance of United Reformed Churches and the Federation of Protestant Churches in Italy. Paolo Spanu, the President of the Baptist Union of Italy, sent a message of encouragement and prayer to the Romanian Baptists. He quoted words from Revelation 14.12 which had often sustained Eastern European Christians in dark days: a call to endurance by believers who obey God's commands and keep their faith firmly in Jesus.

Politically, the climax of the Romanian revolution was the public execution of President Ceaucescu and his wife. His successor, Ioan Iliescu, eventually met a deputation of twelve Baptist leaders on 4 May 1991. This took place during the first freely convened Congress for almost fifty years of over 1,000 representatives of the member churches of the Baptist Union of Romania. There was a euphoric atmosphere as they gave God thanks for the open doors before them, and began to plan for the new era in which they would be able to practise their faith openly. President Iliescu expressed his hope that Baptists would help to rebuild their ruined country, and his confidence that their moral and spiritual values would contribute to the renewal of the nation. Vasile Talos, the Baptist Union President, openly testified to him of the Christian Gospel. Nicolae Gheorghita, the Union's General Secretary, assured him of daily prayer in many Baptist homes and churches for him and the government. On the same date, the Romanian Minister of Foreign Affairs admitted that to exclude faith and religion from national life had been a serious mistake. Knud Wümpelmann, who by now had become the President of the BWA, welcomed this good news, by reaffirming the democratic basis of Baptist life, and therefore their readiness to help.

People have debated, and no doubt will go on debating, how far Gorbachev succeeded or failed. He clearly wished to move away from the rigid communist ideologies of the past, by trying to restore human rights to millions who had been denied them. He strove for disarmament and peace, knowing that the continuing arms race was economically ruinous, even suicidal. He was ready to admit the positive value of genuine religious faith in the life of a nation. In restoring religious freedom to the churches, he opened doors for them into a new age of missionary opportunity. But he did not intend to dismantle the Soviet Union, nor to allow its allies in the Warsaw Pact to break away in political independence. As they revolted one after another, his fair dream turned into a nightmare. The republics which made up the Union of Soviet Socialist Republics declared their independence, and the USSR ceased to be. The Warsaw Pact dissolved, and Comecon, the communist organization for mutual economic and trade support, lost its meaning. In 1991, after an abortive coup to remove him from office, Gorbachev resigned. The political future was plunged into uncertainty; but the religious scene was radically changed and full of promise.[9]

NEW LEADERS FOR A NEW AGE

The impact of these changes upon the EBF was considerable. In fact, they were a searching test for the Federation. They made new ways of thinking necessary and required new structures and policies. They raised questions about the sharing of resources. They even posed problems about maintaining the unity which had for so long held in one family Baptists of the north, south, east and west, and now, for various reasons, came under threat.

A widespread change in leadership was also taking place. During the second half of the 1980s many experienced and trusted leaders died; among them were Stanislav Svec of Czechoslovakia, Joszef Nagy of Hungary, Michal Stankiewicz of Poland, Oswald Tärk of Estonia, Ilia Ivanov of the USSR, and Maurice Farelly of France. News of the death of another former European leader came in March 1988, when Gerhard Claas was killed in a tragic car crash near Lodi, California. He was travelling with others in a pastor's car to a special meeting to raise money among SBC and ABC congregations for the reduction of the BWA's serious financial deficit. He was only 59 years of age, and his death was a sad loss to the Baptist family world-wide. Knud Wümpelmann said of him; 'Dr Claas was both highly respected and deeply loved for his wise and warm leadership. He was a great statesman, a gifted evangelist and an able administrator in one person....We thank God for what Gerhard Claas has meant of encouragement and inspiration and practical help to so many individuals, churches and national Baptist bodies, not least in Europe.' Many EBF representatives were present to pay their tribute to a beloved leader at the funeral service in Volmarstein (FRG) on 30 March.

Several other leaders who had given distinguished service for many years reached retirement, including David Russell, chairman of the Books and Translations Committee, and Glen Garfield Williams, for well over twenty years the General Secretary of the Conference of European Churches and a trusted ally of the EBF family. John Wilkes returned to the USA to serve as director of the Communications

Division of the BWA after thirteen years as director of the European Baptist Press Service. When the changes brought about by Gorbachev's policy took effect, many of the national Baptist Unions were able to hold assemblies and congresses and elect future leaders. This led to the retirement or rejection of some leaders, and the emergence of many new ones. They were much younger and more radical, but they understandably lacked the experience and knowledge of their predecessors. Some appeared to be less strongly rooted in Baptist history and tradition, but maybe this was outweighed by involvement in recent developments and awareness of their own generation's hopes and aims.

The Federation had clearly come to an important time of transition, which coincided with the retirement of Knud Wümpelmann due at the end of 1989. Discussions were already taking place about ways of reducing costs, increasing efficiency and easing the pressures increasingly being put on the General Secretary/Treasurer. At the meeting of the Council at the West German Baptist Familienferienstätte, Dorfweil in September 1988, a Search Committee was appointed to nominate a new General Secretary after consultations with the Baptist World Alliance and the EBF member Unions. It was hoped that a name would be presented to the BWA and EBF Executive Committees in April 1989, so that the new appointee could be introduced at the Budapest Congress later in that year, and be *in situ* as soon as possible after 1 December. The members of the committee were Bernard Green (Great Britain) (chairman), Piero Bensi (Italy), Birgit Karlsson (Sweden), Wiard Popkes (Germany) and Vasile Talpos (Romania). Denton Lotz was added later to ensure thorough liaison with the BWA. The committee was also asked to serve as a Structures Committee, charged with a threefold evaluation of the present activities, future challenges and financial possibilities of the Federation. A discussion document - *EBF: Yesterday, Today and Tomorrow* - was circulated to Council members.

After several meetings, Peter Barber (Scotland) replaced Bernard Green as chairman because of health problems. In July 1989 he was able to bring the nomination of Karl Heinz Walter, which was confirmed by the Executive and unanimously approved by the Council on the following day. Since 1978 Karl Heinz Walter had been pastor of the Bremerhaven Baptist Church and Area Superintendent for North-west Germany. He was also chairman of the West German Baptist Foreign Mission Board. Previously, he had served for six years as Youth Director in the Nordrhine-Westphalia Association, for nine years as Director of the West German Baptist Union Youth Department, and for four years as a pastor in Minden. In addition he had been Secretary and Chairman of the EBF Youth Committee and Chairman of the BWA Youth Committee. He clearly brought wide experience to his new task, which he would be able to commence from 1 December 1989.

A preliminary report of the structures review suggested that consideration should be given to organizing the work of the Federation in four sections: (1) Education and Theology; (2) Mission and Evangelism; (3) Communications and Promotion; (4) Administration and Finance. More time was needed to study this first draft, in order to allow the General Secretary-elect and the retiring General Secretary to share in shaping the final proposals. Council granted the Search Committee a further year to prepare their final report for presentation to the 1990 Council. Meanwhile, it was agreed that in future the General Secretary should have a full-time secretary, a part-time bookkeeper, and chairpersons of committees and/or divisions who would carry more responsibilities and be in close contact. Authority was given for the EBF office to be moved from Copenhagen to Hamburg.

Knud Wümpelmann had served the EBF with distinction for nine years. He had shown himself to be a patient negotiator, a constant encourager, a faithful advocate and a tireless visitor to all parts of the Federation's constituency. His kind and gracious personality endeared him to European Baptists, who trusted him widely and recognized his statesmanlike qualities and deep spirituality. When the time came for him to retire he expressed his gratitude for the privilege of nine years service to the EBF. He shared his optimism that the new openness in the East would grow, that the development of the European Community in the West would continue, and that a new unity between East and West would be established.

At the Dorfweil Council in September 1988, he forecast that three issues would be of major importance: Baptist identity, mission and evangelism, and religious liberty. He went on to ask whether European Baptists permitted freedom of conscience among themselves. 'Do we fully appreciate not only the right to be different, but even the blessing and richness of being a variety of people with very different background and experience and insight?' He maintained that this was essential in the contemporary European situation. In his view, freedom of conscience was a precondition for true unity in the Spirit.

We may wonder whether he had insight into some of the debates, even disputes, that were to arise in the 1990s. His message was most pertinent. With freedom and independence spreading in so many countries previously under strict control, ethnic, nationalistic and theological differences were soon to create such polarization in some areas that Baptist unity would be seriously threatened.

INTO ACTION

Karl Heinz Walter was duly inducted as General Secretary/Treasurer of the EBF and an Associate Secretary of the BWA at a special service in Bremerhaven on 3 December 1989. Gerd Rudzio took part as the representative of the German Baptist Union. The BWA was represented by their newly elected President, Knud Wümpelmann, and the EBF President, Peter Barber, spoke on behalf of the Federation.

The rapid changes in Eastern Europe made it necessary for the new Secretary to act decisively and quickly. There was general political and economic chaos. Freedom was a priceless benefit; but how to exercise it with proper order and adequate resources for all was fraught with difficulty. Trade and commerce suffered, with a consequent lack of food and other necessities. Public services struggled without the accustomed central control. Heating and lighting supplies failed, and the winter was hard. Unemployment, public disorder, crime, and ethnic rivalries added to the hardship affecting vast populations. In this context, the EBF urgently needed to organize substantial aid for the churches with two main purposes. One was to assist with programmes of aid for the hungry, cold, sick and elderly. The other was to provide resources for the many missionary and evangelistic opportunities now open to the churches. Equipment, literature, educational and training facilities, transport, church buildings, bible schools and seminaries were all pressing needs.

At his first Executive meeting in April 1990 Karl Heinz Walter announced plans for the formation of an aid programme to be called Baptist Response-Europe (BR-E). This was the result of an important consultation at Dorfweil three months earlier, when Baptist leaders from Bulgaria, Czechoslovakia, the German Democratic Republic, Hungary, Poland and the Soviet Union had met with representatives from Western Baptist Unions, North American Conventions, the European Baptist Mission and four other international Baptist mission bodies, to consider needs and priorities, and how to meet them. Denton Lotz and Archie Goldie of the BWA, Keith Parker of the SBC Foreign Mission Board and Karl Heinz Walter played a key role in the discussions. The new General Secretary also secured support from the EBF Executive for a proposal to seek registration of the Federation as a Non-Governmental Organization of the European Parliament, in the same way as the BWA was related to the United Nations. This action was a timely reminder that significant change was simultaneously occurring in the West, with the growth of the European Economic Community and development towards European Union. Some of the Eastern Europeans viewed this with uncertainty, even alarm. Others of them were eager to accept the free market economy and have close links with the EEC and NATO. It was vital that the policies and programmes of the EBF should embrace the whole of Europe, be alert to the needs of all its members, and fulfil its role as an inclusive and uniting body..

One of the first BR-E aid projects was directed to Bulgaria and Romania. Both were facing crises through lack of heating, lighting and food; many people were in desperate need. In response to appeals from the Baptist Unions there, it was decided to encourage Western Baptists to gather specifically listed supplies and send standardized food parcels to addresses provided by the Bulgarian and Romanian Unions. Labels indicating that duty exemption had been negotiated were provided to the senders. An emergency aid fund was also established.

In April 1986 the explosion of a nuclear reactor at the Chernobyl Power Station in the Ukraine had let loose a network of disaster far greater than the horrendous results of the atomic bombing of Hiroshima and Nagasaki in the Second World War. There was massive radiation fall-out in many parts of Europe, but especially in the Ukraine, Belarus and surrounding areas. Radiation sickness, polluted earth, poisoned food and water, the spread of cancer, disease and death, and especially the plight of children, born and unborn, created a pastoral and relief task of gigantic proportions. Government was unable to offer anywhere near sufficient technical, medical and humanitarian aid. Here was another task which came on to the EBF aid agenda. More followed, as ethnic and civil strife broke out in some of the newly independent countries, such as Georgia, Azerbaijan, Armenia, and Yugoslavia. To make matters worse, severe floods in Georgia and a catastrophic earthquake in Armenia added to the tale of human woe. Immediate responses were necessary, and within the Baptist family Baptist Response-Europe and Baptist World Aid were the appropriate channels.

Karl Heinz Walter made an extensive tour of Eastern Europe in 1991 with Keith Parker and Paul Montacute (Director of Baptist World Aid). A strategic meeting took place with Vladimir Zots, Gorbachev's Personal Assistant, to discuss the needs of the children of Chernobyl. Out of this grew an imaginative programme of holidays for the children with Baptist families and churches throughout Europe. As many Baptist Unions as possible were urged to plan holiday visits for about twenty-five to thirty children. There has been a widespread and enthusiastic response ever since. Parents have derived joy and peace to see their children return home so much better in health. School authorities have commented on the improvement in their alertness and achievements. Not only has this been an expression of Christian love;

it has also quickened faith in God, given despairing families new hope, and indirectly raised the profile of the EBF. BR-E broke all records in money-raising in 1992, including substantial gifts from the BWA and Southern Baptist Convention.

It would be wrong to give the impression that all was gloom and disaster. The most dramatic feature of the changed face of Eastern Europe was freedom. In country after country our Baptist people experienced a new sense of release. It is impossible to give a complete survey of all that happened; here we will briefly note some illustrations of new opportunities and remarkable progress in the Baptist churches and Unions of the former Soviet Union. More will be described in the next chapter.[10] In Georgia there was considerable growth through open-air evangelism, scripture distribution, and public showings of the film 'Jesus'. But there were not sufficient buildings or money to cope with the many opportunities. Only seven groups of believers had buildings in 1992. Karl Heinz Walter appealed throughout the EBF for large gifts to help build seventeen new churches. Just over two months later he was able to hand over enough for the purchase of houses for many new congregations. By 1998 the Baptist Union there had grown from one church during the days of the AUCECB to forty-nine, with a combined membership of over 5,000.

Baptists in the Moldavia area of Romania doubled the number of believers' baptisms within two years, and reported the building of sixty-five new churches. In the Baltic States of Estonia, Latvia and Lithuania circumstances of growth varied. Lithuania had suffered much discrimination and the confiscation of properties. Also many people had been forcibly moved to the east during the days of Russian domination, thus depleting church membership. As soon as independence came, the Pentecostals separated into their own denomination. Consequently, Baptists numbered only about 160, gathered in four churches and three small groups. Since then they have steadily grown to seven churches with over 420 members. Estonia quickly opened their Seminary in Tartu with a promising number of new candidates for ministry. They were offered the opportunity to share in broadcast religious services. Four of their pastors were called to prison chaplaincies. A building programme for new churches was launched, as also was a scheme for the erection of a new seminary. Latvian Baptists were much encouraged by the number of young people among them. This made their churches lively and growing, with many baptisms recorded. They began to publish Christian newspapers and magazines. These and other evangelistic efforts soon bore fruit, for in 1990 they rejoiced in the news that during the year they had baptized twice as many as had died!

Bulgarian Baptists held their first Baptist Union Congress for over forty years in the Spring of 1991. A highly significant appointment was the election of Theodor Angelov as their new President. His strong, gracious and spiritual leadership was to be a great asset not only to the Baptist Union in his own country, but also to the EBF over the coming years. During the Congress he succeeded in securing access to Bulgarian radio for Karl Heinz Walter to be interviewed about the humanitarian aid programme mounted by the EBF. In September the Federation Council held its annual meetings in the newly built Varna Baptist Church. This coincided with the official dedication of the new church, the first in the country for 60 years. Linked with the Council was a series of evangelistic events at which old legal prohibitions were cancelled and foreign visitors were able to speak and preach without hindrance. At least eighty people responded to Peter Barber's public appeals. Press, radio and television reports gave Baptists more exposure than they had ever known. Within a short time after the Council Theo Angelov, accompanied by Karl Heinz Walter, Peter Barber and Knud Wümpelmann, had crucial talks with the Vice-president of Bulgaria, Peter Semerdjeu, and the Director of the Commission of Religious Affairs, D. Spassov, to discuss questions of religious equality in the proposed new laws, the restitution of church property confiscated by the former communist regime, and the freedom and rehabilitation of prisoners of conscience.

A special joy at the Varna Council was the presence for the first time of three delegates from Moldova, which had been the smallest republic in the former Soviet Union. They told of 186 churches, with 15,000 baptized members, and many children and young people. Within another year they recorded 3,000 baptisms, 26 new buildings and 43 more being built. With government consent they invited the EBF to hold its meetings in Moldova in 1993.

THE SHAPE OF THINGS TO COME

Reflecting on the astounding changes which had taken place in such a short time, Karl Heinz Walter drew the attention of the 1990 Council in De Bron, Netherlands to some major issues facing the EBF. There would be a continuing need of material and financial help for Eastern European churches. This must obviously be an important element in future policy; but he wisely expressed a note of caution not to ignore or neglect other European needs. It was a warning which had been expressed several times over the years by various EBF Presidents - Claus Meister, David Russell and Stanislav Svec. Later it was to be echoed by Paul Montacute on behalf of Baptist World Aid, when the concentration of appeals for Eastern Europe began to reduce concern and gifts for the suffering and deprived people of the Two-thirds World.

A second matter the General Secretary raised was the urgency of the re-evangelization of Europe as a main task. All denominations were discussing this; therefore, it would be vital to be in dialogue with them. We shall see how this became a central issue during the 1990s, with the approach of the twenty-first century in mind. There were a number of ecumenical conferences in which the Federation shared; but there were also misgivings in some Unions, for whom historical and theological traditions made them distance themselves from ecumenical relations. This was one of the tensions likely to threaten Baptist unity and would call for sensitive handling.

A third item was the influence of para-church groups in Europe and their effect on churches and Unions in membership of the EBF. The present situation was both confused and confusing. A veritable flood of world Christian organizations, missions, independent evangelists, publishing and audio-visual suppliers, as well as cults and sects of every hue, rushed into Eastern Europe to seize a new mission field. In retrospect, one has to ask whether this hindered rather than helped. Some of it was undoubtedly sincere and genuine missionary service in a situation where available resources were inadequate for the size of the task. But some of it seemed more like competitive exploitation of a religious market, unashamed proselytism rather than sensitive evangelism. There was evidence of financial incentives with theological conditions attached. Sometimes programmes were imposed which were in no way related to local culture and conditions. Some churches were split in ways that undermined their loyalty to existing denominational membership.

Inevitably, there was adverse reaction. The new governments began to suspect a socio-political threat; some called it 'foreignization', 'westernization', or even 'Americanization'. The Orthodox Church condemned it as proselytism and lobbied for stricter state laws to prevent it. Before long, proposals were being threatened to ban foreign missionaries and preachers, and to make persuasion of people to convert to another religion a criminal offence. The so-called Traditional Churches pressed for state recognition of only the major religions and churches which had always been part of a nation's history. It was not difficult for this to become a persecuting weapon against evangelical churches, including Baptists. The next chapter will indicate the serious problems this caused in the 1990s. The whole phenomenon was considered by the Conference of Evangelism and Home Mission Secretaries from seventeen European Baptist Unions in March 1990.

Two topics necessarily entered the Federation's agenda - 'Europeanization' and 'Baptist Identity'. The former was vital to the shape of future mission and evangelism; the latter was essential for Baptist apologetics in face of false slanders, and to dispel the ignorance of those who condemned and opposed them. Earl Martin, Director of the newly formed Institute of Mission and Evangelism introduced a valuable aid to counteract the influence of the cults. He produced eight booklets of no more than 1,500 words in simple English, giving basic facts about the Mormons, Jehovah's Witnesses, the Moonies, Transcendental

Meditation, Hare Krishna, Scientology, New Age and Islam. From 1991 these were available for any Union which asked for them.

Another complication which had to be faced was of a more positive kind. When the Republics which made up the USSR became independent, they quickly discovered their need for some sort of inter-dependence. The Commonwealth of Independent States (CIS) was the outcome. Similarly, Baptists in the new States were no longer bound together by the All-Union Council of Evangelical Christians-Baptists. They formed themselves into autonomous national Baptist Unions, and most of them sought membership of the BWA and EBF. Many also related together to form the Euro-Asiatic Baptist Federation, which was closely affiliated to the EBF, although it included some groups not in the EBF. Another corporate fellowship known as the Baptist Union of Middle Asia brought together the Baptists of Tadjikistan, Turkmenistan and Uzbekistan, all difficult areas because predominantly Muslim.[11] When all these new groups and Unions joined the EBF they added considerably to the volume of visiting, pastoral care, communication, conferences, meetings, Bible Schools and Seminaries, to be dealt with by leaders, committees and council. In the providence of God this was a happy complication.

An unexpected by-product of this realignment was a reduction in membership numbers. Statistics in the Soviet Union and Romania had been much inflated in the past; now they became more realistic. Thousands of people who had been refused visas to emigrate now left for Germany and the USA. Forty-two thousand Pentecostalists withdrew to form their separate denomination again. The old AUCECB statistics for churches and members were almost halved. Yet, the EBF was still in a growth situation, for many of the new Unions were actively evangelizing and rapidly increasing.

ALBANIAN BREAKTHROUGH

Enver Hoxha. the President of Albania, died in 1985 after forty years of ruling his country with rigid Stalinist Communism. He had kept the nation totally isolated, closing all borders and establishing the first-ever constitutionally atheist state. The process of change after his death was slow, but in 1990 the English newspaper, *The Independent*, one day carried this headline - ALBANIA UNLOCKS THE GATES! Steve Crawshaw reported that Europe's last Stalinist state wished to belong to the world again. His evidence for this assertion included the fact that the Albanian government had decided to join the Conference on Security and Co-operation in Europe, and had renewed diplomatic relations with the USA. The borders were opened to citizens and foreign visitors. Even more significant was an announcement that 'religious propaganda' was no longer a criminal offence.[12]

A democratically elected government took office in 1992 and in the following year introduced a law establishing freedom of conscience and equality of all religions. This provision for *all* religions was a triumph for diplomacy, for there had been attempts to limit religious freedom and activity to the nation's three original religions - Islam, Orthodox and Roman Catholic. However, the usual flood of foreign missions, sects and cults invaded the country, and in order to safeguard Albania's national identity, the new law required leadership of all churches and religious associations to be by Albanian nationals.

In the Spring of 1992 Karl Heinz Walter met government officials who had given the assurance that Baptists were welcome in the country. He presented five goals for whatever work the EBF would help to initiate:

- to respond to needs within the limits of EBF resources;
- to be a channel for Baptist support and aid for the well-being of Albania and its people;
- to follow the model of Jesus Christ - serving God by serving others;
- to establish Baptist Churches made up of Christian believers;
- to undertake special projects in consultation with the Albanian Government - for example, health and hygiene, agriculture, business training, communication.

These steps marked a complete innovation in EBF policy. Normally, work was undertaken in partnership with national Baptist Unions, but until an Albanian Baptist Union could be formed, the EBF sought and was granted permission to create an office in the capital city, Tirana. Two medical missionaries of the Baptist Missionary Society, Chris and Maire Burnett, were called to pioneer the work there. An Italian Baptist pastor, Saverio Guarna, volunteered to serve as evangelist, preacher and church planter. His ministry quickly led to conversions and baptisms, and the gathering of a Baptist congregation in the office premises in Tirana. North of the city, at Lezhe, a farm project with an agricultural consultant was launched. German and Czechoslovak Baptists and the Baptist Men's Movement in Britain generously donated a large supply of wheat seed under the auspices of BR-E. Financial help for the project was also provided by US AID. An EBF conference for children's and youth workers in Budapest asked for volunteers to work in Albania in the summer of 1993. Several teams worked for a month each, harvesting, digging drains and installing school toilets. Another BR-E project was to assist two Albanian schools to obtain educational supplies, equipment and winter heating.

The EBF Executive in Oslo in May 1992 was told that John and Virginia Keith of Canadian Baptist International Ministries (CBIM) were now spearheading the Albanian Project. The Burnetts had become field administrators. Application had been made to the Government for full legal recognition, and for permission to import 100,000 Albanian New Testaments offered by the United Bible Societies. The Executive unanimously resolved to recommend to the Council at High Leigh, England in September that the whole project be endorsed .

By when the Council met, the Government had asked for more information about the official purpose of the EBF. A Statement of Intent, based on Karl Heinz Walter's earlier presentation, but with significant revisions, was presented by John Keith to the Council for endorsement. He commended the work of the General Secretary in initiating the work in Albania, with Chris Burnett as internal co-ordinator. He told of the welcome received from the Minister of

Foreign Affairs who openly admitted the nation's need for spiritual as well as physical reconstruction. The Statement of Intent was:

1. To establish Albanian Baptist Churches.
2. To channel assistance within the limits of suitable available resources.
3. To undertake projects in consultation with Government Ministries.
4. To assist, encourage and equip Albanians to help themselves.
5. To undertake activities in co-operation with other Christian organizations.

John Keith pointed out that progress was urgent because of heavy Muslim activity and the fragility of the political situation. He proposed the appointment of the following as the Albanian Committee: Hilde Sayers (EBWU), Keith Parker (Co-operative Baptist Fellowship), Angus McNeill (BMS), John and Virginia Keith (CBIM) and Chris Burnett (BMS). Council readily approved all these matters and gave authority for a small executive committee of the General Secretary, John Keith and Chris Burnett to have power to act.

* * * * *

In this chapter we have concentrated on the changing face of Eastern Europe, but significant changes and developments were occurring in the rest of Europe. The Middle East was also in ferment, and several more Baptist groups from there were now members of the EBF. By the beginning of the last decade of the twentieth century the Federation had an entirely new look, contained a new generation of leaders, and faced a demanding and considerably different agenda. We must move on to consider how it has been meeting the challenge of the new Europe during the 1990s.

CHAPTER NOTES

CHAPTER SIX   The Changing Face of Eastern Europe
1   Norman Davies, *Europe: A History,* p.1116.
2   Ibid., p.1117.
3   A project in which the EBF Books and Translations Committee shared. See Chapter 8, pp.170-75.
4   For detailed reports and full text of the letter see EBPS 89:230-33, 24 November 1989, pp.1-2.
5   EBF Prayer Calendar 1998: Czech BU - 24 churches, 2510 members
Slovak BU - 15 churches, 1984 members.
6   See EBPS 89:223, 14 November 1989.
7   Jörg Swoboda with Richard V. Pierard (editor): *The Revolution of the Candles: Christians in the Revolution of the German Democratic Republic,* Mercer University Press, 1996. (English translation by Edwin P. Arnold).
8   *Baptist Quarterly,* **37**, pp.410f.
9   An informative and thoughtful analysis of Gorbachev's impact on the churches can be found in Michael Bourdeaux, *Gorbachev, Glasnost and the Gospel,* Hodder & Stoughton, 1990.
10 The following are good sources for information about Baptist progress in the various Baptist Unions during this period: EBPS 90:050, 3 April 1990, 'East Europe Up-Date 1' and 90:072, 4 May 1990, 'East Europe Up-Date 2'. Albert W. Wardin (Editor), *Baptists Around The World: A Comprehensive Handbook*, Broadman & Holman, 1995.
11   The list of new Baptist Unions (BU) and Unions of Evangelical Christians-Baptists (UECB): UECB of Armenia, UECB of Azerbaijan, UECB of Belarus, BU of Croatia, UECB of Estonia, BU of Georgia, Convention of Hungarian Baptist Churches of Romania, UECB of Kazakhstan, UECB of Kyrgyzstan, BU of Latvia, Union of Free Evangelical Churches in Lithuania, Union of Baptist Christians in Macedonia, UECB of Middle Asia, UECB of Moldova, UECB of Russia, Union of Baptist Churches in Serbia (Yugoslavia), BU of Slovenia, All-Ukrainian UECB, Brotherhood of Independent Baptist Churches and Ministries of Ukraine, UECB of Yugoslavia II.
12 This information was taken from an undated cutting.

7

MEETING THE CHALLENGE
OF THE NEW EUROPE

The incoming General Secretary of the Federation, Karl Heinz Walter, described 1989/90 as an historic year - 'the year of the beginning of the new Europe'. It was also a new beginning for many European Baptists. Amid such dramatic change he had a unique opportunity which he immediately seized. He gave several areas of EBF work high priority, such as structuring the Federation for the future, ensuring aid and resources for the new Baptist Unions of Eastern Europe, leadership training, support for the many seminaries and bible schools which were opening, and partnership in mission and evangelism. Significantly, the minutes of EBF Executive and Council meetings throughout the 1990s are long and detailed. This has no doubt been due to the General Secretary's determination to have policies which were thoroughly integrated, explained and recorded, thus giving him a clear mandate for action.

But Europe was not only new because of radical changes in the East; the West had also been transformed. Soon after the Second World War eleven nations formed the Council of Europe in Strasbourg, to pursue the goal of European unity. A sizeable network of organizations was developed to deal with common economic, industrial, commercial and political concerns. The so-called 'Common Market' (or European Economic Community) was formed in 1957 when six of the eleven nations signed the Treaty of Rome. A Council of Ministers, the European Parliament in Strasbourg, the European Court of Justice and the European Commission in Brussels came into existence to further the aims of unity. Their progress awakened hopes of economic, social and political benefits for participating nations, with the result that more applied for membership. Eventually, political union became the stated aim, together with monetary union and a single currency. This vision was embodied in the Treaty on European Union (EU) signed at Maastricht in 1993. Since then the member nations have been learning together, though with mixed results, how to balance the claims of national identity and being European.

So, while Eastern Europe fell apart with the collapse of Communism, Western Europe became increasingly more united. Paradoxically, Baptists in the East now faced an uncertain future, but with a spiritual eagerness to use their new freedom in Christian mission, while in the West many churches of all denominations were declining within a predominantly materialistic and secular society. It could be argued that the West possessed the material and financial resources which were desperately needed by the East, and the East had the spiritual experience and fervour which so often seemed to be lacking in the West. This was a vital aspect of the challenge which the EBF now had to face. How far has it succeeded in creating such unity between Baptists in East and West that there is genuine two-way traffic of mutual support and partnership in Christian mission?

There were other factors which had to be faced. Cold War attitudes still existed in some people's minds. Could the old boundaries be crossed? Cultural and theological expressions of Christian faith and worship in the West sometimes offended evangelicals in the East. This led to some being much more drawn to conservative evangelical missions from the USA and Korea than to Baptists of the West. Muslim influences began to attract, even pressurize, some of the new Euro-Asiatic republics towards Asia rather than Europe. What would this mean for Baptists there? The British Government tended to be insular and therefore cautious towards European Union. Would this in any way hinder British Baptists from being truly European? An even stronger nationalism existed in some of the new republics, fuelling racial hatreds, civil war and the horrors of ethnic cleansing. What effect would this have on Baptists in different ethnic groups within the same nation? When one considers the possible marginalization of Southern European Baptists, the distinctive life and culture of Scandinavian Baptists, and the problems for small Baptist Unions in the continual ferment of the Middle East, what does being the *European* Baptist Federation mean? And how can a Federation with such limited staff and resources meet the needs of such a vast and diverse group of people?

All these questions are relevant to the theme of this chapter and the next two. Hopefully, they will help us to assess the life and ministry of the EBF during the 1990s. We shall then be in a position to see where we are now, and whether there are pointers to how God wants us to move forward into the next century.

STRUCTURES AGAIN!

At the meeting of the Executive in April 1990, Peter Barber presented the Structure Committee's proposals which were approved for submission to the Council with appropriate by-law changes. The main concept of operating through four Divisions remained basic. But it was not proving easy to define the role and relationship to the Federation of a number of committees which were operating with a degree of independence. It was agreed to recommend that the Youth Committee and the European Baptist Women's Union should be directly responsible for their respective areas of work, with by-laws approved by the Council. Finance was also a matter of concern: there was not sufficient income for the Federation's wide spread of work. A complicating factor was the overlap of various financial appeals which competed with one another: for example, for EBF, Rüschlikon, SITE, BR-E, the Youth Committee, and EBWU. A small *ad hoc* committee under the chairmanship of Asbjørn Bakkevoll was appointed to prepare financial proposals.

An unexpected recommendation of the Structure Committee was that the chairman of the Books and Translations Committee should no longer be an *ex officio* member of the Executive. It is not clear why this was proposed, since the work of that committee had been a major feature of the Federation's work since 1980.[1] The committee was already planning to reshape its work to meet the changed circumstances in

Eastern Europe. Their remarkable achievements over the years will be described in the next chapter on theological and Christian education,[2] but it is important to note here the main thrust of their new plans. The chairman, Alec Gilmore, presented them in outline to the Executive in April 1990, and in more detail to the Council in De Bron, Netherlands in September 1990. Since Eastern European Baptist Unions were now free to publish Christian literature, it was necessary to shift the emphasis from providing literature from the West to producing it in the East. This would involve organizing conferences and workshops for writers and translators. Libraries, resource centres, reading rooms, and necessary equipment would have to be financed. Professional training for editors, sales and distribution workers, and librarians would be crucially important. It was essential to encourage each Union to take the initiative and determine its own choices and directions. At the Executive in Varna in the following year Alec Gilmore proposed that the Books and Translations Committee should be changed to a Publishing Consultative Group, which would be responsible to the General Secretary. He also presented draft proposals for its structure, work and necessary by-law changes, to be set before the Council

Two days later the Council approved the final report of the Structure Committee. In future the work of the Federation would be carried on through four new Divisions: Theology and Education; Mission and Evangelism; Communication, Promotion and Fellowship; External Relations. Convenors would normally serve for four years, with two being elected every two years. This would ensure both the possibility of change and a measure of continuity. Since these new structures had already won the support of the BWA they were to be operative forthwith. The Executive was given authority to implement the work of the Divisions.

When Alec Gilmore presented his report, he expressed the hope that the plan for a Publishing Consultative Group would be implemented, although he was aware that the new structures just agreed and the Baptist Response-Europe programme made this difficult However, the President intervened to introduce a unanimous recommendation from the Executive to freeze the proposal about a Publishing Consultative Group. Instead, they proposed that the Books and Translations Committee continue for one more year, complete its present agenda and then cease to exist. Future matters about literature and publishing would be referred to the Divisions for Theology and Education and for Mission and Evangelism, who would be expected to report via the Executive to the 1992 Council.

This was a hard blow for the members of the Books and Translations Committee. They had developed an expert literature service to Eastern European Baptists, in partnership with the Bible Societies, FEED THE MINDS, EUROLIT and a number of gifted Mennonites. It was difficult to see how the new EBF Divisions could match their expertise or raise equivalent financial resources. If they could not, such important work would be in danger of becoming marginalized just as a golden opportunity for new publishing initiatives had arrived. But the decision was final. A number of questions and requests were sent by the committee's chairman via David Coffey to the Executive in Oslo, May 1992. The answer was a letter expressing thanks for past service, but insisting that future work would be best done by the new Divisions. Therefore, the letter stated, it was unnecessary to appoint a new Books and Translations Committee.

New structures invariably call for considerable effort to adjust to different patterns of work. The minutes of 1992-1993 indicate that Convenors and Division members were confused about their roles. Jean-Pierre Dassonville gave up as convenor of the Communications Division in 1993. He had pressed for the appointment of a full-time professional worker for public relations and communications, but no money was available. When a search for funding met with no success, he recommended that a creative network system would be better than a Division. The Council in Moldova agreed.

In the following year, the General Secretary wrote to the Convenors and EBF officers to explain his vision for the operation of the Divisions. He suggested that a core group of five people in each Division should meet with their Convenor between Councils and then share their ideas with delegates at the annual Council. The President, Vice-president and General Secretary would select the core groups. The Dorfweil Council of 1994 considered this process too closed. They were not willing to leave the power of appointment with such a few people. Instead they insisted that an EBF Nominations Committee should bring names of Convenors and Deputy Convenors to the Council for appointment. Those appointed would then work with the Nominations Committee to select each core group

In November 1993 a special meeting of the Executive was held to discuss urgent business about the future of the Rüschlikon Seminary. In the course of the meeting the General Secretary raised an extra item about the possibility of relocating the EBF office. The Baptist Hospital in Hamburg (Albertinenkrankenhaus) was having some construction work done, which would offer more space for the office. He was keen to move the office to the new site and bring the European Baptist Press Service there from Rüschlikon. The EBPS Director, Stanley Crabb, had reservations, but he and his wife were willing to move, if it was so decided, subject to consultation with the SBC Foreign Mission Board. Karl Heinz Walter also requested that Paul Thibodeaux be appointed an associate secretary for three years, to be financed by the Cooperative Baptist Fellowship. He wished him to manage BR-E, to co-ordinate EBF Albania, and to cover the relocation of the Seminary. General approval was given, but before a final decision was made Council members requested that Knud Wümpelmann and a number of other past leaders be approached about possible sites elsewhere.

That suggestion obviously led to no alternative, for when the Executive met in Lisbon at the beginning of May 1994, the move had already been completed. New equipment had been installed, the Crabbs were already there, Paul Thibodeaux was due to arrive by the end of the month, and an Opening Reception was planned for June. Preliminary costs were reported to the Executive. They had been met from the Reserve Fund which now stood at zero, and it would be necessary to make budgetary provision of DM 15,000 annually for four years to restore the balance of the Fund. A generous grant of DM

10,000 was offered by the German Baptist Union. David Nixon warned the Executive that the Federation's finances needed considerable reorganization. A few months later this situation had become more urgent because of further costs arising from the office relocation and a large deficit on the Lillehammer Congress account. It was decided to negotiate a substantial loan in order to help the Norwegian Baptists deal with their creditors. Meanwhile, David Nixon reported that the Finance Committee was not functioning efficiently, and it was necessary for a core group within it to have authority to take action.

Another difficult structural matter was a suggestion that a European Baptist Men's Fellowship (EBMF) be formed. In the restructuring of the 1970s the Men's Committee was discontinued and two laymen were elected to the Council. In the 1980s one of these was David Beaumont of England, who had also been appointed by the BWA Men's Department as one of their two Vice-presidents for Europe. He was a keen supporter of BWA men's work. He faithfully attended committees, conferences and Congresses, and played a key role in Britain for the annual World Baptist Men's Day of Prayer. In 1991 he called together a number of Europeans to discuss ways of forming an EBMF. The BWA Men's Department wrote to the EBF asking for their support. The Council agreed that this should be explored, but a subsequent meeting in Portugal gave no encouragement to proceed further.

David Beaumont would not give up that easily. He wished to find someone who would work with him and replace him when he retired. He took a possible nominee to the BWA Council in Buenos Aires, where his suggestion was accepted. His colleague returned home convinced that he been elected Secretary of the EBMF. Not surprisingly, that caused problems. In September 1995 the EBF officers and Executive refused to recognize the action taken. They insisted that the correct procedure was for men's groups in Europe to liaise together to bring a proposal to the EBF, and only then to take it to the BWA.

This turned out to be impracticable. There was little interest in separate men's work in Europe. Organized men's groups existed in only five member Unions. There was one ray of hope. A promising exchange had taken place between Scottish and Hungarian Baptist men; possibly that could be the start of something new. Certainly the BWA Men's Department thought so, because when David Beaumont retired, they soon announced in an EBPS news item of December 1998 that Kenneth Stewart of Scotland and Marosi Nagy Lajos of Hungary were the newly elected Vice-presidents for Europe. What this will lead to in coming years remains to be seen.

There seemed to be no escape from structural issues! At the September 1994 Executive it was noted that Karl Heinz Walter's term of service was due to end in 1995. An Evaluation Committee was formed, comprising Birgit Karlsson, Theo Angelov, Peter Barber and John Merritt, with a two-fold task to perform:

• to review the work of the General Secretary and make a proposal for the future;
• to assess the effectiveness of the new structures and how they had affected the General Secretary and his staff.

Sadly, Peter Barber died after serious illness and surgery. His place was taken by Gerd Rudzio who presented the Committee's report to the Executive in September 1994. They unanimously recommended, and the next day Council agreed, that Karl Heinz Walter be re-appointed for a second five-year term. The Evaluation Committee also stressed the need for extra computer equipment in the office, and for a complete revision of working procedures and job specifications. A Structure Review Group was set up to expedite these matters. Its members were: Gregori Komendant, Hilde Sayers, Manuel Sarrias, Wiard Popkes, John Passmore, Ryszard Gutkowski and the Officers.

There was to be no easy solution; discussion about structures dragged on relentlessly. As so often happens in such contexts, one is left wondering what might have been achieved in other spheres if the time and money involved had not been devoured by endless structural debates. At the Executive in Sofia in March 1996, the Review Group eventually produced a revised job specification for the General Secretary, another one for an Assistant to the General Secretary, with a specific nomination for the post. After much discussion and inevitable clashes of opinion, pressure to go ahead with these proposals prevailed. Some amendments to the job specifications were requested, and it was finally decided to bring definitive proposals to the Executive and Council in Tallinn, Estonia in September.

As we have already discovered, there was considerable unease about EBF finances. In addition to the recent large Congress deficit, annual accounts continually failed to produce a surplus. Since no one had a clear idea of the likely financial effects of the new staffing proposals, members of the Executive began to ask whether savings could be made by holding Council meetings every two years and by moving the office to the new Seminary buildings in Prague. This received a strongly negative reaction, especially from the General Secretary. Another Core Group was charged with exploring possible economies by reviewing budgetary policy, devising a scheme for membership fees, preparing plans for more active promotion of the Federation, and suggesting possible changes to the structures. Was there any way of breaking out of the vicious circle?

IN CONFERENCE

During the early 1990s there were several important conferences in which the EBF was actively involved. European Christians generally were facing a totally changed situation. Many doors of opportunity, previously closed, were now wide open. Consultation within the Baptist family and the universal Christian Church, was a vital aspect of understanding human needs, sharing resources and discovering God's will for life and mission.

Peter Barber undoubtedly wished to stress this when he told the Council at Varna in 1991 that the EBF had been represented at a European International Consultation in Basel, Switzerland about 'The Common Witness of the Churches of the Reformation in Europe'. Such an event was encouraging evidence of a growing spirit of inter-church co-operation.

For seventeen days in November-December 1991 the Pope invited fifteen leaders of other churches to meet with the European Roman Catholic bishops at the Vatican, to consider together the theme: 'The Re-evangelization of Europe'. Non-Roman leaders were offered fifteen minutes each to address the conference. Karl Heinz Walter was eager to go and asked for the Council's support. He acknowledged that Baptists in Lithuania, Poland, Spain, Portugal and Italy were having difficulties with Roman Catholics. He was also aware that some European Baptists were highly critical of the current BWA/Vatican conversations. But he honestly thought it crucial to go. In his view it would be a gross error of judgement not to be there to use the opportunity to make the Free Church/Baptist voice heard. The Council wisely supported him with no one expressing opposition.

In his address to the bishops and cardinals, he affirmed the desire of Baptists to play their part in bringing the gospel to the peoples of Europe. He stressed Baptist understanding of the centrality and authority of the Bible, and the priority which they gave to evangelistic mission and servant ministry (diakonia). He urged the bishops to take proper care in helping governments to frame new laws, so that there was true religious equality. He asked them not to use their status to deny Baptists such equality, especially in countries where Catholics were in the majority. He shared their concern about the problems caused by para-church bodies and foreign sects. Baptists, he said, were not to be confused with them; nor were Baptists an American church, but had their own European history and heritage. This was why they were committed to the spiritual well-being of their respective countries and were offended when others portrayed them as less than good citizens because they were not part of the majority church..

Having had opportunity to confer with other denominations, it was strategically important for Baptists to consult together about their role in the new Europe. About fifty leaders from twenty-three Baptist Unions assembled in Dorfweil 26-29 January 1992. They included General Secretaries, Presidents, and the senior staff of theological seminaries and colleges. The format of the meetings was not a lecture programme, but genuine consultation. The only input from the front was an introductory address by Karl Heinz Walter, linking their gathering with the Conference of European Protestant Churches in Basel, the meeting with the Roman Catholic Bishops in the Vatican, and the forthcoming Assemblies of European Protestants at Budapest in March and the CEC in Prague in September. In a way that had never happened before, Free Churches, Orthodox, Protestants and Roman Catholics were sharing common ground in preparing for Christian mission in the 21st century. All Baptist Unions in Europe were invited to attend the CEC Assembly, whether they were members or not. The General Secretary urged them to go, and listed some of the issues for Baptists to raise: their understanding of evangelization; the centrality of the Bible; separation of Church and State; diaconal ministries, charity, education and human rights; avoidance of territorial claims.

At the conclusion of the EBF discussions at Dorfweil, which were not always easy because of the wide diversity of convictions, the aim was to draft an agreed statement for circulation to all Unions and theological schools for comment. Then a final statement would be prepared and made available to churches for general use. It would contain specific principles with a short explanatory statement for each one; but it was not to be viewed as a credal document or binding statement of Baptist faith. After this Consultation there were many expressions of appreciation for the spirit of honesty and fairness which prevailed. People sensed a new freedom leading to uninhibited fellowship. Unity, rather than uniformity, seemed to breed a strong desire for mutual help. One participant described this as the strength of the Federation.

Two months later a BWA Church Planting Conference took place in the Derbyshire conference centre, Swanwick, England. It issued a statement entitled: *DERBYSHIRE DECLARATION - A Call to Establish New Churches.* Delegates committed themselves to world evangelization, and specifically the planting of new churches. They felt led to issue a message to world Baptists, calling them to prayer, to creative thinking and innovative methods, consistent with biblical models and open to the guidance of the Holy Spirit. The final section of the Declaration invited 'every Baptist congregation in the world to establish, or to explore the possibility of joining with other churches in establishing, at least one new congregation by 2000 AD.'[3] In fact, such progressive action was already happening within the emancipated Baptist Unions of Eastern Europe, as well as in quite a number of those in the West. Despite the apparent deadlock of structural debates, many developments were taking place in the EBF family, some exciting and others difficult and disappointing. It is impossible to tell the whole story, but we turn now to a representative selection of events which will show the ever-increasing demands being made upon the Federation. They are arranged thematically rather than chronologically.

SERVING THE LORD TOGETHER

In the Middle East

To be Christian in the Middle East is not easy. Baptists are few in number, but they serve the Lord together with courageous faith. Five groups of them were listed in the EBF Directory for 1997: the Egypt Baptist Convention; the Association of Baptist Churches in Israel; the Jordan Baptist Convention; the Lebanese Baptist Convention; the Syrian Baptist Convention. Between them they have almost sixty churches with a total of just over 4,000 members. At the EBF Council in Varna in 1991, Peter Barber was pleased to report that closer links had been established with the Association in Israel. The Council was also delighted to have delegates present from Lebanon and Jordan. Fawaz Ameish of Jordan spoke of the pressures being asserted by Muslims, religiously to win a new generation for Islam, and politically to increase their influence in government, business and commerce. Nabih Haddad of Lebanon qualified this by stating that many Muslims were hungry for God's Word. Evangelical Christian witness was therefore vitally important. There was also urgent need for pastoral sensitivity and support when Muslims were converted to Christian faith, and so were totally rejected by their families and friends. Council members asked for these concerns to be explored by both the Division and the Institute for Mission and Evangelism.

In 1994 the Federation officers decided that more contact with the Middle East Baptists was desirable, in order to understand their situation more clearly and to offer them more support. With this in mind, the EBF Executive met in Cyprus in Spring 1995, to make it easier for the Middle East representatives to attend, and to hold a special consultation with them. Karl Heinz Walter paid a twelve-day visit to Lebanon and Jordan in November of the next year. In Lebanon the sufferings and damage of many years of war were considerable, but churches were being rebuilt and new ones established. The Arab Baptist Theological Seminary in Beirut, under the presidency of Ghassan Khalaf, was attempting to remedy the shortage of pastors and leaders. The Convention's General Secretary, Charles Costa, was exercising an important ministry, in particular by building a bridge with the EBF. In Jordan, the Convention had obtained 250,000 bibles in modern Arabic. The Baptist school had enrolled hundreds of scholars, many of whom were from Muslim families. In the city of Amman they owned a flourishing religious book store. With these resources they were able to evangelize effectively, with many conversions and baptisms, and consequently the growth of new churches. The Jordan Evangelical Theological Seminary, which had been established chiefly through American generosity, had a strategic role.

When Karl Heinz Walter used his visit to describe the work of the EBF and BWA, he was surprised to learn how little they knew. They explained to him that they had often felt isolated and were disappointed that few seemed to grasp how costly it was to be Christian in an area where human rights counted for little. What they heard about the EBF deeply moved them; so much so, that they made generous donations to BR-E, EBF general funds, and especially the Chernobyl children's project.

In 1997 Stefan Stiegler, the co-ordinator of the EBF's Theological Assistance Group-Europe (TAG-Europe),[4] visited the Arab Baptist Theological Seminary (ABTS) to find ways of drawing it into closer fellowship with the other European Baptist seminaries and colleges. He was so impressed by the size and strategic importance of the seminary, and by the full responsibility for it which the Middle East Baptists had undertaken when the SBC Foreign Mission Board decided to close it, that he wrote: 'We must be careful not to forget this part of Europe. The process of uniting Baptists in Europe does not only mean to unite East and West; it also means to unite with our sisters and brothers in the Middle East.'[5] Relationships were further strengthened when the Federation's Executive met in Beirut for the first time in April 1998.

Through Baptist Response-Europe
Year by year Baptist Response-Europe continued to be an important element in EBF work. A summary glance at reports in Executive and Council minutes reveals the large amount of money raised and aid given. For example, in 1991 grants were made for children's Christian literature, pastors' libraries, fax machines, copiers and projectors, to enable churches in the East to use the freedom which *perestroika* had brought. Substantial gifts were also given towards a conference centre in Romania, the Polish seminary in Radosc, and the new church in Varna. The Chernobyl Children's Summer Holidays project has been well supported by many churches and unions. It is likely to go on for a long time, because as recently as September 1998 statistics in one district showed that eight out of ten children were sick. Very many thousands still live in polluted areas. Even ten years after the Armenian earthquake there was desperate human need which could not be ignored. There has been a constantly recurring need for help in financing refugee programmes, medical and nursing care, and food and clothes for people in situations where economic chaos has left them cold and hungry in bitter winter climates.

In 1996 special help was given to the Moscow Baptist Church rebuilding scheme. This was contrary to BR-E's usual policy of not supporting large building projects, but this exception was made because Moscow was considered to be of central and strategic importance. The church members there had collected $40,000; Swedish Baptists had donated $17,000. The 850th anniversary of the city of Moscow would be celebrated in 1997, and it seemed appropriate to achieve the building target by then to allow Baptists to play a worthy part in the celebrations. Initially, BR-E was a means of reacting to emergencies, but it was important to be pro-active too. This has enabled many Unions to establish churches, orphanages, care-homes, training courses, missionary projects and publications, by helping to provide necessary equipment or finance for personnel appointments. By the end of 1998 eleven million DM had been raised in nine years, 63% of it from European sources.

Throughout the CIS Baptists responded immediately to their new freedom for evangelism and church planting. A key factor in this has been the financial support which BR-E has provided for many home missionaries appointed by their Baptist Unions. Numerous stories could be told of the exciting progress they have made. Two must suffice. When the EBF Council was invited to Moldova in 1993 they were overjoyed to hear that the Christian Evangelical-Baptist Churches' Union had recorded 3,000 baptisms in a year. Twenty-six church buildings had been completed and forty-three more were in process. They had also founded a Bible School and a School for Mission. Two years later their President, Victor Popovich, informed the Council held in Sao Pedro de Moel, Portugal, that as a result of the two-year programme of evangelism, with fourteen missionaries sponsored by BR-E, there had been 630 converts and 405 baptisms. Fifty-six mission centres had been opened. The Union was now aiming to provide a well-equipped central headquarters. In addition to hosting the Council meetings in 1993, they received the regional Home Mission Secretaries' Workshop for Eastern Europe in May 1998.[6]

The second story is from Georgia. Once freedom came, this small and isolated group of Baptists launched an intensive programme of evangelism and church planting. At the centre of their work was a large and unusual church in Tbilisi, housing four Baptist congregations in one building - a Georgian Church, a Russian Church, an Armenian Church and an Ossetian Church - each worshipping in its own language, with its own pastor, choir and leaders, and with a combined membership of about 2,500. When ethnic and nationalistic quarrels were breaking out so widely in the new Eastern Europe, this was a significant Christian witness of multi-ethnic co-operation. The Baptist Union's missionary strategy was unique. They created a team of home missionaries and travelling evangelists, financed by BR-E. Some of them would visit an area to hold a series of about twelve teaching meetings. Out of this one or more house groups would be formed and linked with existing Baptist congregations. This would eventually lead to the establishment of another church or mission centre. The work was so successful that they felt the need to create a home mission department in their Union. BR-E agreed to help finance this for the first two years. The EBWU also caught the vision and, through the leadership and personal efforts of Hilde Sayers, a new office was set up with adequate facilities to include guest accommodation.

Karl Heinz Walter was convinced that the geographical isolation of Georgia, their widespread poverty and hardship, and the instability caused by a tragic civil war which led to intervention by the Russian army, made Georgia a situation of special need. Even if this involved more cost, he persuaded the EBF that it was worth it. Over the years the Baptists have been able to build a home for elderly people and launch a home-nursing care scheme with assistance from the Albertinen and Bethel Deaconesses in Germany. For this scheme, and a similar one started in Bulgaria, the EBF has provided bags of medical instruments and medicines, as well as financial help with training. A Theological School for the training of pastors and lay leaders now exists in Kutaisi. This owes much to the devoted work and scholarship of their President, Malkhaz Songulashvili. He was offered much help from foreign missions and para-church groups, but they usually insisted on imposing their own terms and syllabus. He was determined to forge close links with TAG-Europe and the EBF Division for Theology and Education, in order to be able to establish a curriculum relevant to Georgian culture and their Union's theological position. Georgia is a modern example of New Testament teaching that the way to God's Kingdom is often through much suffering. It is also a notable example of the value of the Christian solidarity, encouragement, practical support and genuine partnership which the EBF offers. Boundaries are crossed which would otherwise seem insurmountable.

In the rest of Europe
During the past decade the needs and developments of Baptist life in Eastern Europe have dominated the agenda. Baptist Unions of the North, South and West have not featured anywhere near as much in the minutes or in the news items of the EBPS. This does not mean that they have been passive and static. Many stories could be told of spiritual progress, new missionary ventures, significant milestones reached, and exciting plans and visions for the coming Millennium. But these belong to the histories of the national Unions, rather than to a book which is specifically devoted to the history of the EBF. We should, however, note some examples of the Federation's involvement with other parts of Europe.

From 1991 to 1996 the Youth Committee organized international Bible Schools at Hamburg. Each year from thirty to forty-five students attended for ten days over the Easter period. These events were a popular and worthwhile venture. Oddly, when their venue was changed to Radosc, Poland, in 1997 only three students enrolled; in the following year the response was nil. An attempt to relaunch it was planned for Easter 1999 at the new German Baptist centre in Elstal, near Berlin.

For many years the Belgian Baptists were denied legal recognition in their predominantly Roman Catholic country. Despite much Catholic hostility and public denunciation of them as a sect, they persisted in their evangelical witness and steadily grew. The EBF and BWA supported them in their campaign for recognition and, at last, in December 1997, the Protestant Synod[7] agreed to admit the Baptist Union as a member. This gave them full recognition, which enhanced their status and increased their evangelistic opportunity just a few months before they celebrated their centenary. On hearing the news their President, Samuel Verhaeghe, expressed thanks to the EBF and its General Secretary for their persistent prayer and support.

Such advocacy is often needed. In answer to an appeal issued through the EBPS *Bulletin* of 6 March 1998, European Baptists successfully petitioned the King of Spain and the President of the Spanish Government to lift a ban arbitrarily imposed on religious radio stations. The Baptist Union of Spain was thus able to play an active part with other evangelical Protestant bodies in a pastoral and evangelistic ministry during the Olympic Games in Barcelona. Earlier in the same year the world trade fair EXPO took place in Portugal. The Portuguese Baptists were grateful for the prayerful support and encouragement of their fellow Baptists in the EBF.

When the Government of Estonia instituted a new religious law which discriminated against all church bodies except the Lutherans and Orthodox, the EBF immediately protested and called on its member Unions to give support by writing direct to the Government. A month later the offensive provisions in the law were removed. Some years earlier, through the Baptists of Sweden, Finland and Germany, the Estonian Baptists had been helped to complete their new seminary. Another small group in the Baltic area, the Union of Evangelical Baptist Churches in Lithuania was also supported in its successful application for official registration. It then proceeded to seek to become the tenth religious body recognized by the State since the fall of communism.

In the summer of 1997 a significant conference on evangelism was held at Vallersvik, Sweden. It was sponsored by the BWA Division of Evangelism and Education, in partnership with the EBF and the Baptist Unions of the Nordic-Baltic region. The Scandinavian Baptists were an indispensable agent of EBF support for the Baltic Baptists when they were under Soviet pressure and when they gained their political and religious freedom. The lay conferences and missionary projects which they helped to make possible have had a strong spiritual influence in that region. The 1997 conference was no exception. A group of outstanding Baptist speakers from around the world, as well as representatives from Scandinavia, Estonia, Latvia and Poland, together with David Coffey, the EBF President, and Karl Heinz Walter, were assembled for the occasion. They led sessions and bible studies on evangelism and related issues, such as winning young people for Christ, spiritual gifts, crossing ethnic boundaries, and establishing new churches. The conference was a clear example of the way in which the corporate fellowship and resources of bodies like the BWA and EBF can enrich the life of both local churches and national Unions.

Through solidarity and partnership
This survey of EBF activity indicates that there has always been more to it than offering material and financial aid. Important as that is in times of emergency, it can easily create dependency and a sort of dominance. A much more important need is to express solidarity and offer partnership in ways which encourage fellow Baptists to be themselves. So a crucial element in the Federation's work has been to stand alongside others and allow new developments to grow within their own national, cultural and theological milieu. That involves pastoral visits, spiritual and practical encouragement, and availability for consultation and advice. To be authentic it involves receiving as well as giving, affirming the worth of others who are different from ourselves, and avoiding at all costs the temptation to create uniformity, since there can be such strong unity in Christ even while remaining so different. The Apostle Paul expressed this truth when he wrote to first-century Christians in Rome: 'I long to see you so that I may impart to you some spiritual gift to make you strong - that is, that you and I may be mutually encouraged by each other's faith.'[8]

Successive Presidents and General Secretaries have undertaken their demanding work and travel schedules in this spirit, despite the limited resources and back-up staff available to them. During the 1990s Karl Heinz Walter and his presidential colleagues have been no exception to this pattern of life. They have given themselves without reserve. Their efforts have been supplemented by committee officers and members, and by representative delegates from member Unions who, while attending meetings and conferences, have built lasting relationships of mutual blessing with brothers and sisters in Christ. Often the time spent in personal conversations about joys and sorrows, or trying to help one another understand and face what seemed like an insoluble problem, or forging communication links which have lasted for years to come, has been the most valuable part of the meetings attended.

It is impossible to do justice to the many travels undertaken by the General Secretary during the 1990s. Inevitably, the majority of them were in Eastern Europe, because there the need for solidarity and partnership was the most urgent. He has written fascinating accounts of his visits, in which he describes the appalling difficulties some have had to face, their eager evangelism which has been so fruitful, the sacrificial service being undertaken with such limited resources, and everywhere he has gone, the warm welcomes received and generous hospitality offered, even to the point of embarrassment. Some visits to areas like Eastern Siberia, Belarus, the five Central Asian republics, Albania, Ukraine and Georgia revealed amazing news of Baptist groups unvisited before, or congregations formed of the many new converts being won for Christ. Young leaders were emerging in many places. Resources for training pastors and church members were urgently needed. Some work was being held back because there was a total lack of transport. Out of his many discoveries Karl Heinz Walter has been in a position to mastermind the distribution of BR-E funds to best advantage. He became to many believers an apostolic figure whose pastoral care and patient listening, followed by the provision of necessary partnership and facilities, were a godsend.

The same must be said about the remarkable work of the European Baptist Women's Union, and in particular the visiting programme inaugurated by Hilde Sayers and Julia Gero. Like Karl Heinz Walter, Hilde Sayers has recorded reports of her visits which make exhilarating reading.[9] Wherever she went, she felt that she should spend some time sitting with them and listening to them, rather than always standing at the front to address them. She wrote: 'My visits, in spite of danger, were a great encouragement to them.... I was alongside people, sharing their lives and hardships with them, especially during the cold winters, thus really feeling their needs myself.'[10] Over a period of seven years she was able to visit at least forty of the fifty member Unions of the EBF. This meant that she spent two-thirds of her time away from home - a wonderful way of offering her widowhood in the service of the Lord. It greatly enlarged the scope of the ministry of the EBWU. In many places it opened up churches which rejected the ministry and leadership of women to a transforming experience of their spiritual role. She and her colleagues were eventually invited to preach, to preside at the Lord's Table, to teach leaders and members to evangelize, to lecture to theological students, and to contribute to conferences for pastors. Much of their time was spent in visiting people in their homes, ministering to the sick and elderly, sharing family sorrows and joys - in fact, an holistic ministry of giving and receiving in body, mind and spirit. They exercised an influential ministry among non-Christians, with prisoners, and even with governments. Two outstanding projects were the scheme to help the Baptist Union of Georgia develop a sunflower cooking-oil production and distribution business, and the provision of a tractor for Aliabad in Azerbaijan. The oil project overcame a desperate shortage over a wide area, generating income for the Baptist Union, and creating employment. The tractor enabled church members to provide for their families and serve others around them. Both projects were of a self-help nature, giving dignity and spiritual encouragement to believers and unbelievers alike in a very deprived area.

Solidarity and partnership have undoubtedly been shown to be vital aspects of holistic mission. They have been an effective way to discover and release new people with unexpected gifts and qualities needed in the work of their churches. But not all have yet learned this. In the early days of the new Europe, Alexander Firisiuk, President of the Belarus Baptists, complained that there was not enough opportunity to share information at the EBF meetings. There were too many speeches and conference style lectures. He spoke for many Eastern Europeans from the newly independent areas, who felt that they were being treated as if they had nothing to contribute. They were always being told, and they did not want just to have to sit and listen. Maybe one of the lessons to be learned from the story of the 1990s is that in the East God has raised up a people who, through much trial and tribulation, have emerged with spiritual riches which we in the West, who are 'rich in things and poor in soul',[11] so much need. Is that a goal which the EBF must seek in the future? Has the first step been taken in the unanimous appointment of Theo Angelov of Bulgaria as the next General Secretary, to succeed Karl Heinz Walter in 1999?[12]

Through Congresses
Early in 1992 the EBF Executive began to plan for the 9th European Baptist Congress due to be held in 1994. The invitation of the Norwegian Baptists to hold it in Oslo was accepted. After the exhilarating experience of the 8th Congress in Budapest, it was agreed to put the focus on the family and prepare a programme for all age groups. The chosen theme was 'Together we will serve the Lord', the response of the Israelites to the challenge of Joshua, when they had entered the promised land after their years in the wilderness.[13] As the various committees moved ahead with their plans, the word 'Together' was given more emphasis. They were keen to encourage partnership in the new Europe five years after the breaking down of the Berlin Wall.

Two serious setbacks hindered the preparations. One was the illness and death of Asbjørn Bakkevoll, chairman of the Local Arrangements Committee. This robbed the planning committees of his wise leadership and wide experience, for he was a former Youth Secretary of the Baptist Union of Norway and the EBF, and also Finance Administrator of the Norwegian Union. The other setback was that prices being quoted for Oslo were rapidly escalating. The Local Arrangements Committee suggested that the venue be changed to Lillehammer. Costs there would be cheaper, and the facilities being built for the 1994 Winter Olympics could be booked for the Congress. The Executive gave authority to explore this alternative and to take action if it was considered wise. 1% of BR-E funds was transferred to a Congress Travel and Scholarships Fund. At previous Congresses scholarships had been offered in the main to delegates from Eastern Europe. Such help was still needed, but it was decided this time to add to the list representatives from the Middle East and the smaller Unions far distant from Norway.

A third setback came when Peter Barber, chairman of the Programme Committee, also became seriously ill. John Passmore acted as his substitute when the various committees met in Lillehammer in April 1993. But progress was proving difficult. There was a shortage of finance both within the Norwegian Union and the EBF, and several larger, wealthier Unions were asked to provide interest-free loans to cover advance expenditure. Unfortunately, it proved impossible to cover all the necessary preparation work in Norway. This placed an extra burden on the staff in the Hamburg office, where providentially Paul Thibodeaux, of the Co-operative Baptist Fellowship, arrived with his wife in time to share in the task. Paul became an associate to the General Secretary of the EBF.

Despite these problems, the Congress on 26-31 July 1994 was a memorable occasion with a profound spiritual impact, which led the EBPS report of 15 August to describe it as 'one of the best'. More than 3,000 Baptists from thirty-four countries registered as delegates. It was estimated that at least one-third of them were from Eastern Europe, thoroughly enjoying their freedom to travel and with the years ahead so full of promise. The first ever Albanian Baptist delegate was welcomed with great joy. Each day the programme had three main sessions: in the morning, worship, prayer and bible study in small groups and different languages; in the afternoon, sectional meetings for women, men, pastors, young people and families; and each evening, large public rallies and multi-media presentations, for celebration, inspiration and spiritual challenge. Children's activities were arranged throughout the Congress. An imaginative new feature was the provision of shoulder bags for delegates. Four thousand of these had been handmade and embroidered by people of one of the impoverished Hill Tribes of North Thailand. The EBF had insisted on paying the full price for them, which ensured the tribe's total income for one year. In serving the Lord by serving and helping others, the theme was made flesh in a striking manner.

A similar act of solidarity was expressed at one of the evening rallies. It was planned as an African night. It included a live link with a missionary of the European Baptist Mission in Cameroon. A choir of African refugees from Zaire, Angola and Chad thrilled the congregation with their singing. Paul Montacute of Baptist World Aid launched an appeal for $500,000 for Zairean and Tanzanian refugees. A record offering was given for the suffering people of Rwanda. Note was also taken of refugee situations in Europe, particularly among migrant Muslims and gypsies. A highly emotive moment came when Max Staublis, the General Secretary of the European Baptist Mission, appealed for recruits for their work beyond Europe, and forty people responded.

On another day the new EBF Vice-president, Theo Angelov of Bulgaria, described how the Bulgarian Government had sent spies to the previous Congress, posing as Baptist representatives and reporting back afterwards. This time he and his fellow country men and women were truly free to travel, attend, speak and mix with people of other lands without fear. It was a new and highly emotional experience. But he used this testimony to warn against false illusions, for there were still difficulties. Both Government and the Orthodox Church tried to impose restrictions. There was much public maligning of Baptists and rumour-mongering about alleged drug dealing and danger to children. Several times during the Congress people from different countries gave news of persecution. This made Human Rights an important item in EBF work. Karl Heinz Walter announced that the Federation had recently set up a network of lawyers across Europe to specialize in Human Rights issues, in order to assist churches and Unions being victimized. Denton Lotz reported that a BWA and EBF delegation was to meet the Orthodox Patriarch in Istanbul to discuss these issues. The BWA was also using its status as a Non-Governmental Organization at the United Nations to press for observance of the Helsinki provisions. An appropriate public resolution on religious liberty and human rights was approved by the Congress. It is noteworthy that several speakers in the discussion stressed the need to view this issue as not for Baptists only.

After the Congress a large deficit was declared; it was eventually found to be DM 480,000. This was a crushing blow to the EBF which was already facing financial crisis. Unexpected help enabled the Norwegian Baptists to deal with their creditors without harming their own Union's work, and by 1995 also ensured that the Federation's finances did not collapse. But questions about future Congresses were unavoidable

Almost immediately, the EBF Council had to begin planning for the 10th European Congress in 1999. They accepted an invitation from Slovakia to hold it in Bratislava, where they were assured of excellent facilities, reasonable prices, and government co-operation. The Baptist Union of Slovakia undertook to provide office space, volunteers, a full-time chairman of the Local Arrangements Committee and a secretary. Reg Harvey, who had agreed to serve as chairman of the Programme Committee, submitted guidelines for the committees and a provisional timetable which the Executive approved. However, as time went on, there were signs of growing uncertainty. Some Slovakians were hesitant about the size of the task. The EBF officers realized that the Lillehammer deficit must not be repeated, and some members thought that the time had possibly come to abandon large Congresses for more modest meetings. Yet the Constitution and By-laws provided for such five-yearly events. Who dare risk abandoning it?

At the Council in Tallinn in September 1996 Reg Harvey reported on a feasibility study. Positively, congresses normally resulted in changed lives, enlarged vision, enriched worship, deeper fellowship and expanded mission. 1999 would be a significant landmark both as the golden jubilee of the EBF and as a bridge to the Millennium. But there was one large negative - the cost. The Federation could not afford it. There was no alternative but to insist that all delegates must pay for their own travel, accommodation and food, plus a reasonable Congress fee. Careful budgetary control must be maintained and all extravagance avoided. With that understanding Council unanimously agreed to go ahead. A year later, the full impact of this decision began to be felt. Registration fees would not cover all the cost. Money for initial outlays would need to be gathered from the stronger Unions for a period of two years. There could be no scholarships offered and the office in Hamburg could not accept responsibility for any booking arrangements. Theo Angelov stated that a delegation had held an encouraging meeting with the Mayor of Bratislava and the Slovakian State President and Minister of Culture. On the strength of that, planning went ahead.

When the Council met in Kiev in late September 1998 the situation was 'All change!' The Slovakian Government had imposed high charges for visas for people from the Commonwealth of Independent States (CIS). No contract had yet been signed for the Congress Hall and costs being quoted had risen by 27%. Despite all the hard work put in by the Local Arrangements Committee and the Programme Committee, Reg Harvey regretfully recommended that it was no longer feasible to proceed with plans at Bratislava. He had conveyed this to the Slovakian Baptists, expressing deep regret that such a decision was necessary, and thanking them for their industry and commitment. He then asked Council to accept the recommendation that the Congress should be held in Wroclaw, Poland. The Polish Baptist leaders were willing to make this possible despite the short notice. This proposal was gratefully welcomed.

The theme agreed for Bratislava was retained for the Congress at Wroclaw: BRIDGE TO THE FUTURE - JESUS CHRIST. In the brochure announcing the details of the Congress, Grzegorz Bednarczyk and Ryszard Gutkowski, President and General Secretary of the Polish Baptist Union, stated in their message of welcome:

> Our Baptist family in Poland is not big in numbers, but rather great in spiritual expectations of the evidences of God's grace.....We will pray for other countries of our continent, so our Lord Jesus Christ may be better known and praised in every place in Europe.

Their words express what will worthily celebrate fifty years of EBF work and witness. Once again, boundaries will be crossed as thousands from north, south, east and west come together in the name of Jesus.

CHAPTER NOTES

CHAPTER SEVEN   Meeting The Challenge of The New Europe

1   See pp.75f, 77, 93.

2   See pp.170-175.

3   The text of the Derbyshire Declaration may be found in EBPS 92.058, 31 March 1992, p.5.

4   For details of TAG-Europe see Chapter 8, pp.166-168.

5   For his full report see EBPS 045, 16 May 1997, pp.3f. Also his report on the Jordan Evangelical Theological Seminary in EBPS 076, 21 August 1997, pp.3f.

6   The EBF Prayer Calendar for 1998 reported that the Moldovan Union had 275 churches and 17,200 members.

7   The only Protestant body given legal status by the Government.

8   Romans 1.11-12 (*New International Version*).

9   For her own accounts of them see Hilde Sayers, *The Transition From The Old To The New Europe,* EBWU, 1998.

10   In a private letter to me, 11 February 1998.

11   Words from the hymn by H. E. Fosdick, 'God of grace and God of Glory'.

12   The first EBF General Secretary from Eastern Europe, pastor of the Sofia Baptist Church and President of the Baptist Union of Bulgaria. He served as EBF President 1995-7.

13   Joshua 24.14-21.

PART TWO

MAJOR CONCERNS

THEOLOGICAL AND CHRISTIAN EDUCATION

The writing of history needs to be more than a mere chronicling of events. They are, of course, important for a well-told story; but the writer can never include everything and, therefore, the story is bound to be incomplete. It will be obvious to the reader that the story which has been told so far in Part 1 has omitted some major turning points and crucial issues which have profoundly affected the life of the European Baptist Federation. This has been deliberate, in order that some of the principal concerns encountered over the years might now be addressed in more depth in Part 2.

Our attention will be turned to creative moments when the Federation moved decisively in new directions. We shall come to difficult moments when controversy and the tensions of different convictions threatened European Baptist unity. There have been visionary moments too, leading to the formation of organizations dedicated to particular tasks. Though independent in structure, those organizations have been closely related to the EBF and have considerably enlarged its contribution to Baptist life and mission. In this chapter we turn now to important developments in the sphere of theological and Christian education.

NATIONAL THEOLOGICAL SEMINARIES

In 1920, long before the formation of the EBF, the Baptist World Alliance asked J. H. Rushbrooke of London and C. A. Brooks of New York to undertake an extensive tour of Europe to assess the Baptist situation after World War 1 and present a report to a specially convened conference in London, 19-23 July.[1] One of the urgent needs they discerned was the provision of adequate training facilities for ministers, evangelists and other church workers. A proposal to assist in establishing new national Baptist seminaries was approved. The rapid growth of seminaries was one of the most creative results of the conference, and a sign of what can be achieved when Christians create trusting partnerships and use their resources strategically.

After World War 2, there were again urgent problems in the sphere of theological and Christian education. Some of the seminaries had been damaged or destroyed. Many in lands overrun by Communism were closed or severely restricted. Some students were able to attend the new Baptist Theological Seminary which the Southern Baptist Convention of the USA established in Rüschlikon, Zurich in 1949. A few had opportunity to study abroad, either through the generosity of the receiving college, seminary or union, or with the help of the BWA and EBF. Generally, however, in the East there was much deprivation and little sustained provision of such education. There were a few notable exceptions. Flourishing seminaries in Hungary and East Germany were permitted to continue their work. The All Union Council of Evangelical Christians-Baptists in Moscow devised a correspondence course which operated successfully throughout the Soviet Union for many years, but it had obvious limitations. Although it ensured that many churches had recognized preachers and pastors, it could not provide the quality of training which a full seminary course would offer.

In 1964, the EBF General Secretary, Erik Rudén, informed the Council that there was evidence of a new vitality in theological education. He cited three examples. The Baptist Seminary in Barcelona (later to be relocated in Madrid) had recently re-opened with nineteen students, at a time when there was increased freedom for evangelical churches. A new Baptist theological school in France was to open in October. A seminary had also been opened in Norway. For the next fifteen to twenty years EBF minutes and EBPS bulletins carried news of exciting seminary developments. **1966**: a new seminary, chapel and living accommodation in Novi Sad, Yugoslavia; the opening of the Bethel Seminary in Bromma, Stockholm; European Baptist Theological Teachers decided to hold their annual conference in East

Germany at Buckow seminary. **1967**: plans made for a seminary in Lisbon, Portugal, which was eventually opened in 1969. **1968**: a large intake of students in Poland, Spain and Hungary; tenth anniversary celebrations at the Dutch seminary. **1969**: Danish seminary building dedicated. **1970**: Hamburg seminary's 90th anniversary - buildings being remodelled. **1976**: a surge of new students in Warsaw. **1978**: high enrolments reported in many European Baptist seminaries. **1981**: the possibility of a seminary in Moscow once again being discussed. These examples by no means tell the whole story of the spiritual progress and growth experienced by European Baptists during the two decades. The fact that this all occurred in difficult cold war years is a glowing testimony to the value of the mutual support being developed through the EBF. In retrospect, it is possible to trace the hand of God at work, preparing pastors, teachers and leaders for the many new opportunities which were soon to come when revolutionary changes swept through central and eastern Europe, and the Baltic States, at the end of the 1980s.

Theological seminaries and Bible schools mushroomed in the 1990s in regions previously dominated by Soviet Communism. We have already traced how the republics within the USSR became independent, democratic states, and how Baptists in them formed their autonomous national Unions. Not only did this considerably increase the number of member unions in the EBF; it also led to the formation of numerous Baptist centres of theological and Christian education. At the meeting of the Executive in Lebanon in April 1998 Karl Heinz Walter stated that before 1989 there were fifteen theological seminaries in Europe; now there were more than forty and almost one hundred Bible Schools.

This development merits thorough research in coming years, for it embodies a remarkable phenomenon of spiritual renewal akin to the advance of the early Church in New Testament times. Maybe a cultural boundary [or is it an ideological one?] needs to be crossed by those of us who live and work in the so-called Christian West. Religious commentators on the world church scene have sometimes suggested that we need to look to the new churches in the two-thirds world for vision and spiritual commitment. Equally, it would be reasonable to suggest that instead of turning incessantly to the USA for evangelistic, church growth and charismatic expertise, we should be ready to learn from Eastern European Christians. How and why did they make such progress when they were 'in chains', and how were they ready and able to seize God's moment of opportunity when it came? Although they lacked many of the resources which we have possessed in abundance but often failed to turn to good effect, they have surged forward in a missionary way that has too often eluded us. On the credit side, the EBF has stimulated a generous sharing of resources in their need. Are we as ready to receive in humility what they are now able to give us? Will the Federation use the scholars, teachers and leaders produced by the new seminaries as contributors and not only recipients?

The importance of theological and Christian education world-wide led the Baptist World Alliance to accept Denton Lotz's suggestion to establish a new programme called Theological Assistance Group (TAG). Its first chairman was Andrew MacRae. The purpose of this programme was to give general direction and guidance in the founding of Bible schools, and to assist Baptist Unions in establishing seminaries, planning buildings, developing courses, assembling libraries, selecting and equipping tutorial staff. There were two sections originally, one for North America and the other for Europe. Co-ordination proved difficult and there was uncertainty about their roles and relationship. So the EBF Executive decided that TAG-Europe (TAG-E) should begin to act with its own agenda in a continent where the rapid growth of teaching centres gave it a crucial function to fulfil in the next few years. The membership of the group comprised the four European members of BWA-TAG - Drs John David Hopper, Wiard Popkes, Paul Fiddes and Stefan Stiegler (Group leader). Its work was closely linked with the Theology and Education Division of which Paul Fiddes was Convenor, and it reported regularly to the EBF Executive.

In their early days new teaching institutions needed the help of guest lecturers, professors and pastors. They also needed sponsorship for various projects. Constant contact was necessary; so TAG-E kept up-to-date information about teachers able to help and institutions needing help, and they linked the two. They also kept the EBF informed of literature needs and publishing advice given. Mutual trust was essential. In order to help create this, they organized a Consultation in Cluj-Napoca, Romania in March 1993, for Leaders of Baptist Theological Schools. About twenty people from nine Unions attended it. Session themes included curriculum design, teaching methods, library development, preparing a mission statement, and the spiritual nurture of students. Some excellent ideas emerged from the Consultation. For example, future pastors needed to learn together in community in order to be 'formed' and not just 'educated'. Another was the plea from Bulgaria for the training of Baptist school teachers who would 'keep a place open for Protestants in society' in the new Eastern Europe. The concept of theological education was widened beyond the training of pastors to that of preparing Baptist young people for a wide range of service in society. A vital question was raised whether Baptist colleges should enter into relationships with other institutions such as a secular university. Would this lead to loss of control over the syllabus, or would it give opportunity for Christian witness in the secular 'market place'?[2]

It soon became clear that TAG-E was fulfilling a valuable role within the EBF. It still continues to do so. It does not exist for financial assistance, nor does it initiate education. It has a consultancy task and aims to create networks, through which experience can be shared and partnerships be formed with national leaders, to ensure theological and Christian education which is thoroughly rooted in the local, national context. Stefan Stiegler coined a phrase to use the initials TAG in a different way - 'Teach as Guests'. Teachers from around the world began to be recruited for two-week terms in countries where pastors could be gathered together for seminars. Thus, a former leader of the East German Baptist Home Mission Department and his wife led special seminars on evangelism and church leadership in two places in Lithuania. Also, four Bible Schools in Russia, which were formed to back up groups of new churches spiritually and theologically, have received guest teachers from Canadian Baptists, German Baptists, the Co-operative Baptist Fellowship and the Fellowship of British Baptists.

TAG-E was reconstituted in 1997-8 because of personnel and faculty changes, and especially because Drs Wesley and Cheryl Brown of the American Baptist Churches International Ministries (ABC/IM) were seconded to work with TAG. They had wide experience in team teaching and seminary administration. Based in Prague, they were given a roving ministry, to visit seminaries and Bible schools in Central and Eastern Europe and the Middle East. They quickly won a position of trust after attending the Russian Baptist Congress, the Euro-Asiatic Federation and a German Baptist Assembly. The new TAG members from March 1998 were: Wesley and Cheryl Brown, Othniel Bunaciu (Romania), Andre Heinze (Germany), Toivo Pill (Estonia), Paul Saunders (Lebanon), Martin Scott (Great Britain), Stefan Stiegler (Germany - *Co-ordinator)*, Davorin Peterlin (Croatia - *Convenor of the T & E Division)*, Erroll Simmons (International Baptist Lay Academy), David Brown (SITE), and a representative of the European Baptist Theological Teachers' Conference.[3] When the Group met in Prague in March 1998 they planned a conference for administrators of theological institutions, to be held prior to the European Baptist Congress in July 1999. No doubt its main focus will be to consider issues likely to be of strategic significance in the twenty-first century. In order to prepare for the future, a Directory of Baptist Theological Education in Europe, which was developed in 1994-5 and set up on the Internet at Regent's Park College, Oxford, was revised by the Browns with the intention of creating a new TAG-E website on the Internet by the end of 1998. They also planned to establish a data base of international guest teachers available to help with the development of Baptist leadership in the twenty-first century.

Another network of considerable importance to the theological institutions in the European Baptist family for many years is the European Baptist Theological Teachers' Conference (EBTTC). It first met at Rüschlikon in 1954 and, with much encouragement from the President of the Seminary, Dr Josef Nordenhaug, held two more conferences there during the 1950s. After meeting at Regent's Park College, Oxford in 1961, future conferences met every two or three years at different colleges or seminaries. From the beginning it has remained a conference rather than an organization, a network with a secretary, but no staff. The Secretary has usually liaised with the Principal of the host college to plan each conference programme, including two or three main papers, Old and New Testament seminars, reports from all the institutions represented, and times of worship, fellowship and prayer.

For many years those present were predominantly from Western Europe, because there were few seminaries in the East, and those which existed were seriously hindered by visa and currency restrictions. Representatives from Spain, Portugal and Italy were frequently absent. Finance was a major cause of this, but Southern Baptist Convention influences may also have been responsible for the non-participation of the first two countries. In 1985 the conference met for the first time in Eastern Europe at Warsaw, but this failed to bring about a lasting change. When the new situation of the 1990s came, it was obvious that the EBTTC was too Western in theology and personnel. They actively sought to attract representatives from the East, but the response was very patchy. Several reasons may be suggested: financial restraints, theological mistrust, the attraction of generous offers from foreign mission groups with an evangelical ethos more acceptable to many Eastern European Baptists.

A few years earlier at the EBF Council in Denia, Spain (1982), the EBTTC expressed concern over the haphazard links between the Federation and the BWA Study Commissions. They pressed for more consultation about the Europeans appointed to the Commissions and for more specific reports of their work to be given. They expressed a willingness to help in any way possible, as, for example, relating the work of the BWA Commissions to workshops and seminars at EBF Congresses. Another matter they emphasized was the need to concentrate attention on Baptist beliefs and principles.

The 15th Conference at Rüschlikon in 1992 dealt with the theme of Baptist Identity, in relation to spiritual renewal, leadership, worship, ecumenism, other faiths, and political involvement. It succeeded in bringing together forty-one representatives from twenty theological institutions. Two plenary sessions were devoted to the Dorfweil Statement, *What Are Baptists?* They submitted a number of revisions which were included in the final published version. While their contributions ensured that the document possessed reliable theological substance, they also made clear that it was intended to be used not as a confession of faith but as an agreed statement of the position and direction of Baptists in contemporary Europe. As such, it could be used as a study document in the denomination and as a useful apologetic with governments and other churches. At this conference Wiard Popkes retired from the secretaryship, having served in that capacity since 1976. In a brief retirement speech he described the EBTTC as a place for honest sharing and mutual trust, where people felt free to rethink and float new ideas, without fear of unauthorized publication and with the assurance of confidentiality. In theological and Christian education he saw that it was crucial to provide such 'a protected room'.

CHRISTIAN LITERATURE

Theological and Christian education was high on the agenda at the EBF Council meetings in Italy in 1977. The Eastern European Baptists had referred a number of resolutions to the Executive about patterns of training for their pastors. The need for books was an absolute priority. They wanted to see the provision of mini-libraries in all Eastern European countries, with standard works understandable to lay people. They also wanted help with establishing study courses based primarily on those books.

Three people in particular picked up their requests. David Russell was already involved with the BWA project to publish William Barclay's *Daily Bible Study Commentaries* of the New Testament in the Russian language. He also became a keen supporter of SITE, with its mini-library scheme. A close friend, Alec Gilmore, was an administrator of FEED THE MINDS, an ecumenical agency providing Christian literature for the Third World. He was convinced that the project could be expanded to take in Eastern Europe. The two men formed an alliance to raise money and organize publicity. With the full support of the Baptist Missionary Society, the Baptist Union of Scotland and the Baptist Union of Great Britain and Ireland, they launched EUROLIT. It had three aims: (a) To help churches in Eastern Europe to develop Christian literature; (b) To stimulate Christians in the West to learn more about Eastern Europe, to pray more intelligently and to give more generously; (c) To work openly, respecting the laws of other countries, and to seek to work with them.[4] The other person who had been thinking on similar lines was Denton Lotz. He was working in Europe for the American Baptist Foreign Missionary Society and was linked with the Rüschlikon Seminary. The two others shared their vision with him. On 5 March 1980, he wrote to Gerhard Claas, John David Hopper, Stanislav Svec and David Russell, outlining his plan to propose to the Executive and Council in Paris in April of that year that a Books and Translations Committee be formed to expedite the supply of Christian literature for Eastern Europe.[5] He won wholehearted support for such a scheme, and the committee was established at once, with David Russell as its first chairman. Gerhard Claas became a keen supporter and advocate of their work. He subsequently opened the way for Alec Gilmore to attend EBF Council meetings, and in due course serve on the Executive, thus ensuring a firm place in the Federation for the committee's work.

Christian literature was a controversial issue in the Cold War years. 'Underground' organizations which smuggled bibles and religious books into Communist countries were widely active. Their work had an aura of romance and excitement, which attracted great support all over the world. Undoubtedly, they supplied the Word of God to many needy churches and believers, but there will always be debate about possible harm done to recipients who became prisoners, and even martyrs, through being involved in contravention of unjust laws. From the outset the B & T Committee and its allies made it a firm policy always to stay within the law. Proper contracts, import licences and official State approval of projects, travel and conferences were patiently negotiated. This was the general approach of both the BWA and the EBF. Maybe they lost support among some Christians who mistrusted their theological soundness and gave their support elsewhere. They were frequently accused of compromise, treachery to the Gospel, and infiltration by agents of the KGB. However, they won access to Governments and key Ministers of State, establishing trust by their integrity, and helping Baptists to obtain more standing and freedom than the so-called 'dissidents'. This is illustrated by the fact that on several occasions permission was obtained for representatives of the B & T Committee to undertake a tour of about six Eastern European countries to gather information, plan literature projects and negotiate details with State officials. FEED THE MINDS and its Director received similar co-operation from the authorities.

Alec Gilmore, who eventually succeeded David Russell as chairman of the B & T Committee, once related how, on closer acquaintance with a leader of the Hungarian Reformed Church, he reminisced lightly how on first meeting him he felt that he had been treated with caution. The leader replied: 'I did not view you with suspicion, but I was puzzled because *you* came to discover how you could help *us* to achieve *our* programmes. Everybody else from the West came seeking *our* help to achieve *their* programmes.' His reply was a striking testimony to the integrity and genuine motivation of the committee's work.

Over the years their programme of activities went through three stages. The first was to provide theological textbooks for seminary libraries, and for ministerial and lay training. Catalogues were sent annually to seminaries and denominational headquarters, and grants to purchase books were available within set limits, on the understanding that the choice always belonged to the receiving body A second-hand book service was also operated. Many were collected, listed and made available on request, especially for filling gaps in existing libraries. This service was widely used, as also was a Baptist Book Centre in

Vienna, of which John David Hopper, at one point, served as the Director. It was primarily a literature storage and translation centre. FEED THE MINDS regularly published a Theological Book Review, which was for sale in the UK but free in the Third World. Through EUROLIT and the B & T Committee it was now offered freely to Eastern Europe.

The second stage was to provide cash and training for translation, writing, printing and publishing. Major translation projects which were assisted included the Barclay Commentaries in Polish, the Tyndale Commentaries in Serbo-Croatian for Dobra Vest, the publishing arm of the Baptists of Yugoslavia in Novi Sad, and the Barclay Commentaries in Russian. The Romanian Baptists sought help from the USA in producing a Romanian translation of the Broadman Commentaries, and the EBF B & T Committee assisted by the provision of printing equipment. They supplied a substantial quantity of typewriters, photocopiers, computers, printing machines, paper and printing ink to other EBF member bodies, notably the new Baptist Seminary and Conference Centre at Radosc. The SITE programme of mini-libraries for each student to take home afterwards featured annually in the expenditure of the committee, thanks to the generous support of EUROLIT. A sizeable list of other projects towards which grants were made from 1980 onwards includes hymnbooks, lexicons, concordances, religious education books and visual aids for children, magazines, Braille bibles and a library for young people.

The third stage added training and publishing to the agenda. Indigenous religious writing and publication faced difficulties for years in the communist world, but when hopes of new initiatives began to appear in the mid-1980s the B & T Committee immediately created training opportunities. Many Baptists were enabled to attend two ecumenical seminars for Eastern European scholars, academics and publishers in Oxford. While they were there, they were free to explore the city's book shops with funds available for them to select their own mini-library to take home. When the EBF Council met in Glasgow in 1987 a one-day Baptist translators' workshop was arranged, led by the

EBF General Secretary, Knud Wümpelmann, who was an ardent supporter of the committee, and Walter Sawatsky, a Mennonite scholar and writer, with wide knowledge of Eastern Europe.[6]

A year later a much larger workshop was organized at Rüschlikon, at which a number of ecumenical guests were also present. Among them was Father Verzan, Head of the Orthodox Church Publishing Division in Romania, who warmly chose to worship in the Baptist Church on the Sunday morning. The B & T Committee gave to every participant a Resource Pack on Christian Publishing and Bookselling which it had specially produced for the occasion. In an introductory section, Alec Gilmore stressed that Christian publishing was highly commercial and competitive, and that amateurism or poor quality workmanship were inexcusable. He pointed out that, while modern technology was not always the answer, it was crucial for those who wanted to develop effective Christian publishing to know what was available, what to select and what to reject. From his own professional experience he urged people to recognize the value of co-operation with other churches, whether by sharing equipment and information, or planning united Christian publishing facilities. This was one of the emphases which Knud Wümpelmann was keen to commend.[7]

Through the generosity of the Southern Baptists of the USA and EUROLIT, and the co-ordinating work of the B & T Committee, several Eastern European Baptist Unions were supplied with computerized desk-top publishing equipment in 1990. Practical training and relevant literature were also provided. The Romanian Baptists, in particular, were said to have taken to it 'like ducks to water'! In 1992 the Latvian Baptist Bishop, Janos Eisans, was invited to spend a week at the SCM Press in Britain, learning how Christian publishers operated in the West, as a follow-up to a recent evaluation of the resources available to the Latvian Baptist Union and how they might best use them. These two examples illustrate the sort of help which Eastern European Christians most needed at this stage; namely, help to help themselves. Cash, equipment and training to enable them to write, translate, publish and distribute their own literature in their own languages and for their own culture were now of much greater value than supplies of Christian literature from the West.

A totally new situation, therefore, existed and a radical change of direction in the work of the B & T Committee was necessary. To their credit, they were fully aware of the situation and were soon ready with proposals for future policy. However, as we have seen in an earlier chapter, this was also a time when radical restructuring of the EBF was taking place. The revised make-up of the Executive Committee left no place for the B & T Committee. More significantly, the formation of a Theology and Education Division was judged to be capable of dealing with literature and publishing matters without the need for a separate Committee.

A significant chapter of EBF life thus came to an end. Hopefully, the full story of the committee's achievements will one day be written and published, for it is a remarkable and thrilling story. Their efforts greatly enriched the life and fellowship of the EBF and many of its struggling members. Most of the Eastern European leaders with whom the committee worked are no longer in office. It is important that they are remembered, and that today's and tomorrow's leaders are aware of the debt of gratitude they owe to them. The story would also underline the undeniable importance of good Christian literature in the churches' vital tasks of theological and Christian education, worship and mission.

SPECIAL INITIATIVES

During the past twenty years a number of imaginative initiatives have been taken by other groups like EUROLIT, which have constitutionally been independent of the EBF, and yet have been very much part of its life and work. Three of them have made a valuable contribution to theological and Christian education among European Baptists.

The first is **SITE - the Summer Institute of Theological Education.** When Denton Lotz introduced the idea to the EBF Council in 1978 and became its first Director, it met with immediate support and success.[8]

176 CROSSING THE BOUNDARIES

Within two years the number of students enrolling for the month's study programme had reached at least sixty. From the outset it was closely associated with the Baptist Theological Seminary (BTS) at Rüschlikon and was held there. It was designed for pastors, preachers and church members, and, although open to Baptists from the whole of Europe, was chiefly intended for Eastern Europeans. The syllabus included studies in the Old and New Testaments, Church History, and Systematic and Practical Theology. These were covered by two members of the BTS Faculty who were joined by three visiting professors, one from Eastern Europe, one from Western Europe, and the other from North America. The mini-library presented to each student to take home contained fifty to sixty books - a veritable godsend to most of them, and an incentive to go on reading and equipping themselves for ministry at home. The original scheme included plans for an optional correspondence course spread over three years, but this was not a success. In 1981 a plan was suggested to create a small travelling faculty who would provide seminars and lectures wherever groups of people could be gathered for the purpose. There is no evidence in EBF records that this suggestion came to fruition.

Denton Lotz had to return to the USA in due course. He was replaced by the former General Secretary of the EBF, Ronald Goulding, who agreed to serve for a time as Interim-Director. At a joint meeting of the EBF Executive Committee and the BTS Executive Board at Rüschlikon in October 1980 thanks were expressed to Denton Lotz for the formation and development of SITE. Academically, it was separate from the main curriculum of the Seminary, just as, constitutionally, it was independent of the Federation. Yet both saw it as an indispensable part of their work.

When new structures were established at the time of Karl Heinz Walter's appointment, he was eager to maintain co-ordination and accountability in all the Federation's activities. One way of achieving this was to link every committee or programme with one of the four new Divisions. In 1989 SITE was placed under the wing of the Theology and Education Division, and henceforth reported to Council via that Division. But there were other more significant changes afoot. As we have already seen, the transformation of the Communist world led to the rise of many independent States, freedom of travel, the birth of autonomous and thriving Baptist Unions, and the rapid growth of Eastern European Baptist seminaries and bible schools.

SITE now faced a totally different situation. A thorough reassessment of its policies was called for, and there were several other factors which affected the outcome. First, Robert Frykholm, the Director since 1991 announced in 1994 that he would be returning to pastoral ministry in the USA. Then, the EBF decided to relocate the BTS from Rüschlikon to Prague in the summer of 1995. A temporary home was needed for SITE until it could be established in Prague, and an Acting Director had to be found until the future teaching staff at Prague had been determined and a permanent Director appointed. Fortunately, Dr Harry Moore, who had been Director from 1988 to 1990, was able to fill the gap. The Baptist Union of Poland willingly agreed to allow SITE to be held in June 1995 at the Baptist Theological Training Centre in Radosc.

From 1996 onwards SITE continued its ministry from the new campus at Prague, but with a major change of direction. What began as an annual one-month summer programme of general theological education was reshaped to provide an all-year programme including varied campus courses and regional conferences on strategic issues. David Brown, of the American Baptist Churches/International Ministries (ABC/IM), had become the Director of Continuing Theological Education at the Seminary, and it was decided that SITE should come under his care. He gathered around him a new committee chaired by Sam Pettersson (Finland), which included Bodo Riedel (Germany), Ruth Lehotsky (Serbia), Cornel Ghita (Romania) and Marina Karetnikova (Russia), all of whom played an active part in launching the new scheme. They prepared a Mission Statement for the EBF Council to adopt, which stated that their objective was to strengthen the Unions, institutions and churches of the Federation. With the same letters in the title a new name was devised to indicate the changed nature of their work - the **S**eminary **I**nstitute for **T**raining and Education. Again, the Seminary and the Federation were laying claim to SITE as a part of their work. Yet, oddly, neither included it in their annual budget! Without the generous support of the American Baptist Churches' Board of International Ministries and book grants and donations from sources like FEED THE MINDS, the Society for the Promotion of Christian Knowledge, World Vision International, Baptist World Aid, BR-E and the EBWU, much of the work could not have been accomplished.

The EBF Council in Kiev, September 1998, marked the twentieth anniversary of SITE. David Brown presented an exciting report of the year's work. Two well-attended conferences had taken place in Prague: a week in February for church planters, organized jointly with the Institute for Mission and Evangelism (IME); and three weeks in August with a similar programme to those of previous years on the theme of 'Foundations for Pastoral Ministry'. The first regional conferences were an excellent foretaste of things to come. In May the Director was invited to the Euro-Asiatic Federation's annual meetings in Minsk, to lead discussion on the secular challenge being faced by the churches, how to respond to it in the making of disciples, and how this affected worship and preaching. At Kiev, just prior to the Council, a Media Conference was shared with the Communications Division and, in particular, the EBPS. The visiting speaker was Dr Roger Palms of the Billy Graham magazine, *Decision*. .He also consented to visit several other seminaries while he was in the region. A third regional event was held in November, by invitation of the Hungarian Baptist Unions. It took the form of a three-day travelling conference using two locations in Hungary and Romania, with the primary purpose of offering supportive training for their pastors.

Additionally, David Brown and his wife are able to travel around Europe when needed for consultation and teaching. In 1998 they spent ten days in Romania exploring the possibility of regular training events for pastors. They also spent seven days in Wales. Their plans for 1999 include:

- teaching sessions for Russian pastors in Estonia;

- an IBTS campus conference in partnership with the EBF Youth Committee for the training of youth trainers in each Union;
- the annual three-week study programme on 'Foundations of Pastoral Ministry', with the emphasis on biblical studies;
- four regional conferences with the help of members of the EBTTC on 'Baptist History and Identity'. These are designed to clarify what being Baptist essentially means, in order to heal the tensions and disagreements which have arisen during the past nine years as Baptists in Central, Eastern and Western Europe have become aware of the many differences between them.

The second special initiative to note is the **Lay Conference Committee.** Dr Gordon Lahrson, the ABC representative in Europe in the 1960s, had first suggested a Lay Academy in Scandinavia.[9] The idea was discussed at the EBF Council in London in August 1966, when a committee was set up to investigate it further. Discussions dragged on for several years without result until Ronald Goulding convinced the Council in 1969 that it was hard to justify the expense of a Baptist Lay Academy building, and harder still to guarantee viable use of it through the year. He suggested that it would be wiser to explore the possibility of linking a Lay Academy with an existing Baptist institution. At this point a key figure emerged in the person of Sven Svenson, the Editor of the Swedish Baptist newspaper, *Veckoposten.* He drew up aims and guidelines for organizing lay conferences which were to be clearly linked with the EBF, but arranged by a committee of Danish, Finnish, Norwegian and Swedish representatives.

A generous grant from the ABC enabled the scheme to be launched in 1970 with its first Lay Conference on the theme 'Dialogue with the World'. It was held at a diocesan centre near Stockholm and attracted over sixty people from sixteen nations. After such an encouraging start, conferences were held annually for over twenty years. In his published account of the activities of the Lay Conference Committee, *Building Bridges*, Sven Svenson explained that there were two major reasons for planning such a programme of lay training. One was to explore fresh forms of evangelism in the context of the need for renewal of the church's life, not only in outreach but also in social responsibility. The other arose from the harsh reality of Cold War years which he described as 'a Europe with closed borders'. Such boundaries needed to be crossed. Christians were being called to take the initiative in finding ways of achieving dialogue and fellowship between East and West.[10]

There is no doubt that the conferences made an immense contribution to the work of the EBF and were esteemed highly among neighbouring Eastern European Baptists. Eventually, it was possible to hold conferences in East Germany, Poland, Hungary, Lithuania and Latvia. A selection of the issues covered over the years indicates their worth. In 1971 there were two conferences; the first in Tølløse, Denmark considered 'Renewal in the life of worship', the second in Gothenburg, Sweden brought together secular and religious journalists to deal with issues of Christian journalism. After considering 'Missions Theology and Third World Development Policy' at Vallersvik, Sweden in 1973, they went on to meet in the following year at Schmiedeberg, East Germany to explore 'Christian Life and Work for Church and Society'. Among future topics were Peace and disarmament; Education in school, church and society; Care of the elderly; The ministry of the laity; Ethical problems in our time; Baptist identity and relevance; The Church in the year 2000. When European Baptist Congresses were held at Hamburg (1984), Budapest (1989) and Lillehammer (1994), no conferences were arranged. Instead, sums of money were made available to the EBF to assist Eastern European Baptist lay people to attend the Congresses.

By 1994 it had become clear that the changed situation in Europe raised serious questions about current needs and future policy. After discussing several different approaches, and an abortive attempt with the EBF Youth Committee to hold a Baltic/Scandinavian youth conference, the Lay Conference Committee decided in autumn 1996 to discontinue its activities and transfer its funds to the EBF for the benefit of lay training in Europe. A number of conditions were also agreed, in accordance with the originally approved Guidelines, providing for consultation with the founding donors, ABC, and the use of the funds primarily for the same purposes in northern Europe, the Baltic region and Poland. It was hoped that SITE projects, and therefore the ministry of David Brown of the ABC, would be within this remit. With that understanding, the closure of the Lay Conference programme is in no way to be viewed as a failure. Having effectively met an urgent need in the days of the Iron Curtain, it has generously handed on its resources for others to meet a different situation in new ways. This, surely, shows a genuine seeking of the Kingdom of God, in contrast to some projects in Christian history which have seemed more like personal or corporate kingdoms to be jealousy guarded.

The third special initiative in theological and Christian education is the **International Baptist Lay Academy (IBLA).** A proposal was made to the EBF Executive in September 1987 for an International Baptist Lay Academy to be established at Pec in Hungary. Recognizing that lay training had high priority among Eastern European Baptists, Knud Wümpelmann persuaded the Executive to refer the matter initially to the Baptist Unions in the East for consideration. A year later, with the support of the Executive, Dr Keith Parker presented to the Council a paper proposing that an academy should be set up in Budapest as an Eastern branch of the Rüschlikon Seminary. The city was a good central location, surrounded by lively churches which could be drawn into the practical aspects of the courses, and easily accessible by both East and West. The Hungarians were eager to sponsor such an institution. They would be able to house twenty-eight students at their Seminary for three months each summer, and when the extensions currently being built were completed that number could be increased to over forty. Dr Laszlo Gerzsenyi was willing to serve as Director.

Keith Parker explained that teaching at the academy would be based on the lay pastor model widely operative in Eastern Europe. This could also be useful to the West in situations where full-time pastors could not be financed. He went on to describe the type of courses in mind, such as music ministry, local church leadership, evangelism training, and English language study. The last-mentioned would make international contact and communication more possible. It would also allow wider theological reading and considerably improve translation skills. Hopefully, the academy would serve as a bridge for SITE and further study at Rüschlikon and other seminaries. Teaching staff would be drawn from Eastern Europe. Their presence would ensure the growth of more trust between the BTS and Eastern Europeans. Difficulties with travel visas were less likely to occur.

Another major benefit would be that Budapest was a strategic place for the development of Christian literature in a Socialist cultural context. Co-operation with the EBF Books and Translations Committee would be easy. Similarly, the academy would be able to liaise with the Youth and Children's Committee in teacher training, manuals for teachers and youth leaders, and the production of Sunday School lesson materials. This would help to counteract the growing impact of international free-lance and sectarian activities which were far from helpful. Keith Parker finally indicated that the Southern Baptist Convention's Foreign Mission Board would probably be willing to second a missionary couple to undertake associate directorship and English teaching. He hoped that the Council would accept these proposals and agree to initiate discussions, so that the Academy could open in 1990. During the ensuing debate doubts were expressed about long-term financial implications. Some of the Eastern Europeans questioned how their national Unions would be affected. Generally, Council members felt that the project was much more likely to win support if a consultation document with full financial projections and reports could be made available to member Unions after the first twelve months. When the vote was taken there was overwhelming support for the proposal, with none against and only three abstentions.

Karl Heinz Walter was pleased to report to the September 1990 Council in the Netherlands that the International Baptist Lay Academy (IBLA) was established in Budapest and had opened its doors for the first time in July. Ninety students had been enrolled. After this encouraging start, there was an alarming drop in the second year: only thirty-six people attended. This did not reflect a lack of confidence in IBLA, for the records of its work in subsequent years tell a better story. Errol Simmons, of the International Mission Board of the SBC,[11] took over from Laszio Gerzsenyl as Director. He was soon able to report that more than eighty women and men from twelve countries had participated in the 1992 sessions. By 1994 the total number of students since the formation of the Academy had grown to three hundred and fifty from twenty-one countries. Teachers were being recruited from near and far, often with their travelling costs and incidental expenses covered by their Unions or Mission Boards. Several Unions and Conventions had made scholarships available for some of the students. The European Baptist Women's Union had also made generous grants for this purpose. A number of partnership arrangements had been made to provide English teachers and a secretary/bookkeeper.

IBLA was rapidly becoming an important institution, fulfilling the vision which led to its birth. Extra accommodation had to be rented at a nearby girls' boarding school for the female students. Over the next year or two, additional courses were organized in the spring and autumn. A correspondence course was also launched for those who had been awarded the IBLA Certificate of Studies and wished to go on learning at home. An extra member of staff was appointed to co-ordinate this.

It soon became clear that the EBF must do some hard thinking about more adequate accommodation and greater financial resources. This grew urgent when the Hungarian Baptist Union indicated that the growth of their own Seminary's work necessitated the termination of the lease on the use of their premises by the summer of 1994. Temporarily, IBLA moved all its operations to Szigetszentmiklós, near Budapest, where it secured a three-year lease to share the premises of the local Baptist Church. The SBC/FMB could no longer supply scholarships; also their promised funding of the Academy was unlikely to continue indefinitely; certainly not beyond September 2000, when the Director and his wife would be returning to the USA. This made consideration of future staffing an additional major item for decision.

While all these issues were arising the debate was taking place about the future of BTS at Rüschlikon and the possible move to Prague, which eventually occurred in 1995. At the EBF Council in Kiev in September 1998, Erroll Simmons outlined the situation which IBLA was now facing. The lease at Szigetszentmiklós Baptist Church had been extended until the end of 2000. This ensured the continuance of the work for the time being. In faith he was still travelling around Central and Eastern Europe, and the Middle East, promoting the work of the Academy, but plans for the long-term future must be settled as soon as possible. 1999 will be a crucial year in which at least three possible options must be considered:

- To continue as at present, hoping to secure future use of the current accommodation and trying to negotiate further staffing and finance with the SBC/IBM.
- To move IBLA to Prague and let it become an integral part of the IBTS; this would involve radical changes to the nature of the Academy and call for different staffing and financial arrangements.
- To terminate the work of IBLA - surely an unthinkable disaster?

There are several points of uncertainty and tension which call for early clarification. For example, when the Structure Committee presented its report in 1989, IBLA was placed under the care of the Theology and Education Division, with an executive committee appointed by the EBF. Yet, the initial proposals had suggested that the Academy would be an eastern branch of the Rüschlikon Seminary. At Oslo in 1992 the EBF Executive had to appoint some new members to the IBLA committee. They did this on the understanding that it was one of the Federation's committees, not an integral part of Rüschlikon. However, at Lillehammer in the following Spring, Wiard Popkes stated that IBLA had been a satellite of the BTS from the beginning and came under its Board of Trustees. A document about the future of the BTS, which was discussed at the same meeting, stated that one of the Seminary's tasks was to provide lay and continuing theological education through IBLA, SITE and TAG. Another problem arises from the obvious overlaps in the programmes of these and other groups like the Institute for Mission and Evangelism.

Whatever the outcome of current discussions, the work already done has been of undeniable value, by giving excellent training and cross-cultural experience which have strengthened European Baptist unity at a time when it was under threat. The contributions made to local churches, national Unions and the EBF by those who have been trained at IBLA are full of promise for years to come.

THE INTERNATIONAL BAPTIST SEMINARY

On 5 September 1949 an historic event occurred at Rüschlikon, Zurich. The Baptist Theological Seminary instituted by the Foreign Mission Board of the Southern Baptist Convention welcomed its first thirty students from twelve European countries to begin their ministerial training. In practice the Seminary was intended to be international and has attracted students from all parts of the world. But its primary aim was to be a centre of academic excellence with a gifted theological faculty at the heart of Europe. When the Southern Baptists offered to fund it, they generously suggested that European Baptists would not need to contribute while they were facing the immense costs of recovery from the devastation of war. However, European Baptists were invited to be part of it from the outset by choosing from among themselves able Baptist leaders to serve as a Board of Trustees.

Another historic event took place a month later, on 9 October, when the special Committee of Seven met at the Seminary to draw up the draft constitution of the proposed European Baptist Federation. Once the Federation was born, the Seminary played a key role by becoming for many years the venue for conferences, committees and various Baptist groups and agencies. A constant stream of trained pastors, teachers and leaders has flowed out into churches and unions. Because of their common roots and their experience of closely-knit community life, they have been able to work together across national barriers with harmony and strong mutual trust. Since the Seminary used English as its basic language, they have also been able to communicate freely in the councils and committees of the EBF. Successive Presidents and members of the Faculty have also played an influential part in EBF and BWA affairs.

In the 1970s circumstances arose which necessitated several critical decisions about the future. There was a growing wish to 'Europeanize' the Seminary. As national seminaries increased in strength, fewer students were registering for courses at Rüschlikon. Some Baptist Unions pointed out that the high life-style there could not be maintained by students when they returned home; nor could it be afforded as costs rose. The Foreign Mission Board also faced financial difficulties because of their increasing commitments at a time when the American dollar fell in value from 4.35 Swiss Francs to 1.60 in six years. In 1977 they announced that they might have to close the Seminary in 1979. EBF General Secretary, Gerhard Claas, immediately said that this would be a disaster for European Baptists. The BTS was a 'Father-house' for them. It had fulfilled a vital role in healing wounds and creating new relations between East and West since World War 2. He declared: 'They know each other. They trust each other, and they love each other.' It would be wrong to undermine such a benefit. He asked for discussions with the FMB, in order to explore the possibility of joint administration. His request met with a positive response.

The Mission Board promised to continue support in the future if there was more European input. They would limit their own contribution to a maximum of $300,000 in 1979, add an extra $5,000 a year until 1983, and continue to support their missionary personnel in the Faculty. Their most radical proposal was to offer the Seminary for the use of the EBF for the next five years, with the Federation being responsible for the administration. Eventually, a joint agreement was reached, identifying the FMB as the holders of the property and the EBF as the sponsoring body. An Executive Board, answerable to both bodies, was appointed; also an Administrative Committee including one representative each from the Faculty and the students. In future, Presidents and Faculty members were to be nominated by the Executive Board and Faculty, but appointed jointly by the EBF and FMB. To aid the process of 'Europeanization', future missionary personnel would only be appointed subject to EBF approval. The Council in Vienna in September 1978 accepted these proposals, whereupon Gerhard Claas thanked the FMB for all that they had done over the years. He reminded the members of Council that European Baptists would have to contribute at least 100,000 Swiss Francs in 1979.

Soon afterwards, Isam Ballenger resigned from his Acting Presidency and was replaced by Ronald Goulding. The EBF Executive identified his two major tasks; to seek a permanent Professor/President, and to promote the Seminary as a European Baptist Centre which would provide facilities for Anabaptist studies, as well as conferences and courses for SITE and the Education and Evangelism Committee. They hoped that as soon as a new President was found, Ronald Goulding would remain as the leader of the conference centre. Student numbers and finances ebbed and flowed during the 1980s. Health problems and other personal circumstances led to a succession of five short presidencies between 1982 and 1986. This was not good for the stability of the Seminary, and almost inevitably there was a financial crisis in 1986.

In the midst of this, a debate took place at the EBF Council in Glasgow when the BTS Executive Board and Faculty sought approval to set up an Institute for World Mission, Evangelism and Church Growth. Many expressed unease about this. The Director and most of the finance would come from the Foreign Mission Board. Would this lead to FMB domination and control? How big would the Institute be? Would it be an integrated part of the Seminary? Was it wise to launch such a project in the current financial situation? Council members were adamant that personnel and aims must be under the Federation's control. They would only accept the American offer if European independence was not threatened. Negotiations continued in the coming months with the result that the 1987 Council in Italy approved the guidelines and gave the go-ahead for the Institute to be established. It was inaugurated in April 1988 as the Institute for Mission and Evangelism (IME), with Dr Earl Martin as its Director.

In the same month, when the EBF Executive met at Rüschlikon, members were informed of a large deficit in the Federation's accounts, which had seriously depleted their reserves. This was in addition to the financial straits of the Seminary. The Unions would have to increase their annual contributions by fifty per cent or drastic cuts in structures and activities would be necessary. Faced with this dire situation John David Hopper, who had been appointed as Seminary President in 1987, addressed the EBF Council at Dorfweil in September 1988, in a way that can now be seen as visionary and prophetic. After reminding his hearers of Rüschlikon's major contribution for thirty-nine years as 'a hub of Baptist life in Europe', he set out his vision for the future. He longed for the BTS to possess both academic excellence and evangelistic passion. He wanted to see a greater international dimension by offering places to students from Africa, Asia and South America. Master and doctoral research facilities should be available for those who had done initial training at their national seminaries, and there should be room for furlough studies for missionaries. Sabbaticals for national Baptist leaders and scholars ought also to be encouraged. At the same time, he wanted to strengthen the conference programme, working closely with the IME and with IBLA, which was due to begin in Hungary in 1990. Such a diverse curriculum would require full co-operation and support from the EBF and FMB. He considered the appointment of a Development Officer necessary, in order to raise money to stabilize the accounts and invest for future staffing and scholarships. Finally, he urged the two parent bodies to place this on their agendas as a matter of urgency, and he asked for comments from the Council.

The Rüschlikon Executive Board recommended asking the FMB for permission to mortgage the property to clear the deficits and then continue operating with support from the Mission Board at the present level. They also suggested that from 1992 there should be a steady reduction of their subsidy so that in twenty years it no longer existed. If these suggestions were unacceptable, they recommended the sale of the Seminary and relocation elsewhere. In contrast, the EBTTC pleaded for an all-out attempt to retain Rüschlikon and find ways of establishing stronger relations between unions and seminaries, so that a central theological institution could be kept in a neutral country acceptable to East and West. By facilitating greater co-ordination in theological education, it could be a focus of Baptist unity.

The EBF Executive had received these various views in advance, and now brought to the Council four recommendations:

1. that the time had come for the EBF to become the owner of the Seminary in accordance with the FMB policy of indigenisation.
2. that the proposal to mortgage the premises be endorsed for the two reasons already stated and for any other purposes as the Executive Board deemed necessary.
3. that the EBF valued the long-term partnership with the FMB, and wished to maintain it, but also endorsed the recommendations about steadily reducing subsidies over twenty years from 1992, or permission to sell and relocate.
4. that they welcomed the President's future vision, and asked the Executive Board to take steps to redefine the future.

The first recommendation was carried with none against and one abstention. The other three were carried unanimously. To prepare for ownership of the property a legal foundation would need to be created. The necessary steps were prepared. Arrangements were also made for a Board of Trustees to be elected on the recommendation of the EBF Executive and answerable to the Council.

After conferring with the FMB trustees, agreement was reached in accordance with the above recommendations. The necessary legal documents were signed, and the property was transferred to a BTS Association composed of Swiss Baptist citizens, who would hold the property on behalf of the EBF. On Sunday, 28 May 1989, Dr Keith Parks, the President of the FMB, handed over the key to the EBF General Secretary as a symbol of the transfer of ownership. Three days of consultation followed, to agree future goals, a new charter and by-laws, all of which were to be taken to the Council for approval.

A number of conditions were attached to the final agreement. Among them was the promise to consult with the FMB before any sale of the property. The proceeds of such a sale must be used for Baptist theological education in Europe. More controversial was the FMB's request that the new Charter should include a written statement of European Baptist principles to be accepted by all members. This would be expected to express a biblical commitment to which all Seminary teachers would be required to subscribe.

In September 1990 at De Bron, Netherlands, the EBF Executive objected to such a requirement. They authorized a letter to be sent over the signatures of Wiard Popkes (Chairman, Board of Trustees), Peter Barber (President, EBF), and Karl Heinz Walter (General Secretary), stating that Baptists in Europe should determine the question of European Baptist Identity, and that they welcomed the diversity which currently existed among them. The letter pointed out that it was not common practice in Europe to require Baptist professors to sign a credal statement, although theological views were explored in selection interviews. They considered that the statement of purpose already printed in the Seminary brochure was adequate, but they pledged further work on Baptist Identity. During that Council meeting the first Annual General Meeting of the BTS Rüschlikon Association was held. Those present readily affirmed John David Hopper's future vision and plans.

All seemed to be progressing favourably. Excellent Council meetings took place in Bulgaria in September 1991, combined with the joyous opening and dedication of the new church in Varna. Karl Heinz Walter described the meetings as a highlight of the year; probably one of the highlights of the whole history of the EBF, because there was almost a complete attendance of the member Unions, as they celebrated the new age of freedom. However, the euphoria was shattered two weeks after the Council, by another 'bombshell' from the SBC/FBM. At a meeting in Richmond, Virginia, the Trustees of the Foreign Mission Board decided, without giving any notice or opportunity to consult, to defund the BTS, Rüschlikon from 1 January 1992. The reason given for such drastic action was that the Seminary had invited Dr Glenn Hinson, Professor of Church History at one of the Southern Baptists' own seminaries in the USA, to be a guest lecturer during the autumn semester. Some Southern Baptists considered Dr Hinson to be a liberal scholar. The conservative fundamentalists on the FMB Board of Trustees had secured a 35-28 majority for the defunding action.

As soon as he received the news, Karl Heinz Walter notified all the Baptist Unions in the EBF and received a strong reaction against what many saw as an 'illegal act', bearing in mind the solemn agreement they had made with the Federation in 1989.[12] The American action did far more than threaten the financial stability of the Seminary. It shattered the confidence which European Baptists had in the integrity of the Southern Baptist Convention. Many Unions began to question their own relationships with the FMB. Further still, the affair started a debate about American mission agencies in general, and strengthened the determination of Europeans to take over major responsibility for mission in Europe. At the same time there were many expressions of sympathy for FMB missionaries serving at Rüschlikon and elsewhere. Some of them had devoted themselves to European Baptist work for many years. They were valued colleagues, and this action was seen as disrespect for them and their ministry. The Board of Trustees sent a statement to the Trustees of the Foreign Mission Board accusing them of an action that was 'highly irresponsible and morally indefensible'. In it they drew attention to moral, missiological and theological issues which far outweighed the financial ones. They urged the FMB Trustees to reconsider their decision.[13]

Early in December Karl Heinz Walter, Wiard Popkes and John David Hopper were invited to further discussions in Richmond. Despite their strong and honest responses to the demands of the FMB they were unable to reverse the decision. In fact, the earlier vote was confirmed by an even larger majority.[14] Probably an even more worrying development was that the Board stated its intention to use the money being withheld for theological education in Eastern Europe. That could only mean one thing - parallel, competitive mission, which was bound to cause division by exporting the theological battles of the Southern Convention to the membership of the EBF.

1992 turned out to be a crucially important year for the future of the Seminary and the policy of the EBF. In January during the Dorfweil Consultation about the future role of Baptists in the new Europe, a session was set apart to discuss the Rüschlikon crisis. Despite strong feelings of hurt and anger, it was agreed not to prolong the fight with the FMB, but to accept what had happened and move forward in partnership with other American Baptists. A statement was drawn up to send to Dr Keith Parks (FMB President), the Revd William Hancock (Chairman, FMB Trustees) and the Revd Steve Hardy (Chairman, European Trustees of FMB), setting out five elements for any future partnership: 1. Mutual respect. 2.Spiritual freedom. 3. Moral integrity. 4. Genuine consultation leading to mutual consent. 5. Reciprocal sharing.[15] Karl Heinz Walter made the following unambiguous comment: '...any Baptist mission group, including the Foreign Mission Board, which cannot accept partnership on the basis of these elements, will not be welcome within the EBF.'

Month after month steps were taken which began to give the future a totally new look. In February fifty Southern Baptists who belonged to the Co-operative Baptist Fellowship (CBF), made up of moderate evangelicals who support alternatives to the Southern Baptist Convention because of its extreme fundamentalism, visited Rüschlikon to affirm the Seminary. They promised the same financial support as the FMB had previously pledged, and to hand over a first instalment of over $219,000. Meanwhile, Isam Ballenger (FMB Vice-president for Europe) resigned, and Keith Parker (FMB Director for Europe) joined the CBF and became its Co-ordinator of Mission in Europe. In April John David Hopper and his wife, who were President and Director of Public Relations at the Seminary, resigned from the FMB after twenty-seven years of service. They were immediately commissioned by the CBF to continue their work, with the promise of full financial support. The EBF Executive accepted this offer in May, and at the same time agreed to begin discussions with the German Baptist Union about the possibility of BTS sharing their planned new centre in Berlin. The Board of Trustees was also authorized to look for other potential sites.

In early September at Hamburg, seven EBF and six FMB leaders met to try to re-establish relations after the 1991 breakdown. They drew up what became known as the Hamburg Agreement which was conciliatory in tone, yet firmly endorsed the five elements of the Partnership Agreement. It acknowledged the harm done by the defunding conflict, testified to their joint experience of forgiveness, and also addressed the urgency of Baptist unity in a continent which had suffered so much from national and international divisions.[16] This was ratified by the EBF Council at High Leigh later in the month and by the FMB Trustees in Richmond in October. At High Leigh two highly memorable moments occurred. The new FMB Vice-president for Europe, Samuel James, was warmly welcomed by the Council. In the words of the Hamburg Agreement: 'They recognized in him the kind of attitude to mission and Christian spirit which should lead to fruitful co-operation between the FMB and European Baptists.' He was given the opportunity to address the Council. The second moment was when, in his presence, a partnership agreement with the CBF was approved, and Cecil Sherman was able to speak to council on their behalf.

The scene was now set for a series of important and historic decisions to be made which radically changed the course of theological and religious education within the EBF, and took the Rüschlikon Seminary to an exciting new home. The happenings of the next five or six years could fill a whole book. No doubt one day someone else will write it. Here we must be content with a summary of the main events. The first was at the EBF Executive meeting in Lillehammer, Norway, April 1993. Seminary finances were clearly in a critical state. Consideration of two actions was imminent: to move from Rüschlikon to a less expensive, but strategic place, and to capitalize the present buildings and site to make that possible. A draft document from the Joint Committee of the EBF and the Seminary Board of Trustees was presented and discussed. It described a future pattern of education and training for the Seminary which would be very different from what had existed from the beginning. It was intended to meet contemporary needs in the radically changed continent now confronting the EBF. After amendments arising from the discussions, a comprehensive document, to become known as the Lillehammer Statement, was sent out in July to all the EBF Unions, for them to consider before the Council in Kishinev, Moldova in October.[17] When the Council met it approved a proposal for the BTS to move from Rüschlikon, for the new role of the Seminary based on the Lillehammer Statement to be affirmed, and for Berlin and Prague to be the primary sites for consideration. The debate was lively and prolonged, with some strongly opposing views expressed, but when the vote was taken there was a clear majority in favour, with only one against and several abstentions.

A special Executive meeting took place at Baptist House, Didcot, England in November 1993, to update members on the merits of the two alternative locations. The Italian Baptists tried to introduce Rome as a third option, but without success. Instead, they were assured that their anxiety about theological and ministerial training in the South would receive co-operative attention in the future. A decisive vote to go ahead with further negotiations about Prague was then made.

At Lisbon in May 1994 John Biggs, Vice-chairman of the Seminary Board of Trustees, explained to the Executive the reasons for a firm recommendation to move to Prague. He and Paul Fiddes reported on academic and programme issues. David Nixon identified the legal steps to be taken and the need to act quickly for financial reasons. When Karl Heinz Walter gave details of the responses from the forty-five member Unions, it seemed that the debate was going to start all over again from the beginning. Wisely, he pressed for the vote to be taken; the move to Prague was agreed with no one against and only one abstention. A supplementary recommendation was also approved to give the relocated seminary the name 'The International Baptist Theological Seminary (IBTS) of the EBF'. Having brought matters this far, the Joint Committee ceased to exist, to make way for a Relocation Committee, chaired by John Biggs and comprising representatives of the EBF, the Seminary, the Czech Baptist Union, the legal holding body and an architect from Western Europe. A Steering Committee was also created to act for the Federation in the sale, purchase, and associated financial and legal arrangements.

Three major steps remained to be taken: (a) the sale of Rüschlikon and negotiations with the Swiss Baptist Union about the future use of the chapel; (b) the purchase of the site and buildings at Prague, the move, and satisfactory attention to the needs and courses of current students; (c) rebuilding and refurbishment of the new premises, establishing the new seminary structures, and dealing with future arrangements for present and future staff. All this necessarily involved a large volume of organization and work which kept all concerned at full stretch until the move was completed. An adequate mortgage was raised on the Rüschlikon property to enable the Jeneralka site in Prague to be purchased forthwith. It was a large site, already containing twenty-two buildings. These could be refurbished and changed into an excellent suite of premises for the Seminary, easily accessible from the city centre and airport. It would be a larger place, with funds for scholarships, ample family accommodation, and facilities to include conferences and satellite bodies in its regular programme. All previous debts would be cleared, the new premises fully paid for, and endowments for the future secured. In every sense IBTS would be in a position to play a leading role in assisting the churches, unions and theological institutions of Central and Eastern Europe.

The move, which was a colossal exercise, took place between 17 May and 26 July 1995. The Seminary was able to open for the new academic year in the autumn with a student complement of twenty who moved from Rüschlikon and thirteen newly joining them. Such a satisfactory situation could never have been possible without the magnificently sustained effort over a long period of nearly 1,300 volunteers from the wider Baptist family, some from Europe, most from North Carolina, all of whom met their own costs and shared in many types of hard work on site.

In order to maintain contact with all interested parties, the EBF arranged a special consultation for Union leaders, the Seminary

Faculty, and representatives of all European seminaries, colleges and bible schools, to be held in September 1996 during the annual Council meetings in Tallinn, Estonia. The agenda included papers on the Prague Vision, the Lillehammer and Hamburg agreements, and the financial situation. Some basic questions were also prepared for group discussion. The situation was not easy. Numbers attending were disappointing. There were still many differences of opinion, not so much about the move as about the changes in the nature of the Seminary. John Biggs prepared a report and statement afterwards to present to the Council in the form of recommendations. When these were approved they were referred to the Seminary Board of Trustees for action. Dr Biggs also presented the final report of the Relocation Steering Committee - another large task well done.

Unfortunately, John David Hopper's health began to deteriorate after what had been a very strenuous ten years of Presidency. He needed to return to the USA for major heart surgery, and in 1997 he decided to retire and hand on future leadership to his successor. Walter Füllbrandt also retired from Chairmanship of the Board of Trustees and was succeeded by Keith Jones, Deputy General Secretary of the Baptist Union of Great Britain. On Sunday, 20 April 1997, an Official Opening and Thanksgiving Service for the New Campus of the IBTS was held in the historic Bethlehem Chapel, part of the Ceremonial Hall of the Czech Technical University in Prague.[18] Karl Heinz Walter preached the dedicatory sermon on verses from Philippians 2, linking the new role of the Seminary with Christ the Servant, building bridges between east and west, north and south. He pointed out that the Prague location put the Seminary within 1,000 kilometres of most of the European Baptist family. On the previous day a dinner had been held in the Seminary dining hall, followed by a meeting in the Vinohrady Baptist Church in Prague to honour Dr John David and Mrs Jo Ann Hopper on their retirement. Speeches of appreciation for their long and faithful ministry in Europe[19] were given by Walter Füllbrandt, Theo Angelov, Knud Wümpelmann, Wiard Popkes and Kent Blevins. In reply, both uttered some wise and encouraging words. Jo Ann Hopper stressed the desire of European Baptists to know each other and to work together. 'That', she said, 'is the ministry of IBTS.' John David Hopper reminded his hearers that it is essential for God's people to come together in mutual trust, with a readiness to learn from one another. He concluded, 'What a richness, what a diversity, what an amazing family we have as Baptists!'

Two months later the Seminary suffered a serious set-back. Dr Stefan Stiegler, Professor of Hebrew and Old Testament at Hamburg Seminary, was unanimously nominated for the Presidency of IBTS by both the Faculty of the Seminary and the Search Committee of the Board of Trustees. However, before all the responses to his nomination had been received from member Unions, Dr Stiegler withdrew his name because of disagreements which had arisen between him and the Faculty, leading him to feel that he no longer had their support. There was an immediate outcry about this throughout the EBF. Faced by many questions and criticisms, the Board of Trustees convened a special meeting in Hamburg to consider what action to take. After much discussion they decided that it was right to take a deeper look at the future pattern and purpose of the Seminary in a very changed Europe, and to prepare a report to be presented to the next meeting of the EBF Council.

Despite this set-back, the Prague Campus was a hive of activity during the summer. During June and July five SITE conferences were held there, with subjects as varied as 'Foundations for pastoral ministry', 'Working together in the local church', 'United in Union ministry', 'Executive management for Union administrators' and 'Music leadership in the local church'. The Institute for Baptist and Anabaptist Studies, led by Dr Phyllis Rodgerson Pleasants hosted two events: in August, the Ecumenical Summer Seminar on 'The religious heritage of Prague', and in September, a working group of the church historians in the European Baptist Theological Teachers' Conference (EBTTC) who were preparing a book about Baptist perspectives on 'The Priesthood of Believers'.

At the end of September, the EBF Council assembled in Novi Vinodolski, Croatia. A most important item on the agenda was the comprehensive report of the IBTS Board of Trustees presented by Keith Jones. This was contained in almost four pages of the Council's report book and   was supplemented by an additional document, *Forward from Tallinn*. The latter document had been prepared to explain the Board's proposals for refocusing the academic programme of the Seminary in the light of the substantial discussions at the previous year's Council in Estonia. The chief aim was to make Prague the hub of a network of national seminaries to facilitate more effective mission and identity in Europe. The Federation's President, Theo Angelov, presented a resolution from the Executive supporting the Board's proposals. This would involve discontinuing several of the current academic courses from July 1998. The main programme would concentrate on Baptist and Anabaptist studies, human rights, missiology, spiritual growth and formation, continuing professional development for pastors and leaders already trained in national seminaries, and continuing education through such bodies as SITE and IME. Research facilities and doctoral studies would still be available. A new approach would be to start courses for 'teaching the teachers to teach', thus providing opportunity for academic and educational growth for staff members of national seminaries. Karl Heinz Walter explained some of the concerns which had been raised and the implications of the changes being proposed. Although there were some unanswered questions and opposing viewpoints raised in the ensuing debate, Council gave a clear mandate to the proposals by a vote of sixty-six in favour and six abstentions.

The Board of Trustees met again in November and clarified many of the points raised.[20] Meanwhile, David Nixon was appointed as Acting Co-President with Dr Kent Blevins, and the Search Committee set about the task of finding a General Director (not a President) to lead what would be known as the Directorate of the Seminary. When a General Director was in place other Directors would be sought for the following areas of work: Baptist and Anabaptist studies, Mission and Evangelism, Adult education, Human rights, Spiritual life and development, Administration, and Library services. Dr Elizabeth Green (Italy), Chair of the Academic and Student Affairs Committee, was charged to co-ordinate the establishment of a panel of consultants in all the major theological disciplines, in order to ensure regular development of the library for Baptist scholarly and doctoral research.

Controversy and intense opposition from the student body and existing Faculty still remained. They posed major questions to the Board of Trustees for its meeting in April 1998. There was also a meeting between the Board and the students. Clearly neither approaches managed to assuage their fears, for in May a special publication was issued by the students and members of the Faculty entitled *The Missing Link,* claiming to show 'the other side of the coin'. The Board believed it had adequately answered criticisms that the changes had been made in haste, that the theological excellence of the Seminary was being dismantled, and that the international campus culture would be lost. Students and staff remained convinced that their complaints had not been answered.

Encouraged by the clear mandate given at the Council in Croatia, the Board of Trustees and the EBF Executive proceeded to nominate the Revd Keith Jones as the Rector. This title was considered more appropriate to the European academic scene. The member Unions decisively voted in favour. The Board and Executive also accepted a suggestion which had come from several quarters that they should appoint a Director of Biblical Studies. Dr Davorin Peterlin, the Academic Dean and Director of Graduate Studies at the Evangelical Theological Seminary in Osijek, Croatia was appointed Pro-Rector, Academic Dean, and Director of Biblical Studies. Reinhard Geissler, the current interim Business Manager, was appointed Director of Finance and Administration. His wife, Ingrid, was already serving the Seminary as Public Relations Manager. Dr David Brown, who had been part of the IBTS team for three years, concentrating on the SITE programme and integrating it into the total work of the Seminary, was appointed Director of Continuing Education.

In the Summer 1998 edition of *The Link* Keith Jones announced that from September 1998 the Seminary would be offering MTh degrees in both Biblical Studies and Baptist and Anabaptist Studies. By September 1999 they expected to be offering Master degrees in Missiology, Human Rights and Pedagogy. Supervision of doctoral studies and partnership with the Theological Faculty of the Charles University for their Magister degree would also be provided He confirmed that the Seminary's degree courses would be for accredited degrees of respected European and American universities and institutions, and thus maintain worthy academic status.[21]

The Seminary will celebrate its Golden Jubilee in 1999, recognizing fifty years of excellent service in Europe since it was first launched in Switzerland in 1949. BWA Council meetings will take place in Dresden, Germany, in July, followed by the EBF Council and European Baptist Congress at Wroclaw, Poland, 18-25 July. These events will no doubt make space for recognition of the Seminary's achievements over the years. At the Congress the IBTS itself will share in an exhibition of theological education in Europe and organize several seminars. They hope that many alumni and others will then travel on to Prague to participate in special celebrations there on 26-27 July.

Earlier in this book we explored how the EBF was meeting the challenge of the new Europe. The Prague Seminary is vitally involved in that process. To quote from the Mission Statement of its Directorate, it is pledged to *'offering a place where Baptists and other Christians gather for study, reflection, spiritual renewal, worship, and fellowship, and where cultures, traditions, and different practices of our Baptist faith are accepted and celebrated in a loving Christian community.'*[22] Such a pledge deserves the prayer of Baptists near and far - 'Amen, Lord! So may it be.'

CHAPTER NOTES

CHAPTER EIGHT Theological and Christian Education

1 See Bernard Green, *Tomorrow's Man: A biography of J. H. Rushbrooke,* Baptist Historical Society, 1997, pp.72-84. Also *Baptist Work in Europe,* the report of the Commissioners of the Baptist World Alliance, London, 1922.

2 Among the TAG-E papers is a printed report of the Consultation. See also pp.33-34 in the book of reports for the EBF Council in Moldova, September 1993.

3 The new group formulated a Mission Statement which was printed on p.50 of the report book for the EBF Council in Kiev, September 1998.

4 This is a summary of a letter sent by David Russell (5 January 1985) to William L. Wipfler, Director of Human Rights, Overseas Ministries Division, National Council of Churches, Riverside, New York, USA.

5 See Chapter 4, p.75.

6 Walter Sawatsky was a graduate student in the Canada-USSR Cultural Exchange Programme in the early 1970s, a research scholar at Keston College's Centre for the study of Religion and Communism (1973-76), the director of the Mennonite Central Committee's East/West Research Office in Neuwied, West Germany, and author of *Soviet Evangelicals Since World War II,* Herald Press, 1981.

7 He once commented to Alec Gilmore that what the EBF valued in the FEED THE MINDS and EUROLIT contact was the ecumenical commitment.

8 See Chapter 4, p.69.

9 Ibid., pp.69-70.

10 *Building Bridges* was published in Stockholm, October 1996. Further details can be found in EBF minutes and EBPS bulletins.

11 The new name of the former SBC Foreign Mission Board.

12 Only the BU of Romania wrote in support of the American action.

13 See EBPS 91:168-9, 4 November 1991.

14 Ibid., 91:199, 12 December 1991.

15 For the Partnership Statement text see EBPS 92:026, 3 January 1992.

16 For the Hamburg Agreement text see EBPS 92:151, 14 September, 1992.

17 The relevant documents may be found in the 1993 EBF Council report book, pp.43-52.

18 Bethlehem Chapel is a rebuilt replica of the fourteenth-century chapel in which the Czech Reformer and martyr, John Hus, preached.

19 They served from 1965 to 1997 in Rüschlikon, Yugoslavia, Austria, and then back to Rüschlikon and on to Prague. John David Hopper learned eight languages in order to be able to communicate freely in all parts of Europe.

20 For more details see EBPS 085, Bulletin 13, 2 October 1997; ibid., 103, Bulletin 16, 14 November 1997; and the IBTS magazine, *The Link*, No.92, Autumn 1997, pp.1-2.

21 *The Link,* Summer 1998 issue, also included news of the opening ceremony on the Prague Campus of the Abbey Christian School for Teaching English. The School is a branch of a Baptist institution in London, which teaches English in a Christian residential setting, for international students needing it for missionary work and professional or personal purposes.

22 The full text of the Mission Statement was published in *The Link,* No.94. Autumn 1998, p.8, and EBPS 112, Bulletin 16, 7 October 1998.

9

ISSUES OF CHRISTIAN MISSION

Certain major issues run like continuous threads through the patterns of EBF life over the years. We need now to look at them in more depth, in order to understand their importance, to trace the different ways in which European Baptists have responded to them, and to attempt to discern their place in present day priorities.

MISSION AND EVANGELISM

In *What are Baptists?,* the study paper issued by the EBF Division for Theology and Education in 1993, two statements are basic to this issue. One declares:

> We believe that every Christian disciple is called to witness to the Lordship of Jesus Christ, and that the Church as a part of God's Kingdom is to share in the whole mission of God in the world.

This makes clear that mission and evangelism are personal and corporate obligations at the heart of all Baptist life and work. It is important to distinguish the meaning of the two words. Evangelism is the spreading of the Gospel of Jesus Christ as Saviour and Lord, in order to bring people to faith in him. The above document comments that mission always includes evangelism. But mission also lays upon us a wider task; for God calls us to 'share with him in his work of creating justice, social welfare, healing, education and peace in the world.'

The second statement declares:

> We affirm the need for personal faith in Jesus Christ and for discipleship in his likeness.

It goes on to affirm that personal trust involves 'repentance towards God the Father and renewal of life by the Holy Spirit', and is enshrined in our practice of believers' baptism.

Whenever Baptists consider these issues, there are differences of emphasis and practice. In earlier chapters we have occasionally found that this has led to controversy and division; but the predominant feature of the EBF story is the constant attention given to our missionary and evangelistic responsibilities. In almost all the meetings of the Executive and Council, and certainly at all the Congresses, they have been essential parts of the agenda.

Three of the four purposes of the Federation, set out in the original constitution, laid the foundation for this: 'to stimulate and co-ordinate evangelism in Europe' - 'to provide a board of consultation and planning for Baptist mission work in Europe' - 'to stimulate and co-ordinate where desirable the missionary work of European Baptists outside Europe'.[1] Therefore, it is no surprise to discover that the theme of the 1st European Baptist Congress at Copenhagen in August 1952 was 'Baptists and the Evangelisation of Europe'. In fact, as we shall see later in this chapter, the main evangelistic effort in the early years was in overseas missionary work through the formation of the European Baptist Missionary Society. In Europe most effort had to be put into post-war relief and reconstruction, and to renewing contact and healing broken relationships with those sisters and brothers in Christ whom war put on opposing sides. It was not until the 1960s that a modest beginning was made with an **EBF Evangelism Committee**. It arranged a number of conferences for pastors and lay people. The five-yearly Congresses always included missionary and evangelistic seminars, addresses and rallies. Periodically, the BWA offered programmes for their members around the world to use as they felt led. The EBF commended these to the churches and Unions, and tried to link their own agendas with those of the Alliance.

When Ronald Goulding ceased to be General Secretary and moved to Washington to become Director of the newly formed BWA Division of Evangelism and Education, the EBF committee became the **Evangelism**

and Education Committee. It was more a resource centre than a programme planner, until in the late 1970s two matters arose which caused people to question the nature of its future work. At the Vienna Council of 1978, a report was given of good work being done by Dr Bill Thomas as an evangelist at large in Austria, West and East Germany, France, Netherlands and Norway. He had been sponsored by ABC International Ministries who were finding it increasingly difficult to finance him. He does not seem to have been linked specifically with the EBF, but he obviously hoped that they would contribute towards his work. When the Council met a year later in Brighton it heard that ABC/IM intended to withdraw him from Europe. Members of the E and E Committee were eager for his work to continue but could not see how this was financially possible. They were already pressing for the appointment of Bill Wagner of the SBC/FMB as Director in Church Growth and Conference Planning, to be funded from America. At the same time a US/European youth exchange was being canvassed, also with the promise of FMB financing. Both ideas failed to win Council's support. One wonders if this was due to uneasiness about growing American influence, which was a question raised periodically in the EBF. Or was it prompted by financial limitations?[2]

During 1981 there was evidence of growing co-operation between the E & E Committee, the Youth Committee and the EBWU. Structural changes within the Federation had also led to a system of Council appointments to the committee, with members being carefully drawn from north, south, east and west. Annual consultations with the delegates of the Unions present at Council meetings encouraged more direct input. At the Denia Council in 1982 Knud Wümpelmann urged that evangelism be regarded as a top priority, but the main responsibility for it rested with local churches. The task of the EBF and the Unions was to offer help, encouragement and support. He wanted to see more liaison between the EBF and BWA committees in achieving this. Presumably he also intended to make it clear that the Federation should not become a mission agency in itself.

Discussions continued about patterns of mission and evangelism in the future. At the 1983 Council a resolution was passed stressing the importance of inter-church relations and common witness. In 1984 there was the first reference in the minutes to Church Growth, and many encouraging signs of commitment to it. This pressure for more specific policies came to a head in a recommendation brought to the Council in Glasgow in 1986 by the Executive Board and Faculty of the Rüschlikon Seminary. They proposed the establishment of an Institute for World Mission, Evangelism and Church Growth. The recommendation was approved, but not without serious questions from a number of key people. What would be its effect on the future work and programmes of the Seminary? How big would the Institute be and how would it be integrated with the EBF and Seminary? How would it be financed? To whom would the Director be answerable? The minutes indicate that the unease was not about mission and evangelism, but the recurring fear of independent organizations financed and controlled from America. When the debate came to an end, one of the conditions of the approval given was that the EBF would retain its independence and have freedom to determine the personnel and aims of the Institute. They wanted to ensure a European approach, with a wide theological spectrum, and awareness of the variations of culture and environment in the many member Unions. They were not willing to import a foreign pattern. Moreover, they wished to press the point that the primary responsibility for mission and evangelism rested with the Unions and churches. It is interesting to note how this debate anticipated the issues which had to be faced when Communism fell and evangelical and mission groups from all over the world flooded into Eastern Europe.

Draft proposals for the Institute were agreed at the 1987 Council in Italy. They expressed four main principles:
1. To have a dual focus, centring on the Seminary Campus and looking outward to the horizons of Europe.
2. To fuse Christian scholarship and evangelistic passion.
3. To enhance missiological studies in the Seminary.

4. To provide training and research in mission and evangelism for churches, unions, conventions and missions.

The **Institute for Mission and Evangelism (IME)** was inaugurated in April 1988 at Dorfweil. Earl Martin was installed as the first Director. Five months later he reported that a Seminar had been held at Rüschlikon to introduce the range of programmes for different groups in the EBF. He spoke of a 'perceived eagerness for the re-evangelization of Europe'. After the crisis caused by the defunding of the Seminary by the SBC Foreign Mission Board, the CBF offered to accept financial responsibility for the IME from 1993. Earl Martin left Europe in 1994 and was succeeded by another member of the CBF, Don Berry.

Around this period there seems to have been some confusion and overlap in European Baptist activity. In addition to the IME, there were conferences for Home Mission Secretaries and International Mission Secretaries. The Muslim Awareness Committee was active in training people for witness among 'strangers in the midst'. SITE and IBLA also included similar topics in their programmes. When the EBF introduced its new divisional structures a **Division for Mission and Evangelism** was formed. Its first convenor, David Coffey, stated in Varna at the 1991 Council that one of its priorities must be discipleship, over against nominalism. Two months later he spoke of Europe as being on the verge of a new mission era. He followed up these comments by proposing to the Executive in Spring 1992 that thought should be given to creating an Inner-European Missionary Agency to co-ordinate Baptist efforts to reach the vast unevangelized areas of Europe. Although the idea was agreed in principle, there were doubts about financing it. There were also questions about the extra work which would be involved for the EBF office and General Secretary. A proposal to call it an Institute for Mission in Europe (IME) obviously raised discussion about its overlap or integration with the existing IME. Eventually, the new proposals were dropped and the original IME continued with the same terms of reference and a Director with the same job specification. Even so, there continued to be many groups organizing missionary and evangelistic conferences and courses. Their enthusiasm was highly commendable, but there were occasions when the right hand did not seem to know what the left hand was doing! This was apparent when Hans Guderian, the current Director of the Division for Mission and Evangelism, complained to the Executive that he had not even been invited to the conference on 'Church Planting for the 21st Century' organized by SITE and IME.

At the Council meetings in Novi Vinodolski and Kiev in 1997 and 1998, he attempted to draw together all the efforts being made, by seeking to classify the specific concerns and wishes among Baptists in all parts of Europe, and then posing what he described as 'open questions regarding the future'. He listed four specific concerns:
1. Opportunity to share about mission and evangelistic activities.
2. National mission strategies and the development of an overall European strategy.
3. Possibilities for a missionary work and life style among Muslims.
4. Closer and better co-operation between Home and Foreign Mission.

Then he posed his 'open questions':
- Do we want to have an Institute for Mission and Evangelism also in the future?
- How does the EBF want to nominate a candidate as new Director of Missiology?
- Whom does the EBF want to nominate as new Director for Missiology?

The outcome of these concerns and questions will be fundamental to the future nature and shape of the EBF; so fundamental that one may wonder whether in the next century it will remain a Federation of Baptist Unions or become a European Missionary Agency.

The distinction implied by the question in the previous sentence is illustrated by the **Albanian Project.** An earlier chapter described the beginnings of Baptist work in Albania in the early 1990s, following the downfall of Communism.[3] The method of EBF involvement was totally different from normal. The usual pattern was to work in partnership with national Baptist Unions. Since there was no Baptist Union in Albania, the Federation took the initiative as a mission agency, and with the Government's permission set up an office in Tirana. From there they began to evangelize and plant churches. They offered the service of medical missionaries, teachers in the international school, a farming project, a language school, help with school equipment and heating, and various other practical projects. This could only be done with the support of other Baptist Mission agencies, who were willing to serve under the umbrella of the EBF. Careful liaison with Government Ministers was also crucial.

The first service was held on Sunday, 11 September 1993. Over seventy people were present, forty of whom were Albanians. The work developed well, so that by September 1995 a report to the EBF Council could point to one hundred and two baptisms in the Tirana congregation. Thirty-three more in the group linked with the farming project at Lezhe were baptized in the sea. Several gypsy groups were among these. Volunteer teams recruited by the EBF Youth Committee ran summer Bible Schools and Clubs.

Several important needs had emerged by then: for example, a Nursing School in Vlora urgently required refurbishment, the EBF Centre needed to be adapted to make Christian education work possible, and the construction of a road into the mountains was essential if remote rural populations were to be reached. A new law was passed in 1992, insisting that the leaders of all churches and religious associations must be Albanians. The EBF and its missionary partners declared their intention to hand over the work to Albanian leaders as soon as possible, and to change their role to one of support and service under them. This called for sensitive ministry. They also had to be vigilant about their vocabulary, for Muslims found such words as 'mission' and 'missionary' aggressive and threatening. In the Spring of 1996 it was reported to the EBF Executive that the two churches in Tirana were flourishing - The Way of Hope Baptist Church and the Freedom Baptist Church. Another congregation was growing in Bregu. There was also the group at Lezhe, and now bible study and services were taking place in Laprak, where a site would soon be needed for a meeting place to be built. Negotiations were taking place concerning the formation of an Albanian Baptist Union.

Birgit Karlsson, recently appointed to the Chair of the EBF Albanian Committee, asked the September Council for their prayers as steps were taken to bring local people on to the committee and to begin handing over responsibilities to nationals. She underlined how important it was for all parties involved to co-operate with one another and with *whatever* form of Albanian Baptist Union was formed. Unfortunately, the SBC/FMB had withdrawn from the committee to work with Campus Crusade in independent church planting. This had led to an urgent meeting between Karl Heinz Walter and John Floyd about honouring the Hamburg Partnership Agreement. The FMB continued to act independently, but at least agreed to encourage churches to join the proposed Baptist Union and not form a second one.

Two new bodies were established during 1996. One was the **Baptist Foundation of Tirana (BFT)** which took over the ownership of the Tirana Centre buildings and supervised their activities and finances. The other was the **International Baptist Cooperation in Albania (IBCA),** intended to co-ordinate the work of the various mission partners. John Passmore of the British BMS was its first Convenor. The two bodies were bound together by a covenant. Later, Karl Heinz Walter explained that the formation of these bodies was a step towards Albanian Baptist independence. The number of missionaries would gradually reduce, EBF would give way to IBCA and simply have one representative serving on it, and the Albanian Committee would cease to exist. Future links would be through Albanian Baptist membership of the Federation.

An unexpected national crisis suddenly placed heavy leadership responsibility on inexperienced church members, and led to their rapid growth to maturity. Civil strife and angry public protests about the economic condition of the country produced violent anarchy, which made it necessary for foreigners to leave the country for several months, until order was restored. The churches were left without missionaries, and their work had to be undertaken at local and national level by church members. Their response to the situation, and the gifts which emerged in some of the potential leaders, gave the EBF and its partners the confidence to take the next steps towards a national Baptist Union. In September 1997 the Albanian Committee decided to recommend to the Council that the EBF's role should be phased out, if circumstances permitted, from 1 January 1998. BFT and IBCA would then become the responsible administrative channels. Meanwhile, Albanian Baptists were granted associate membership status in the Federation.[4]

But more trouble arose. Fierce fighting broke out between Serbs and Albanians in Kosovo near the Yugoslavia/Albania border. Thousands of Albanian refugees fled back over the border, in desperate need of food and clothing, shelter, medical supplies and attention. The Evangelical and Protestant churches in Albania, including the Baptists, worked together to create an adequate aid programme. Many families took refugees into their homes. It was a tremendous drain on their resources and energy, but again they revealed their Christian commitment and growing spiritual maturity. The public impact of their inter-church co-operation for the benefit of people in need, whatever their religious affiliation, and even if they had none, was considerable.

When the EBF Council assembled in Kiev in September 1998, a delegation of Albanian Baptists was present. Among them were Freddie Golloshi, one of the pastors of Freedom Baptist Church, Tirana; Jonathan Steeper, Director of the Baptist Centre; Saverio Guarna, pastor of the Way of Hope Baptist Church, Tirana; and Adnan Pula, an elder of the Way of Hope Church. News was given that four churches had already begun to discuss the formation of a Baptist Union. A provisional covenant had been prepared and taken back to the churches for ratification. The EBF document *What are the Baptists?* was accepted as the basis for a Constitution. In a month's time the union was likely to be formed. To the joy of all concerned the Council voted to accept the Union as a provisional member. This would be reviewed in three years and, if the Union was fully operative and functioning satisfactorily, it would have its full membership affirmed in 2001.[5]

On the human level, we speak about structures and policies, and these have been an important factor in the development of Albanian Baptist work. It remains an exciting and difficult situation, in which all concerned deserve prayerful support. The EBF leaders have shown wise insight in finding the way to launch a pioneering mission where no Baptists existed, and in willingly beginning to step back to allow a national Baptist Union to be born. In looking at what has happened at a much deeper level, we express wonder and praise for what God has done. In a land where an evil regime tried to imprison the minds and souls of its people and to shut God out, the Lord has opened the doors and crossed the boundaries to bring the Gospel to many people, and to build his church.

A similar testimony to the grace of God at work must be given as we briefly explore the missionary work of European Baptists outside their own continent. As early as the inaugural meeting of the EBF in Paris in 1950, surprise was expressed at the wide range of missionary work being undertaken abroad. Before long a small group was appointed to see how this could be co-ordinated and supported. The **European Baptist Missionary Society**, as it was originally called, was formally established at the EBF Council in Munich in 1954.[6] Within three years four missionaries were serving in the French Cameroons and nine European Baptist Unions were members of the Society. By the mid-1960s the number of missionaries had grown to twenty-seven.[7] In 1965 a new field opened in Sierra Leone, to be followed in the early 1970s by Liberia and Argentina.

The Society's first two Directors were Dr H. Mascher and Dr Helmut Grundmann. When the latter reported to the EBF Council in 1978, he pointed out that with the development of political independence for many former colonies, autonomous churches and conventions were coming into being. Native churches were undertaking more and more responsibility, including the determining of the areas, nature and duration of the Society's work. Such integrated partnership under the control of national conventions and local churches was not without its problems, but this was the policy being positively pursued. In keeping with this decision the EBMS dropped the word 'Society' from its name and became the **European Baptist Mission (EBM).** It was also given non-voting membership of the EBF Council and reported annually to it.

Some other significant changes took place in this period. In 1979 a missionary society known as Missionary Actions in South America (MASA), founded eighty years earlier by a German Baptist pastor, entered into partnership with the EBM. The Director then started to report under the title EBM/MASA. Helmut Grundmann retired in 1982, to be succeeded by Horst Niesen. By now the Mission had eighty-two European missionary personnel from eleven Unions. A few years later the first two missionaries from East Germany were commissioned for service, amid great joy and thanks to God for another triumph of his grace.

A new feature appeared in the 1988 annual report with the title, 'The Foreign Mission Work of the Nordic Baptist Unions'. It told of extensive work being undertaken by the Baptist Union of Denmark (in Rwanda, Burundi and Thailand), by the Baptist Union of Norway (in Zaire and Nepal), by the Baptist Union of Sweden in partnership with others (in ten countries in Asia, Central America and Europe), and by the Orebro Mission. The Swedish speaking Finnish Baptist Union had no separate missionary work, but some of their personnel were in partnership with the Danish and Swedish Baptists. Alongside this report, Reg Harvey pointed out that the British Baptist Missionary Society (BMS) should also have opportunity to report on its work. This was agreed.

Hans Guderian, the present Director of EBM/MASA, gave a most encouraging report to the 1998 Council in Kiev. He told of visits to India, South Africa, the Central African Republic, Peru, Bolivia and Cuba. Future developments are planned in all those countries. He spoke of the tragic problems in Sierra Leone, torn apart by civil war. He also gave details of the EBM's move from Bad Homburg to the new Baptist Education Centre in Elstal, near Berlin. In conclusion, he outlined several positive goals for the coming years:

- to build closer contacts with member Unions in the EBF, especially among the Eastern European countries;
- to open up new paths for partnership mission among unreached people, like the Mingrels in Georgia;
- to explore joint operations with other European and non-European Baptist mission agencies in ways that will allow more strategic use of shared resources.

PEACE AND DISARMAMENT

Bearing in mind that the EBF began soon after the Second World War, with the hope of bringing together European Baptists whose nations had been torn apart by strife, it is no surprise to find that very soon in its life peace was on the agenda. A major proportion of its life was covered by the prolonged years of the Cold War between East and West. The menace of the nuclear arms race, the debates about the deterrence theory to justify it, and the constant propaganda war between East and West put Christian churches and leaders of all denominations in a difficult position. From a biblical point of view, peace and peace-making were fundamental to their understanding of God's saving purpose for humanity. Yet each country's government naturally justified its own policies, and many expected, or even insisted, that Christian delegates to international conferences would defend their nation's position. For a long time it was generally assumed that Baptists from the East were under obligation to make patriotic speeches as a condition of securing a passport and visa to travel. In the same way, Baptists from the West tended to suspect that the Christian Peace Movement was communist inspired and to be treated with caution.

No doubt, there was an element of truth in both positions, but it was by no means the whole truth. The horrific sufferings of war, the massive proportions of death, destruction and deprivation that it left behind, and the crippling economic costs of the arms race at a time when there was so much human need, created a widespread abhorrence of war. The threat of a nuclear holocaust intensified the search for peace. In both

Walter O Lewis, USA
General Secretary 1950-55

Henry Cook, Great Britain
President 1952-54,
General Secretary 1955-59

Bredahl Petersen, Denmark
President 1950-52

Manfredi Ronchi, Italy
President 1954-56

Hans Luckey, Germany
President 1956-58

F. Ernst Huizinga, Netherlands
President 1959-60

Erik Rudén, Sweden
President 1958-59,
General Secretary 1959-65

Ronald Goulding, Great Britain
President 1960-62,
General Secretary 1965-76

Baungaard Thomsen, Denmark
President 1962-64

Michael Zhidkov, Russia
President 1966-68

Jacob Broertjes, Netherlands
President 1964-66

Rudolf Thaut, Germany
President 1968-70

Andrew MacRae, Scotland
President 1970-72

José Goncalves, Portugal
President 1974-76

Claus Meister, Switzerland
President 1972-74

Alexei Bichkov, Russia
President 1976-78

Gerhard Claas, Germany
General Secretary 1976-80

David Russell, Great Britain
President 1980-81

Knud Wümpelmann, Denmark
President 1978-80,
General Secretary 1980-89

Stanislav Svec, Czech Republic
President 1981-83

David Lagergren, Sweden
President 1983-85

Vasile Talpos, Romania
President 1987-89

Piero Bensi, Italy
President 1983-85

Peter Barber, Scotland
President 1989-91

Karl Heinz Walter, Germany
General Secretary, 1989-99

Birgit Karlsson, Sweden
President 1993-95

John W. Merritt, EBC
President 1991-93

Theodor Angelov, Bulgaria
President 1995-97
General Secretary 1999-

David Coffey, Great Britain
President 1997-99

The EBF Council in Kiev, 1998
Karl Heinz Walter, General Secretary, David Coffey, President,
Theodor Angelov, General Secretary elect, Ole Jörgensen, President elect

East and West there was a genuine, popular longing for peace. Year after year, prayers for peace were offered in churches all over the world.

Christians increasingly believed that they must be a major voice for peace. If they were not, was it not possible that the world powers would continue their political battles to the point of utter disaster? Against this background, we will now survey the involvement of the EBF in issues of peace and disarmament.

In September 1959, Henry Cook, the EBF Secretary, introduced a debate in the Executive on his report of the Prague Christian Peace Conference which he had recently attended. He must have made quite an impression, because a committee was appointed to keep peace issues under regular review. Their terms of reference required them to take account of sociological and ideological factors, to keep themselves informed of conditions in East and West Europe, and to study the principal convictions of the Christian Church about peace with God and with one another. They were also encouraged to confer with the BWA and other denominational and ecumenical bodies. Resolutions for discussion at Councils and churches, and for distribution to the press, would be expected from time to time.

Four years later the new EBF President, Baungaard Thomsen of Denmark, reported on his visit to one of the Prague Peace Conferences. He was convinced that EBF representation at these events was most important. Eastern European Baptists were always present, taking an active role in the discussions. They expressed disappointment at the poor response of the West. A serious result of this was that statements emerged which were highly critical of the USA and NATO, without any questioning of Soviet foreign policies. A stronger Western presence could challenge this imbalance.

Nuclear testing became a major issue in the 1970s. The European Baptist Women's Union drew up a firm resolution for debate at the BWA Congress, objecting to the production, testing, detonation and use of nuclear weapons Unfortunately, they tabled it too late for inclusion in the programme. Undeterred, they forwarded it via the Swedish Ecumenical Council to the World Council of Churches. It was taken up later by the BWA Council in 1977 and wholeheartedly approved. When the EBF Council met in Italy in the autumn of that year it readily endorsed the Alliance's action. At the 6th European Baptist Congress in Brighton in 1979, Dr Glen Garfield Williams, General Secretary of CEC, preached a timely and memorable sermon at the closing service on 'Jeremiah - Prophet for Our Age'. Delegates from all quarters of Europe recognized it as a word from God, a word of judgement and challenge to the Churches in the face of the nuclear threat.

During the 1980s conferences multiplied. On the whole they were organized by other bodies, but the EBF usually sent representatives who reported back and helped to develop a growing commitment to peace and disarmament. For many years the chief initiatives came from Eastern Europe, but in the mid-1980s decisive steps were taken ecumenically to establish an International Christian Peace Research Institute in Sweden, to be known as The Life and Peace Institute. The concept had been introduced at the 'Life and Peace' Christian World Conference in Uppsala, April 1983. The Institute was to be run by an international Board. It would not attempt to speak for the churches, but to serve them. It was to be a centre for research not for demonstrative action. Fundamental to its purpose was to be an independent body which would not seek to promote any policy on behalf of a government or church.

Just over two months later, the EBF held a Peace Forum at Sjövick, Sweden. Contributors included Ambassador Olle Dahlén (a leading figure in the Life and Peace Institute), Carl W. Tiller (BWA), and Christian Wolf (GDR). The Forum urged governments to take steps towards the abolition of nuclear arms and to implement the Helsinki Act of 1975. They also called upon Baptists to work and pray more earnestly for peace, to try to dispel the apathy and false enemy image that often prevailed, and to promote international Christian relationships wherever possible. Their appeal won unqualified support at the EBF Council meetings a month later in Södertälje, Sweden. These positive moves must have been pleasing to the members of the Youth Committee, who had reported to the Council in Spain in 1982 about an international youth gathering at Burg Feuerstein, Nürnberg, where a 'Challenge for Peacemakers' had been prepared and publicized.[8]

The momentum was maintained at the EBF Council and Congress at Hamburg in 1984. Knud Wümpelmann welcomed the formation of the new Institute and saw it as a sign of the growing commitment to peace. Baptist Unions and churches in Western Europe, which were once hesitant, were now keenly pursuing the matter as part of their prophetic calling as Christians. He asserted that another promising sign was that peace conferences in Eastern Europe had become more balanced. It was an opportune moment to introduce a resolution on peace and disarmament. Council readily agreed to submit it to the Congress, where delegates also warmly adopted it. In the name of Jesus, the Prince of Peace, they resolved 'to work for peace among the nations by means of prayer' and 'to counteract the forces that make for war'. The resolution went on to denounce war in all its forms and described nuclear war as an affront to God's purpose for the world. Other issues included were the arms race, the waste of global resources which it caused, and the threat it posed to the whole human race. Addressing the work of member Unions and local churches, the resolution ended with a call to them to make representations to their respective governments and to focus attention on these issues in the coming International Year of Peace (1986).[9]

In August 1988 a second Baptist Peace Conference took place at Sjövik. This time it was an international one, involving the BWA as well as the EBF. One hundred and seventy people attended from twenty- seven countries; all six regional fellowships of the BWA were represented. Speakers pointed to the lack of constant Baptist involvement with peace issues in history, and to the tensions which have always existed on the question of the use or otherwise of violence to resolve conflict. Yet, there had always been Baptist individuals and groups vigorously urging non-violence. In the daily Bible studies on 'The God of Peace as expressed in the Trinity', Dr Noel Vose of Australia, the President of the BWA, said: 'Peace is the very nature of the Triune God. Therefore, peace like love ought to be in the nature of the Church as well.' A final statement urged Baptists world-wide to affirm peace as a crucial biblical concern and to raise awareness of the Baptist heritage of peace-making.

Thankfully, the European scene changed radically for the better during the 1990s. The old Cold War tensions ceased to dominate life and thought. But there are still political situations which lack stability, and there is strife in parts of Europe, the Middle East and beyond. There is no room for a complacency which assumes that peace issues are no longer essential on BWA, EBF, Baptist Union and local church agendas. Is this a time to consider what place positive peace making should have in Baptist policies of the coming century? And is this a critical human concern where inter-church co-operation would be more appropriate and effective? More boundaries to be crossed!

HUMAN RIGHTS AND RELIGIOUS LIBERTY

Through all their history Baptists have grappled with the issue of Church/State relations, involving questions of religious liberty and human rights. Their understanding of the Gospel and their theology and practice of the church have led, on the one hand, to independence and dissent, and, on the other, to denunciation and persecution. Previous chapters have contained illustrations of how this affected the EBF and its member Unions in earlier years, especially during the Cold War. We now briefly recall those times, but go on to examine developments during the 1980s and 1990s.

Successive General Secretaries have found this a crucial aspect of their work. In 1964, Erik Rudén explained to the Council that he wanted to make representations at the political level on behalf of Baptists in the Balkans, Romania and Bulgaria. But he felt that closer links with American and Western European Baptists were needed, in order to give an international emphasis to his efforts. It has always been strategically important that Baptists are seen as a global body, part of the universal Christian Church. In 1967, Spanish Baptists were victims of the Roman Catholic Church's attempt to use the civil powers to harass non-Catholics by stricter laws. Ronald Goulding felt there was no alternative but to travel to Spain for direct negotiations with both government and church officials. Advocacy for the persecuted, backed by the prayers of fellow-Baptists, was one of the reasons for the EBF's formation. At Glasgow in 1970, Council delegates were told that Knud Wümpelmann was investigating better ways of gathering and acting upon information about issues of religious liberty and aid for persecuted Christians.

When Baptists claim religious freedom it is never out of self-interest. They uphold the right of every person to believe or not: whether they are Christians, Jews, Muslims, or of any other faith, they have a human right to practise and express their faith freely. It was true to Baptist principles, therefore, when the AUCECB, with the EBF and Baptist leaders from various countries, appealed on behalf of the imprisoned Georgi Vins and the Initsiativniki, although they had separated from the AUCECB, and were hostile to the EBF and BWA. Towards the end of March 1978 a delegation of EBF leaders was received in Moscow by Mr Victor Titov, Deputy Chairman of the Council for Religious Affairs in the Soviet Union.[10] They shared in exceptionally frank and honest discussions about denials of religious liberty, and the difficulties the authorities were causing over the registration of local congregations. In particular, they expressed the strong concern felt by Christians all over the world about the Soviet Union's harsh treatment of religious dissidents. As Baptist leaders they appealed for leniency towards Georgi Vins.

By the 1980s a plentiful supply of international declarations and documents was available to assist advocates of human rights in their work. Two examples of this are to be found in EBF records of that time. Thorwald Lorenzen, of the Rüschlikon Seminary, addressed the EBF Council in Dorfweil in 1981 on the theme, 'The Bible and Human Rights'. He aimed to relate biblical faith to the modern concern for human rights. He used the word 'modern' because he wanted to go beyond an abstract moral ideal to what he called 'an emerging universal ethic'. He saw this growing out of the 1948 Universal Declaration of Human Rights and the two Covenants which became international law in 1976: the International Covenant on Economic, Social and Cultural Rights, and the International Covenant on Civil and Political Rights. His address contained a strong biblical and theological emphasis on the Christian doctrine of man and woman. Created in the image of God, they had great worth in the sight of their Maker, and God's saving love in Jesus Christ gave them a dignity and destiny which no power on earth had the right to deny or threaten. Therefore, human dignity was not an optional extra, but an essential part of the whole mission of the Church. He closed his address as follows:

> Where God's grace arrives, human dignity is restored; there a new humanity is taking shape; there seeds of hope are sown. Modern human rights may be seen as signs of God's providence. Let us therefore as part of our evangelical concern to restore man's distorted dignity, support and help to implement human rights. And we do that in the hope that in our active engagement for the least of his brethren we are ministering to Jesus Christ himself.[11]

A public resolution on human rights and the use of torture, passed at the Hamburg Congress in 1984, was in similar vein. It quoted Article 5 of the Universal Declaration of Human Rights: 'No one shall be subjected to torture or to cruel, inhuman and degrading treatment or punishment.' After setting out some of the issues, the resolution urged the EBF Executive to bring their concern to the notice of the BWA with a view to a world-wide Baptist response.[12]

When the Communist empire suddenly collapsed, all religions regained their freedom and Christians dreamed of spiritual revival. Baptists in Central and Eastern Europe found many new opportunities and experienced remarkable growth. But all was not well. The influx of foreign sects and the independent activities of many evangelical groups, without any consultation with the churches which had borne the brunt of the hard years, led ecclesiastical and political authorities to react with new laws and prohibitions, with denunciation and sometimes violent opposition. Once again, freedom was under threat. Baptists were among those singled out for public attack. In God's providence, the work done in the 1980s made them more prepared for action.

At the Varna Council (1991) some important strategies were agreed: to be constantly vigilant; to build good relations with State authorities; to promote a clear Baptist identity, in order to avoid being confused with foreign sects and para-church groups. In 1992, defence of religious liberty was even more urgent in some parts of Eastern Europe. David Coffey promised to contact the British Government's Foreign Office about developments in Russia and to arrange for a delegation from some of the CIS republics to accompany him to the Foreign Office during the EBF Council in September, to tell their own story.

By November 1993 the situation in Bulgaria was described as 'desperate'. Oppression and intimidation were widespread. At a meeting specially arranged to consider the future of the BTS at Rüschlikon, an emergency debate took place about Bulgaria. Three specific actions were approved. One was to ask the BWA to approach the Bulgarian Ambassador via the White House. Another was for David Coffey to arrange for the Baptist Union of Great Britain to complain to the Bulgarian Embassy in London. The third was for Jim Smith (CBF) to confer with Keith Parks about a personal approach to ex-President Jimmy Carter. All three were fulfilled, but in a report given to the Executive in Lisbon in May 1994 there was little evidence of any positive response. It was time for the EBF to take new steps. A Task Force on Human Rights was set up, under the chairmanship of Thorwald Lorenzen. It included Anatoly Pchelintsev of Russia, Ebbe Holm of Denmark, Theo Angelov of Bulgaria and Per Midteide of Norway. Its work was put under the wing of the Division for External Relations. At the Dorfweil Council in September several plans for action were outlined:

- to collect detailed evidence of human rights violations;
- to create a BWA/EBF network of lawyers to give advice;
- to produce an information brochure and prayer material;
- to promote the ideal of religious freedom for all people.

Council also agreed to establish a Day of Prayer for Human Rights and Religious Freedom on the second Sunday in December. This was so well supported in 1994 that it became an annual event.

Thorwald Lorenzen soon moved to Australia, after years of notable service within the EBF and at Rüschlikon. Ebbe Holm succeeded him as chairman. Under his leadership, the Task Force worked with vigour and urgency. A book on human rights was commissioned and published in Bulgaria for circulation to Baptist Unions. A Newsletter was also launched. The Chairman built a useful link with the Institute of Human Rights in Denmark, which offered to finance the training of one person for the EBF. By early 1997 he was able to announce to the Executive in Bratislava the formation of several groups for young people in different countries - Sweden, Belgium and possibly Austria. He went on to give information of a Seminar on Human Rights due to be held in Prague in October.

At this point in the meeting, one of those frustrating discussions occurred which arise when an organization has limited finance and leaders have to question good ideas. Karl Heinz Walter pointed out that the Task Force was appointed to gather and circulate information. There was no budgetary provision for the extra work being undertaken, and they had no authority to speak publicly in the name of the Federation. He felt that the group's work needed to be integrated into the EBF's general programme. President Theo Angelov urged that some way must be found to encourage the Task Force, even if there was no budget for them. Other members too were eager to encourage them. They suggested that Ebbe Holm be given opportunity to meet with the Executive.

It is clear from the minutes that when the Executive met again in Croatia in September 1997 there was still disagreement and uncertainty about the purpose of the Task Force. At the Council a day or two later, Karl Heinz Walter moderated a Forum on Human Rights. Leaders from Russia, Georgia, Armenia, Israel, Lebanon and Macedonia gave first-hand accounts of the situations they were facing. The general picture was of a considerable deterioration in the areas of religious liberty and human rights. Laws were becoming harder in ways that helped Orthodox and Roman Catholics to fight against the Protestant and Evangelical churches. Public attacks were common. Arrests and interrogations were beginning to reflect the old days of Communism. In the Middle East Christian Arabs were hemmed in by pressures from Muslims on the one hand and Orthodox Jews on the other. Delegates sensed that letters to governments, and even talks with them, were not enough. Long-term, it was necessary to persuade capable Christians to become more active politically and gain influence in parliaments. Political pressure at such levels was likely to bear more fruit. The EBF should use all avenues open to it (for example, the European Union, the European Council, and CEC), to press for religious freedom and the protection of human rights. Meanwhile, the prayer and support of local churches in all Unions should be actively sought.

At the close of the Forum a resolution on Religious Freedom was unanimously passed. With it, the External Relations Division released details of a five-step procedure for action to be circulated to all member Unions. This embodied methods which were likely to go a long way in clarifying the role of the Task Force on Human Rights.

1998 was the 50th Anniversary of the United Nations Universal Declaration of Human Rights. The EBF Council in Kiev passed an appropriate resolution to acknowledge that, and to pledge its own ongoing concern for human rights issues. The resolution reminded members of the good networking resources of the EBF and BWA which had now been established, and which they should use whenever human rights issues made it necessary. The EBPS *Bulletin* of 26 November 1998 contained several important items on this subject. One surveyed the whole European scene, identifying nineteen countries where violations of human rights and religious minorities were rife. A second described how the EBF works in human rights matters. A third gave precise details about actions for European Baptists to take and the resources available to help them. The fourth supplied the full text of the Kiev Council's resolution.[13]

True to its historic traditions and, even more important, to its biblical mandate, the EBF continues to include such work in its understanding of Christian mission. As 1997 brings us towards the end of one millennium and the beginning of another, plans are in hand for another Human Rights Forum in the autumn.

INTER-CHURCH RELATIONS

The EBF has often tended to find difficulty with ecumenical issues because of the wide variety of convictions in the Baptist Unions which it represents. Some engage in inter-church activities with a natural ease, though never with full doctrinal agreement. Others feel obliged, as a matter of Gospel integrity, to reject Catholicism totally, and to withdraw from participation in any event or body which includes Roman Catholics. Others prefer not to enter into partnership with Orthodox, Roman Catholic and State Churches, because they have suffered so much at their hands. Yet others testify to the warm and creative fellowship which they enjoy with such churches. After years of honest dialogue they have had full opportunity to bear their Baptist witness, and to learn from the traditions of others, so that all have discovered the others' real character rather than their common caricatures.

These differences need to be respected. Unity among Baptists depends on accepting diversity, for their strong biblical principles include liberty of conscience. A Baptist Union, Federation, or Alliance can never bind the conscience of a member church. Therefore, ecumenical decisions are ultimately a matter for the local church. Bodies like the EBF are under obligation to try to communicate to other denominations what Baptists believe and feel, and vice versa. In order to do this adequately they need to be involved in inter-church relations.

Two different comments from EBF leaders in the 1970s illustrate this point well. When Andrew MacRae came to the end of his two years as EBF President, he reminded the 1972 Council in Novi Sad that there were many different views of ecumenism. He affirmed the need to learn that 'We have more in common with the most heretical

Christians than with the most friendly atheists!' Some years later, no doubt creating a sense of horror in some delegates, Gerhard Claas reported to the 1977 Council in Italy that he had been to Rome for the Conference of Secretaries of World Confessional Families. This had included an audience with Pope Paul VI. But he explained that this was favourable to Baptists, for the Roman Catholic Church was placing new emphasis on the significance of the local church. Therefore, in Europe they were seeking bilateral talks with Baptists, whom they saw as major examples of the doctrine and practice of autonomous local churches.

From that viewpoint, it is possible to see positive value in ecumenical involvement, for it gives Baptists opportunity to testify openly and unashamedly to their faith. As early as 1966 Ronald Goulding included in his General Secretary's report the comment that ecumenical partners often asked about Baptists. They seemed unable to understand the Baptist position, and therefore it was highly important for Baptists to be there among them to communicate their view of Church and Gospel. Those who have represented the EBF at various ecumenical events over the years have faithfully done that. Günther Wagner was often the spokesman of the EBF and BWA in bilateral and multilateral conversations. In 1982 at Denia, Spain, he presented to the Council an informed paper on the progress of such dialogues since the Faith and Order Movement began in 1927.[14] He spoke again at the 1985 Executive in Lisbon, to describe the part played by the BWA in them, and to give details of talks due to begin with the Lutheran World Fellowship in 1987. Thorwald Lorenzen, Wiard Popkes, Nils Ingelson and Knud Wümpelmann were to be members of the Baptist team.

Another Baptist in a key ecumenical role was Glen Garfield Williams, a Welsh Baptist, who for twenty-five years served as General Secretary of the Conference of European Churches (CEC). During his time CEC grew into a fellowship which included members from Anglican, Eastern Orthodox, Protestant and Old Catholic traditions. He wrote an important article in 1979 entitled 'European Baptists and CEC'.[15] In it he showed his sensitive awareness of what he called 'unresolved tensions among Baptists on ecumenical issues and involvement'. At that time, Baptists of Denmark, East and West Germany, Great Britain, Hungary, Italy, Poland, Sweden, Switzerland and the USSR were members of CEC. The Baptist Union of the Netherlands had been in membership but later withdrew. Good contacts existed with the Baptist Unions of Bulgaria, Czechoslovakia and Romania. Some well-known individual Baptists served on CEC's Advisory Committee: Irwin Barnes (Great Britain); Arthur Mitzkevich (USSR); Benjamin Fedichkin (USSR). Other Baptist participants up to 1979 included Otmar Schulz (West Germany), Karlo Kjaer (Denmark) and Claus Meister (Switzerland).

Although he held no office in the EBF, Glen Garfield Williams was a trusted friend, and throughout the Cold War years did much to plead the cause of Baptists who were under attack. In 1979 he persuaded CEC to share with the EBF in a project to give pension help to Italian Baptist pastors and their widows. When he retired in 1986 and then died in 1994, EBF leaders paid warm tribute to the excellent work he had done.

During the 1970s and 1980s, David Russell, Alexei Bichkov, Knud Wümpelmann and others were frequently involved in inter-church conferences on such issues as disarmament and peace, international confidence-building, human rights, refugees and asylum seekers, the evangelization of Europe, Christians/Jews and Christian/Muslim relations. Whether they went as representatives of their national Unions or from the EBF, they often gave reports to the EBF Executive and Council, thus making sure that members were not left in ignorance about ecumenical affairs.

In 1982 the Faith and Order Commission of the World Council of Churches published *Baptism, Eucharist and Ministry*. It was an agreed statement of over one hundred theologians from virtually all the major church traditions in the world, who had met in Lima, Peru. It was offered for the common study and official response of the churches at whatever was the appropriate level of authority for them. European Baptist Unions in membership of the WCC were invited to send copies of their response to the EBF. This was a golden opportunity to feed into the world ecumenical scene current Baptist understandings of the theology and practice of these three fundamental subjects. Hopefully, it also helped to resolve some of the tensions caused by disagreements between Baptists who opposed or supported inter-church relations. The replies of the AUCECB, the BU of Scotland and the BU of Great Britain and Ireland were circulated by Knud Wümpelmann to all member Unions of the Federation. In a covering letter of 16 August 1985, he expressed his hope that this material would be helpful to Baptists in their own relations to Christians of other denominations.[16]

The radical changes in Europe early in the 1990s, and the consequent reactions of the different churches to each other, gave a new importance to inter-church relations. CEC organized a conference in 1992 on 'The Role of the Church in the New Europe'. Since this was a topic currently being discussed in the EBF, Karl Heinz Walter did all within his power to persuade Baptists to attend it. Two years later the BWA and EBF were invited to meet the Orthodox Ecumenical Patriarchate in Istanbul and the Russian Orthodox Patriarch in Moscow. CEC also helped to arrange meetings with other Orthodox leaders of some of the CIS nations. These talks probably did not achieve all that was hoped, but they were a decisive step forward in building relations, which could lead to better understanding and face-to-face discussion of major issues. One comment which arose from them was the timely reminder that the steadfast faith of the Orthodox Church was a strong defence against Islamic militancy. Another example of the worth of the meetings occurred in 1996. In Russia an old document was republished and widely distributed, attacking Baptists as 'the most pernicious sect'. When this was raised with the Patriarch in Moscow he assured those who complained to him that he stood by his word to recognize Baptists as one of the traditional churches in Russia.

Because of the Baptist understanding of the church, membership of CEC was open to individual Baptist Unions rather than to the EBF. Eighteen Unions were already members. Early in the 1990s, CEC's Central Committee took steps to allow such bodies as the Federation to become Associate members. As such, they would be able to share in discussions and be aware of the matters dealt with, but would have no vote. At the EBF Executive in Dorfweil in 1994, a recommendation was approved for the Council to decide on an application for such membership. But at the Council meeting the Division for External Relations asked for time to consult all the Unions, and the proposal was withdrawn. This action caused a delay of two years. The Tallinn Council (1996) approved an application for Associate membership, but for some reason this did not take place. The subject, with all its tensions, was raised yet again at the Council in Croatia in the following year. Keith Jones reminded Council that the decision had been constitutionally made at Tallinn and it was out of order to debate it again. This was agreed; the application was made, and CEC formally accepted the EBF as an Associate Member in September 1998.

This section has indicated that inter-church relations still cause strong differences of conviction among Baptists. It is crucial that these are not allowed to destroy the unity that has been such a distinctive mark of the EBF for the past fifty years. Hopefully, without surrendering fundamental beliefs, Baptists will continue to recognize among themselves and in the wider church the rich variety of God's grace. According to Scripture, God's eternal purpose is to gather together *all* things into one in Christ.[17] We should pray for his desire to be in us, and that his Spirit will show us how to pray and work for its fulfilment, for in Church and world there are dividing boundaries that need to be crossed.

CHAPTER NOTES

CHAPTER NINE   Issues of Christian Mission

1   See Chapter 1, p.11.

2   It is interesting that Bill Thomas found ways of continuing his work. But when he tried twice more in 1980 and 1989 to become an official EBF evangelist he met with a negative response.

3   See Chapter 6, pp.131-4.

4   Associate membership allowed them to attend EBF Council meetings, but without a vote.

5   For a fuller report see EBPS 113, 7 October 1998, p.4.

6   See Chapter 2, pp.24f.

7   There were 2 Finnish, 5 French, 2 Swiss, 16 German and 2 Dutch.

8   The text of it is included in the EBF Council minutes for 1982.

9   The full resolution was printed in the report booklet published after the Congress, pp. 76f.

10 The members of the delegation were Gerhard Claas (Secretary-elect, EBF), David Russell (BUGBI), John Merritt (EBC), Theo van der Laan (BU of the Netherlands), and Knud Wümpelmann (BU of Denmark).

11 Thorwald Lorenzen's paper was printed and made available after the Council. Other contemporary European Baptist writings on religious freedom and human rights, which were consulted in the preparation of this chapter, include: Alan Scarfe, 'A Call for Truth: An Appraisal of Rumanian Baptist Church-State Relationships', an article in the *Journal of Church & State,* Vol.21, No.3, 1979; D. S. Russell, an unpublished paper on religious freedom, containing a good summary of important legislation and international statements, prepared for the British Council of Churches' Human Rights Commission, 1988; D. S. Russell, 'Church/State Relations in the Soviet Union' - recollections and reflections on the 'Cold War' years, 1995, *Baptist Quarterly,* 36, No.1, pp.21-28; Nigel Wright, *Power and Discipleship: Towards a Baptist Theology of the State,* the Whitley Lecture, 1996-97, Whitley Publications, c/o Regent's Park College, Oxford. (He also wrote a short paper, 'The Theology of Religious Liberty', for a debate on the subject at the BUGB Council in March 1994, following the EBF Human Rights Consultation at Dorfweil, January 1994.)

12 The full text was printed in the Hamburg Congress Report Book, pp.77f.

13 EBPS 135, 136 &137, 26 November 1998, pp.4-8.

14 Copies of Günther Wagner's paper are still useful source documents for details of historical development and bibliography.

15 See *Baptist Quarterly,* 28, pp.52-58.

16 The Lima document is *Baptism, Eucharist and Ministry*, WCC Geneva, 1982, Faith & Order Paper No.111. A useful Report on the process and responses is *Baptism, Eucharist and Ministry 1982-1990,* WCC Geneva, 1990, Faith & Order Paper No.149.

17 Ephesians 1.9-10.

PART THREE

THE WAY AHEAD

10

LOOKING TO THE NEXT CENTURY

Two resolutions approved at the EBF Council in Kiev in September 1998 were about the year 2000. Both opened with these words: 'The Council of the European Baptist Federation, meeting in Kiev, Ukraine, September 23-27 1998, anticipates a special celebration of the anniversary of the birth of our Lord Jesus Christ in the Year 2000...'

The first went on to affirm the biblical principle of Jubilee, by which debt is forgiven, slaves are freed and redemption is made real. It lamented the burden of debt carried by the world's poorest nations, and expressed support for the worldwide campaign, *Jubilee 2000,* aiming to secure for them a debt-free start to the new millennium. In conclusion, it urged the Baptist Unions of the EBF to join the campaign and make their respective governments aware of Baptist commitment to the Jubilee principle. The second lamented that we live in an age of moral failure, marked by social and economic conflict, and in danger of a 'spiritual Chernobyl!' It urged European Baptists to use every opportunity given by the Millennium celebration for mission and evangelism, boldly proclaiming the Word of God as the only word for our times. It encouraged EBF members to co-operate more closely in prayer, support and encouragement in the shared mission of God.

These resolutions expressed a basic truth about the patterns of Christian mission needed for the future. Our concern must be for Kingdom issues as well as Church. Personal faith in Christ and individual conversion remain essential to our understanding of the Gospel, but working for peace, justice and social righteousness is also necessary. Our churches and Unions should prepare their members to demonstrate their faith in the affairs of everyday life. Christians are needed in politics, commerce, education and many other realms. They must be our missionaries there, and we must support and pray for them. So the 1999 Congress theme is about the Bridge of Jesus Christ into the life of the world and all humanity, Similarly, the title of this book is about the Church, like its Lord, bearing its witness and fulfilling its calling on and across the boundaries of life.

In his presidential report to the Kiev Council, David Coffey gave two examples of what this can mean. He spoke of Dr Tadeusz Zielinski, a member of the Katowice Baptist Church in Poland, who is now a Member of Parliament. He is a theologian who lectures on Protestant Dogmatics at the Ecumenical Seminary, and a lawyer who helped to write the religious liberty clauses in the new national Constitution. The second example was Ivan Grozdanov, President of the Macedonian Baptists. Despite the threat of severe sanctions against religious liberty in his country, he is widely respected as a pastor and as a University Professor, and his open witness among students has led to the greatest number of converted chemistry students that David Coffey has met in all his travels! Both men show the value of committed Christians in key places *outside* the Church.

The EBF has many signs of encouragement for the coming century. The newly independent nations are young. Many of the older church leaders have died or resigned; their successors are much younger than has been usual in earlier generations. They are bringing to their Unions a new enthusiasm, and an understanding of contemporary needs and culture, which will undoubtedly lead to changes. How far will they be allowed to do this? In some areas of the world, the enthusiasm of younger leaders has been quenched by their elders, who have seen it as their calling to hold fast to old traditions. Baptist identity will be of crucial importance, and hopefully this book will help to explain the rich heritage into which they have entered, and reasons for issues and questions that others may raise. How far will they be ready to maintain the unity of the Spirit in the bond of peace between the generations and the different sections of our European family? These are not rhetorical questions, but pointers to patterns of fellowship which the EBF will need to foster. The Young Leaders' Conference which the Federation's officers arranged at Prague in January 1999 was a strategic step forward.

Other signs of hope can be seen in the new beginnings of the IBTS in Prague, with its plans for co-operation with the growing network of

Baptist Seminaries and Bible Schools throughout Europe. There are also the developing programmes of IBLA, SITE and IME, and the Prefab Churches project for more rapid and affordable church planting. In the year 2000 the Youth and Children's Committee intends to hold a Conference for Youth Workers in the churches, in order to help each nation to build its own strategy for mission among young people.

The EBWU has launched exciting new forms of service in some of the Eastern and Middle East countries in recent years. They have put alongside their fellowship, prayer, fund raising and leadership training courses what Hilde Sayers described as 'the Diaconia part of our mission'. This has been so blessed and used by God that some Baptist Unions which were firmly opposed to the ministry of women are now openly welcoming it. How appropriate it was that the Kiev Council also passed a resolution recalling with gratitude the part played by women in the history and development of the EBF. It ended by urging the member Unions of the EBF 'to encourage women to play their full part in the life of local churches and their Unions, modelling biblical principles of partnership between men and women.'

Financial restraints have frequently handicapped the EBF and some of its newer and smaller Unions. Many people who could benefit from sharing in conferences and assemblies are not able to because former scholarship provision has had to be severely reduced. Looking ahead, a question that probably needs to be asked is whether the EBF is becoming too programmatic. Has it become so involved in running programmes that, with its financial and staffing limitations, it lays too heavy a load on those who serve it? Ought more stress to be laid on assisting Unions and churches in their own programmes?

Ole Jörgensen, the present EBF Vice-president and General Secretary of the Danish BU, proposed in 1998 that larger, wealthier Unions should establish partnerships to enable smaller and poorer Unions to participate more fully. This echoed what Karl Heinz Walter had suggested several years earlier, that East and West, and South and North should generate and encourage bilateral exchanges within the EBF. Co-operative networking and living in each other's situations would be a valuable learning experience.

In autumn 1999 Karl Heinz Walter will retire from the General Secretaryship after almost ten years of devoted service. His lecture at the Dorfweil Council in 1994 ('Where do we stand? Where will we go together? What will our role be in Europe?'), and a further lecture at the Croatia Council in 1997 ('The Future of the EBF, in view of the political, social and cultural new developments in Europe'), illustrate the quality of thought and commitment which he has given to the task. He has served in one of the most remarkable periods of European Baptist history. His successor will be Theodor Angelov of Bulgaria, the first Eastern European to serve in this office. Son of a Baptist pastor who suffered long imprisonment by the Communist regime, he became a beloved pastor and evangelist himself, and is currently President of the Bulgarian Baptists. Prior to being ordained he was highly qualified in the field of biochemistry. He will be welcomed into office as one who is likely to play a significant part in enabling the Baptists of Eastern Europe to contribute to the EBF the rich spirituality and evangelistic zeal which have been typical of them through many years of hardship.

The last words of this book shall be from Claus Meister of Switzerland, addressing the European Baptist Congress in Zurich in 1972:

> We begin to realise that economists, social sciences and many secular organisations have stolen from the church a subject on which Christians should be the specialists: the future. We must regain the responsibility for this, our own subject. We are quite willing to learn from futurologists, although we cannot trust many of their presuppositions. New structures for the life of our churches must be found. But all of this we must not do in desperate seriousness, but in the almost hilarious confidence that God has already opened the future which we responsibly shape. With this conviction...we call you to this openness for the future which is first God's future and only then ours.

Index of Persons and Places

Index of Persons and Places

Index of Persons and Places

Index of Persons and Places